BEYOND THE AREA STUDIES WARS

The Middlebury Bicentennial Series in International Studies

 ⌘

MICHAEL GEISLER, SUNDER RAMASWAMY, NEIL L. WATERS
SERIES EDITORS

The Middlebury Bicentennial Series in International Studies comprises interdisciplinary anthologies that delineate, analyze, and compare the various encounters of national and regional cultures with global phenomena of the post–cold war era. Anthologies gather together original or seminal articles dealing with a particular theme from a wide range of perspectives. They seek to generate discussion of that theme as well as understanding of its specific expressions within particular cultures. The central aim of the series is to focus on each volume's subject the combined light of scholars who might not ordinarily find themselves in association with one another.

BEYOND THE AREA STUDIES WARS

Toward a New International Studies

Neil L. Waters, editor

Michael Geisler, Sunder Ramaswamy, Neil L. Waters
series editors

MIDDLEBURY COLLEGE PRESS

Published by University Press of New England

Hanover and London

MIDDLEBURY COLLEGE PRESS

Published by University Press of New England, Hanover, NH 03755

©2000 by Middlebury College

Printed in the United States of America

5 4 3 2 1

James N. Rosenau, "Confessions of a pre-Postmodernist: Or Can an Old-Timer Change Course?" is from *Postmodernism and Its Critics,* copyright © forthcoming by Darryl S. L. Jarvis. Reproduced by permission of Greenwood Publishing Group, Inc., Westport, CT.

Library of Congress Cataloging-in-Publication Data
Beyond the area studies wars : toward a new international studies / Neil L. Waters, editor.
        p. cm.—(The Middlebury bicentennial series in international studies)
Includes index.
    ISBN 1–58465–074–5 (pbk.)
    1. Area studies. 2. World politics—Study and teaching. 3. International relations—Study and teaching. I. Waters, Neil L., 1945–
II. Series.
D16.25.B5   2000
907'.2–dc21   00–009483

CONTENTS

BEYOND THE AREA STUDIES WARS

Introduction

❦

WE ARE IN the midst of a technological revolution which has combined with the collapse of cold war barriers to bring about an unprecedented level of mobility of capital and information. The implications of that mobility—called, generically, globalization—seem to point to an emerging congruence of economic systems and, some scholars maintain, of political systems and even social systems as well. Yet at the very moment when political borders and nation-states themselves seem to matter less, people prove adept at finding new ways to reassert their particularity on a scale small enough to provide satisfaction. The means include rediscovered ethnic identity, intentional revival of "traditional" culture, and, alas, the deliberate reincarnation of long-buried grievances. The results can range from benign (the preservation of Ainu culture in Japan) to horrific ("ethnic cleansing" and genocide in Bosnia, Kosovo, and Rwanda). In the year 2000 the world seems to be in the grip of centripetal and centrifugal forces simultaneously.

International Studies programs have proliferated on American campuses over the past decade, expressly to prepare students to operate effectively in the post–cold war world: to live and work in and among individual cultures and in a global arena constantly changing and being changed by those cultures. Are International Studies programs up to the task?

An honest answer has to be predicated on the state of International Studies and of its component disciplines. The purpose of this volume is to provide an overview of both, to investigate the issues that make cooperation between and within disciplines difficult, and to suggest that the intellectual rifts that have pitted area studies experts against

Neil L. Waters, the volume editor, is Kawashima Professor of Japanese Studies at Middlebury College.

globalists, economists against anthropologists, postmodernists against rational choice advocates, are resolvable within the arena of International Studies.

Some clarification of terms is necessary in order to proceed. Just what is International Studies? The term as used in this introduction is not limited to international relations, which in the United States is a subdivision of the discipline of political science and refers to formal relations between nation-states. International Studies here means programs of study that deliberately incorporate trans-regional and even global phenomena and theories into what would otherwise be area studies programs. Area studies, in turn, is used here to denote multidisciplinary research institutes and academic majors at the undergraduate and graduate levels organized around the study of regions defined in the United States in large part by the conditions of the cold war: East Asia, Russia and Eastern Europe, Latin America, Europe, sub-Saharan Africa, the Middle East and North Africa, South Asia, Southeast Asia, Australia and Oceania.

International Studies is thus a hybrid of generalizable and particular knowledge, and its usefulness as an arena to resolve disputes that roil the waters of academia in the United States and elsewhere depends in part on the proportions of the blend and the will of the participants. Those are delicate variables, which differ from one program to another. Yet most International Studies programs enjoy one structural similarity that makes optimism possible: they are inherently multidisciplinary, and their members must communicate across disciplinary lines. Indeed, the need for communicability itself is what makes new directions in research and teaching possible and even likely in such programs. Academics who participate in International Studies programs have no choice but to abandon their insular disciplinary argot in order to explain themselves to colleagues and to students. In a very direct sense, International Studies programs act as intellectual crucibles, bringing together an array of scholars from different ideological and disciplinary camps who might otherwise tend, or even prefer, to ignore each other.

Crucibles, of course, can yield dross more easily than gold, and there is no reason to assume that the International Studies crucible must yield intellectual gold. But I think it is possible to identify the more volatile ingredients in the International Studies crucible and to note that their volatility is on the wane, and hence the chances for gold are fairly good. The active ingredients are the local/global dichotomy, the political science–oriented debate over rational choice theory, and the effects of postmodernism, which have appeared in virtually every discipline associated with International Studies.

These three phenomena affect each other, but I would like to treat them *seriatim.* The first is itself a product of changing conditions in the wake of the cold war and began with an attack on the capacity of pre–cold war area studies programs to prepare students for the post–cold war world. One aspect of these attacks is essentially geopolitical; the division of the globe into area studies entities (the Middle East, Russia and Eastern Europe, etc.) on the basis of U.S. interests and cold war concerns no longer makes sense, and different, more fluid lines that take into account diaspora communities and other sources of identity not necessarily tied to the nation-state should be adopted.

Another and related criticism is that area studies programs ignore what is generalizable about the human condition and that the post–cold war forces of globalization—multinational corporations, instant bank transfers, interdependent stock markets, the world wide web, increasingly universal access to the same standardized news and entertainment, international trade agreements—are themselves the proper objects of study. A few who focus on globalization go so far as to assert that study of individual or regional cultures, languages, and histories are a needless distraction from the grander task of studying and understanding the globalizing, and essentially homogenizing, forces that subject humans in almost every culture to the same stimuli. A proper theoretical understanding of these phenomena, they argue, can render economic and political choices predictable, whatever the cultural milieu.

It is hard to counter the charge that the cold war era demarcations of areas themselves are dated and form an impediment to the study of migration, cultural interaction across area studies boundaries (for example, Turkey and Europe), multinational corporations, and other phenomena that resist geographical limitations. The point was driven home in late 1994 when the president of the Social Science Research Council cited pressure from traditional donors such as the Ford and Mellon foundations to attack the Social Science Research Council's area-by-area funding of research. Indeed, in 1993 the Mellon Foundation had nearly abandoned its funding of area-based research and sought instead to fund "themes that resonate in the cultures of several regions."[1]

When foundations speak, people listen, and the new priorities of the Mellon and Ford foundations had an immediate effect on research proposals. Yet these events did not spell the end for area studies programs in the United States. Area studies experts argued that there was a dangerous overemphasis on macrostructural similarities between cultures. What makes the focus on similarity dangerous is the construction of models that paper over very real ethnic, cultural and linguistic rifts that nevertheless reassert themselves historically, often in the forms of ethnic strife, separatism, or other varieties of rediscovered identity. Indeed, events in

Bosnia soon underscored the arguments of area studies specialists for deep cultural, and linguistic knowledge.

The net result of the 1993–1994 tilt by key foundations toward global and transcultural studies was to precipitate a search for a proper balance between global and area studies. In fact, the Ford Foundation underwrote this search through its "Crossing Borders: Revitalizing Area Studies" grants, which it awarded to institutions demonstrating innovative approaches to area studies. The reverberations were not confined to research centers and area studies institutes; they were felt in leading American undergraduate institutions as well. Several had already tried to link area studies programs together into what were usually termed International Studies majors; more did so after 1993. Indeed, it is largely because Middlebury College was one of these institutions that the editors of this series have taken International Studies to mean what it does here: an institutional orientation and an academic major that consciously seeks to strike a balance between in-depth area studies (language training to the advanced level, multidisciplinary focus on an area, overseas study in that area) and phenomena that have trans-regional or even global effects.

The search for a balance between the generalizable and the particular seems to hold some prospects of disciplinary and ideological peace. Mark von Hagen, director of Columbia University's Harriman Institute, put the case succinctly: "We've heard from the extremes on both sides: those who deride regional studies as atheoretical, cold-war driven, and anachronistic in a global era; those who defend a way of approaching the multiple subregions of Eurasia that resists comparisons and shrinks from anything that smells ever so faintly of theory. We may be approaching a consensus in the major social sciences and humanities faculties that there is no real knowledge of theory without knowledge of place, and no real knowledge of place without knowledge of theory."[2]

Yet it would be too much to say that peace is at hand. Pushed and pulled by internal disciplinary and ideological constituents, International Studies programs at all levels can easily tilt too strongly toward the "global" end of the spectrum and lose the invaluable contributions of the humanities in the process. They can also slip back to business-as-usual area studies and lose the connections and comparisons between regional entities that study of global forces entails.

Additional vulnerabilities for International Studies and area studies stem from ideological/methodological movements that seem to threaten the unity of component disciplines. I will comment here on two of them that seem to be polar opposites: rational choice theory and postmodernism.

Rational choice is a school of thought whose origins are in the field of economics, where it remains alive and well. There it is grounded in the fundamental assumption that people make rational economic decisions based on their own individual self-interest. This in turn is the launching point for a range of corollaries and analytical, usually mathematical means to understand and predict economic behavior. The term itself, however, is most often applied today to a group of scholars within the field of political science who sought to utilize methods to analyze political behavior similar to those that economists used to analyze economic behavior. They focused on the rational calculations of individuals in settings characterized by incomplete information and social constraints to interpret and, hopefully, to predict the political choices of groups. The first substantial wave of rational choice political scientists burst upon the scene about twenty-five years ago. Most but by no means all of this group tended to be politically right wing (perhaps a consequence of the focus on property rights as an explanatory incentive for political choices), and many were convinced of the universal applicability of their methodology. A second "generation" of rational choice scholars, dating to the mid-1980s, continues to have a major effect on scholarship in several political science subfields, including international relations. Their positions on the political spectrum tend to be less predictable.[3]

What makes a few rational choice advocates a problem for international studies and especially for area studies is their connection of the rational choice axiom that people make choices according to their own best interests with the "globalization" perspective that there is a growing similarity of economic imperatives—and by extension political imperatives—around the world. The resulting synthesis is that people everywhere can make a finite—and shrinking—number of choices, whatever culture they come from. It is a simple corollary that specific cultural studies—the soul of area studies—are likewise shrinking in importance.

Yet, if the version of rational choice offered by Margaret McKean in this volume is any example, there seems to be nothing inherent in the primary rational choice assumptions that is hostile to area studies. McKean's version seems thoroughly housebroken, and it seeks to support rather than undermine in-depth, culturally specific, and linguistically proficient research. Some iterations are more destructive toward interdisciplinary research and pedagogy, either because they insulate themselves in an exclusionary jargon or insist that humans are *always* rational, rather than that rationality is one of several aspects of human nature. Nonetheless, even some of these more virulent versions have begun to make their peace with area studies.[4]

While rational choice has primarily affected the discipline of political science—vital to any International Studies program—postmodernism has had an effect on most of the disciplines associated with International

Studies. Postmodernism begins with the premise that virtually all human relationships, even language itself, are inherently hierarchical and therefore act as agents of oppression. Since all disciplines as well as all people must rely on language, the postmodernist premise challenged the epistemological undergirding of one discipline after another. The disciplines represented by the contributors to this volume have begun to make a recovery and usually a partial accommodation, but if disciplines were people, they would still be nursing hangovers.

Ironically, although postmodernism can be viewed as the polar opposite of rational choice, it too, in its extreme forms, is inimical to area studies. Where rational choice practitioners perceive an underlying rational structure to human decisions, the postmodernist perspective is antirational and deconstructionist, and tends to view all structures of human relations as reducible to illegitimate hierarchies for preserving and enshrining the power of one group over another. Postmodernism in the United States, which depended heavily on the ideas of Claude Levi-Strauss, Michel Foucault, and especially Jacques Derrida, appeared first in the field of literary criticism and found especially hospitable ground in syncretic disciplines such as postcolonial studies, women's studies, and culture studies. To many, Derrida's zeal to unmask hierarchies, his celebration of the differences in non-Western societies rather than their similarities to Europe, and his underlying concern for justice (a concept strangely exempt from deconstruction) proved appealing.[5] Why then has academic postmodernism not found an especially hospitable home in area studies?

I think there are three main reasons. One is explored in some depth by the anthropologist Richard Perry in this volume: thoroughgoing, in-depth research on non-Western cultures tends to uncover complex social structures not readily reducible to hierarchies of power. Another, related reason is that postmodernists who see the West as the principal bastion of class, gender, and race discrimination and who would like to use non-Western cultures as a foil to these ills can do so only if they don't look at the latter too closely. Finally, as David Gibbs writes in this volume, postmodernists in their struggles to free language from its inherent hierarchical nature have developed a specialized jargon and a seemingly amorphous style that is all but inpenetrable to even the most determined outsider.

Once again, the insistence on communicability characteristic of multidisciplinary International Studies programs prevents them from adopting the more extreme iterations of postmodernists. But this does not mean that International Studies and the disciplines that take part in International Studies or area studies programs are inoculated against the influence of postmodernism or, for that matter, its opposite, rational choice. What the need for communicability does seem to imply is that the extreme versions of both of these positions are routinely rejected. Several of the chapters included in this volume are permeated with postmodern views: justice is consciously and unconsciously foiled by social and linguistic hierarchies; assigning "agency" to reified entities such as nations inhibits understanding. Yet none of these chapters, even the one by Ravi Palat which takes area studies sternly to task, adopts the self-insulating extremes of postmodernism. Several acknowledge the postmodernist position that language inherently cannot convey the thoughts of one person to another with complete fidelity, but insist that reasonable approximations ("accuracy" for Richard Perry, "checkableupableness" for James Rosenau) allow life, and research, to go on.

What all this suggests is that the ongoing controversies surrounding the local/global dichotomy, rational choice theory, and postmodernism have deeply affected International Studies programs, area studies, and their component disciplines, but have not proved fatal; indeed, they may actually strengthen such programs. Their survival, however, does not mean that they are free to return to business as usual. Most programs in the United States remain vulnerable to the charge of America-centrism because the cold war–generated definitions of areas persist, even as the world remakes itself. Some are still open to the charge of insularity, characterized by ignorance of forces, movements, beliefs, and technologies that cut horizontally across regional demarcations. And all will have to contend with a brand-new variety of America-centrism, grounded in the belief that the contemporary economic and military dominance of the United States is a permanent condition to which all must adjust. If postmodernism and history have one point of tangency, it is in the warnings they provide against this sort of arrogance.

Still, if the nine essays comprising the bulk of this volume are any indication, the dominant note is positive. The authors are a disparate group, representing seven disciplines associated with International Studies (political science, history, economics, languages, sociology, anthropology, geography) and a range of ideological positions. Yet they all have at least one point in common: they all in one way or another decry the rifts that insulate academic disciplines from each other and sometimes subdivide individual disciplines as well. They insist that the rifts within disciplines must be healed and the chasms between disciplines must be bridged. Some describe their own fields as salvageable or redeemable or emerging from a period of internal warfare or external siege. Most have prescriptions to bring academic battles to a halt. Most insist that International Studies, or "new" area studies, must establish a balance between the particular and the generalizable, the local and the global, empirical evidence and theory.

It is not, I suspect, too much to say that the balance itself yields a fundamental realization: humans operate at and are affected by several levels at once, from family to community to country to region to globe, and their behavior cannot be understood, and certainly not predicted, from a single one. In different ways different essays in this volume call for a zoom lens: Ian Barrow's investigation of agency, John Agnew's distress with the bifurcation between constructed and "real" geographies, Paul Streeten's impatience with abstractions from reality—all bespeak the inadequacy of approaching human behavior from a single perspective. The contributions in this volume demonstrate that there is much to be done both within and between individual disciplines that comprise International Studies programs. Yet the essays in the aggregate yield a note of implicit optimism—that a multilayered, multidisciplinary investigation of human behavior is not only necessary but possible.

Notes

1. Jacob Heilbrunn, "Everywhere Does Global Thinking Threaten," *Lingua Franca,* May/June 1996, pp. 49–53.

2. Quoted in Robert E. Clark, "Worlds," *Columbia: The Magazine of Columbia University,* Winter 1999, pp. 23–24.

3. See Donald P. Green and Ian Shapiro, *Pathologies of Rational Choice Theory* (New Haven and London: Yale University Press, 1994).

4. Christopher Shea, "Political Scientists Seek to Lower the Volume in Debate over Area Studies," *Chronicle of Higher Education* (September 12, 1997), p. A23. For the origins of the debate, see Robert H. Bates, "Letter from the President: Area Studies and the Discipline," *APSA-CP* (Newsletter of the APSA Organized Section in Comparative Politics) (Winter 1996), pp. 1–2; and Christopher Shea, "Political Scientists Clash over Value of Area Studies," *Chronicle of Higher Education* (January 10, 1997), p. A13.

5. See Mark Lilla, "The Politics of Jacques Derrida," *New York Review of Books* 45 (June 25, 1998), pp. 36–41.

PART ONE

Issues Beyond the Disciplines

DAVID N. GIBBS

Is There Room for the Real World in the Postmodernist Universe?

ꞈꞈꞈ

A MAJOR THEME of this article is the unoriginality of postmodern thought,[1] and we will begin by noting the unoriginality of postmodern thought with regard to the question of language. It is a familiar postmodern observation that language helps to construct our thoughts and, at least in a certain sense, our realities. It is interesting to note that the issue of language and its capacity to distort perception was a central concern of George Orwell, who emphasized the salience of language in ways that anticipate postmodern writing. Perhaps Orwell's most memorable analysis can be found in his 1946 essay, "Politics and the English Language," in which he made the following observations: "Now, it is clear that the decline of a language must ultimately have political and economic causes . . . But an effect can become a cause, reinforcing the original cause and producing the same effect in an intensified form, and so on indefinitely. A man may take to drink because he feels himself to be a failure, and then fail all the more completely because he drinks." Evidently, the notion that subject and object can be mutually constituting and that language constructs reality to some extent is not particularly new.[2]

Orwell went on and noted how the use of phrases, clichés, and jargon

Editor's note: David N. Gibbs is Associate Professor of Political Science, at the University of Arizona. "Is There Room for the Real World in the Postmodernist Universe?" takes aim at the potential of jargon to obfuscate. The author is particularly concerned about the involuted jargon of postmodern scholars, and his essay constitutes a full-blown attack on what he terms the epistemological relativism of the postmodernist position. For Gibbs, the postmodernists are destined by their own internal logic to fall to the Scylla of extreme relativism—what he terms the "Timothy McVeigh paradox"—or the Charybdis of unoriginality.

words not only serve to confuse substantive issues but, more actively, to dull mental activity:

When one watches some tired hack on the platform mechanically repeating the familiar phrases—*bestial atrocities, iron heel, bloodstained tyranny, free peoples of the world, stand shoulder to shoulder*—one often has a curious feeling that one is not watching a live human being but some kind of dummy: a feeling which suddenly becomes stronger at moments when the light catches the speaker's spectacles and turns them into blank disks which seem to have no eyes behind them. And this is not altogether fanciful. A speaker who uses that kind of phraseology has gone some distance towards turning himself into a machine. The appropriate noises are coming out of his larynx, but his brain is not involved as it would be if he were choosing the words for himself.[3]

Orwell was, of course, writing in a different era and political context, referring to the type of language that one found in political parties at the time, but it is easy to see that his points could be generalized. Anyone familiar with recent academic milieux, especially in the social sciences and humanities, can readily appreciate the widespread use of technical jargon and its potential to obfuscate. One may wonder what would happen if the papers presented at academic conferences were "unpackaged": If the ideas were translated into plain English, what would they look like? Would the ideas contain any real content, once stripped of their verbiage, or would they seem devoid of meaning?

Once in a while, someone manages to cut through the morass of words and expose the underlying issues at stake. Such an event occurred in 1996, when Alan Sokal, a mathematical physicist, raised the issue of meaning in postmodernism through rather unorthodox means. He drafted a postmodernist interpretation of quantum physics that was actually a parody, one that contained numerous (and intentional) errors of fact or interpretation. The parodic article was then submitted to the journal *Social Text*[4] for a special issue on cultural critiques of science, in order to determine whether the journal editors could recognize the article's flaws. The article was in fact accepted by the editors, who evidently failed to detect the joke, and it was published as a serious article. Sokal later revealed that the whole matter was a hoax and that the article's acceptance demonstrated (in his view) the intellectual bankruptcy of cultural critiques of science and of postmodern thought more generally. The whole affair generated an impressive amount of press coverage in the United States, Britain, and (most recently) France, producing one of those rare cases of an academic controversy that achieves wide recognition in the popular press.

The purpose of this essay is to explore the significance of Sokal's prank and in particular to examine the validity of one of Sokal's main points:

that postmodernism is a form of epistemological relativism that denies any possibility of truth or knowledge. The relativism issue formed a central part of the controversy surrounding the Sokal hoax, and of all the points raised in the *Social Text* article, it was the following that gained the most attention:

Many scientists, especially physicists . . . still cling to the dogma imposed by the long post-Enlightenment hegemony over the Western intellectual outlook, which can be summarized briefly as follows: that there exists an external world, whose properties are independent of any individual human being and indeed of humanity as a whole; that these properties are encoded in "eternal" physical laws; and that human beings can obtain reliable, albeit imperfect and tentative, knowledge of these laws by hewing to the "objective" procedures and epistemological strictures prescribed by the (so-called) scientific method. . . . It has thus become increasingly apparent that *physical "reality," no less than social "reality," is at bottom a social and linguistic construct.*[5]

The implication of the above paragraph is perfectly clear: What is considered to be "reality" (note the quotation marks) exists in people's minds but has no objective existence. Accordingly, the widespread *belief* that there is a real external world—one that exists independently of people's imaginations and is governed by physical laws that operate irrespective of social or cultural conditions—is a myth.

Now it is important to bear in mind that Sokal wrote the above as a parody. Nevertheless, Sokal has argued that these statements accurately reflect the core of postmodernist thought; the willingness of the *Social Text* editors to publish an article containing such statements, without serious argumentation, demonstrates that such views are widely accepted. Sokal expresses incredulity at the postmodernists' acceptance of relativism, noting that "[t]here *is* a world; its properties are *not* merely social constructions; facts and evidence *do* matter. What sane person would contend otherwise?"[6]

Numerous writers, including Stanley Fish, Stanley Aronowitz, and Sandra Harding, have all argued that Sokal's claims represent a straw man argument, one that resembles postmodern epistemology only as a caricature.[7] With regard to Sokal's specific claim that postmodernism accepts epistemic relativism and casts doubt on the existence of physical reality, Fish responds forcefully. He writes of "the improbability of the scenario [Sokal] conjures up: Scholars with impeccable credentials making [relativist] statements no sane person could credit. The truth is that none of his targets would ever make such statements."[8] To be sure, the relativism charge is an old one and has been raised many times before the Sokal controversy (although never so dramatically). When the issue of relativism has been raised in a polemical context, defenders of postmodernism have always denied the charge. In 1982, for example, Richard Rorty commented: "'Relativism' is the view that every belief on a certain topic, or perhaps on *any* topic is as good as every other. No one holds this view. Except for the occasional cooperative freshman, one cannot find anybody who says that two incompatible opinions on an important topic are equally good. The philosophers who get *called* 'relativists' are those who say that the grounds for choosing between such opinions are less algorithmic than had been thought. . . . If there *were* any relativists then they would, of course, be easy to refute."[9]

In what follows, I will argue that postmodernism is at base characterized by an ambiguous epistemological stance: On the one hand, postmodernists often do argue positions that are clearly relativist in nature, claims to the contrary notwithstanding, and affirm that on any specific question there exist multiple truths; that there is no consistent, reasonable basis to accept or reject any one of these truths; that, above all, knowledge is *purely* the product of the unique social conditions, interests, whims, and linguistic practices of the individuals or groups that purport to generate knowledge. "Reality" (even if it is said to exist) cannot play any significant role in the construction of socially and linguistically mediated truths. On the other hand, postmodernists adopt a much more moderate position, which (in contrast to pure relativism) may be characterized as follows: Interpretations of social or physical circumstances are *partly* the product of the social conditions, interests, whims, and linguistic practices of the individuals or groups. In this latter formulation, our understanding of reality is influenced by social and linguistic distortions *and* by the existence of real social and physical circumstances. This latter perspective, which we will term the social construction approach, argues that objective analysis is problematic and difficult to achieve, given the extrascientific factors that distort perception; but the possibility of objective knowledge remains potentially achievable, at least in some circumstances.

We thus have two distinct and mutually exclusive approaches to epistemology, the relativist approach and the social construction approach. Postmodernism, it will be argued, reflects a basic ambiguity and an unwillingness to clearly select between these two approaches. This ambiguity constitutes the core of postmodernist approaches to knowledge.

Postmodernism and Relativism

Before I discuss at length the ambiguous features of postmodernism, I will argue that there certainly is quite a bit of straightforward relativism in at least certain variants of postmodernist thought. Rorty's contention that "no one" affirms a belief in relativism is inconsistent with a sizable body of literature. It is easy to come up with examples from the works of some of the most distinguished figures. Let us consider the analysis of Jacques Derrida, where he purports to deconstruct the autobiographical writings of Jean-Jacques Rousseau:

There is nothing outside of the text [emphasis in original]. And that is neither because Jean-Jacques' [Rousseau's] life, or the existence of Mamma or Thérèse . . . is not of prime interest to us, nor because we have access to their so-called "real" existence only in the text and we have neither any means of altering this, nor any right to neglect this limitation . . . in what one calls the real life of these existences "of flesh and bone" beyond and behind what one believes can be circumscribed as Rousseau's text there has never been anything but writing; there have never been anything but supplements, substitutive significations, which could only come forth in a chain of differential references, the "real" supervening and being added only while taking on meaning from a trace and from an invocation of the supplement, etc. And *thus to infinity*.[10]

Much of this certainly sounds relativistic in the extreme; none of the statements here admits any qualification whatsoever. Notice too how the word *real* appears twice in quotation marks. One is left with the overall impression that reality literally does not exist except as a figment of Rousseau's or the reader's imagination ("there is nothing outside of the text," "there has never been anything but writing"). With reality abandoned, the reader is free to undertake an infinite number of readings ("and thus to infinity"), all of which presumably are to be accorded equal weight. Nor is this the only instance in which Derrida presents "reality" in relativistic terms. In a later essay he writes: "there is no such thing as truth in itself. . . . Even if it should be for me, about me, truth is plural."[11] Note that he does not write that the ways that we *interpret* truth are plural but that truth itself is plural.

Let us pause for a moment to consider the significance of these facts. It may be argued that Derrida is just posing and does not literally mean what he is saying. Perhaps Derrida is arguing a much more moderate position, for example, that a combination of incomplete information, vagueness of language, and human fallibility often produce misinterpretations, and such misinterpretations are more common than is widely assumed to be the case. When he writes of "multiple truths," he does not mean this literally; he is suggesting that circumstances can sometimes lead different people to *interpret* truth in multiple ways. This is surely a much more reasonable—and more conventional—view than the idea that there are literally multiple truths.

So it may be that Derrida is simply exaggerating in order to make his point; this is a possibility that I will deal with later. For the moment, we will stress that Derrida's statements do sound relativistic. And Derrida is not alone in proffering such views. Jean Baudrillard, to take another example, celebrates the idea of multiple realities in his witty book *The Gulf War Did Not Take Place,* which argues that there was such a high degree of propaganda issuing from official sources during the 1991 Persian Gulf War and such manipulative images from the mass media, that "reality" disappeared into a series of "hyper-events" that took place on television screens. Thus: "[w]e have gone in a week from 20 percent to 50 percent and then to 30 percent destruction of Iraqi military potential. The figure fluctuates exactly like the fortunes of the stock market. 'The land offensive is anticipated today, tomorrow, in a few hours, in any case sometime this week . . . the climatic conditions are ideal for a confrontation etc.' Whom to believe? *There is nothing to believe.*"[12] Relativistic language permeates the entire essay: "*Everything* is therefore transposed into the virtual"[13]—and presumably nothing is left that can still be called real. The very title of the book underscores the central theme: the relativity of truth. Of course, much of *The Gulf War Did Not Take Place* is ironic humor; and yet, after reading the essay, one is left with the impression that Baudrillard is at base quite serious. Expressions of relativism are not confined to this one essay. In *Simulacra and Simulation,* Baudrillard rather bluntly states, "I am a nihilist . . . I observe, I accept, I assume, I analyze the second revolution, that of the twentieth century, that of postmodernity, which is *the immense process of the destruction of meaning,* equal to the earlier destruction of appearances."[14]

More recent writings in the social sciences also manifest relativistic proclivities. Consider, for example, Murray Edelman's *Constructing the Political Spectacle.* Edelman analyzes how political images are constructed by the mass media and generate information that serves the interests of powerful social groups or individuals. Accordingly, public discussions of what is and what is not to be considered a social "problem" worthy of attention; which foreign countries are to be considered as external "enemies" and which are not; or the role that political "leadership" can play in resolving the identified problems or confronting the purported enemies are all highly subjective matters requiring definition. The ways that such matters are defined in the mass media are essentially arbitrary in quality. Edelman displays considerable insight and depth in his analysis of such constructions. However, he refuses to render any definitive judgment about whether these seemingly manipulative constructions are true or false according to some standard of objectivity. Even the most outrageous or propagandistic media images that he describes do not, in his view, represent falsehood or distortion; they represent instead some of the many ways that "truth" can be defined. Edelman adopts an explicit and unmitigated relativism, in which reality is irrelevant to the construction of reality and no interpretation can be accorded greater weight than any other interpretation. Edelman is perfectly frank about the resulting relativism, and he defends the relativist position against possible criticisms, noting, for example, that "relativist positions are not uniquely vulnerable with respect to verification or falsification."[15] Since Edelman has largely given up any possibility of understanding the world according to objective standards, he also acknowledges the meager possibilities of seeking to change it through any form of political action: "Direct political action through voting and lobbying can help bring modest and temporary changes, but are more effective as psychological balm for those who engage in them than as agencies of lasting and significant change."[16] Epistemic relativism thus resolves into political and social nihilism.

It is easy to come up with many similar examples. Peter Novick has written a lengthy (and fascinating) history of the historical profession, emphasizing how objectivity has been little more than a "noble dream" among historians. Novick qualifies this point and disavows relativism, agreeing with Rorty that no serious observer really believes in the relativist position and that charges of relativism are invariably off base; then he contradicts himself and writes of literary critic Roland Barthes as follows: "By the time of his *S/Z* (1970) he saw the 'text' as without *any* determinate meaning or boundaries, *irreducibly* plural, an *endless* play of signifiers."[17] If ideas can be "irreducibly plural" and can constitute an "endless play of signifiers," then what we are left with—whether Novick likes it or not—is relativism. Similarly, Fredric Jameson, in his classic essay, writes of "a society of the image of the simulacrum" in which there is "a transformation of the 'real' [in quotation marks once again] into so many pseudo-events."[18] At another point, Jameson proceeds to analyze E. L. Doctorow's novel *Ragtime* by noting: "This historical novel [*Ragtime*] can no longer set out to represent the historical past; it can *only* 'represent' our ideas and stereotypes about that past."[19] Once again, we note the lack of qualification. Jameson does not argue that our understanding of the past through reading *Ragtime* is achieved *partly* on the basis of preconceived ideas or stereotypes; instead, he goes much further and argues that the *only* basis of understanding the past through this novel is preconceived ideas and stereotypes. In yet another postmodern classic, Jean-François Lyotard writes: "All we can do is gaze in wonderment at the diversity of discursive species, just as we do at the diversity of plant or animal species," and presumably there is no epistemological basis for resolving this diversity by determining which discourses are the more accurate or the more truthful, according to some standard. If any such standard for discriminating among ideas does exist (or could exist), Lyotard makes no mention of it. Lyotard further concludes that "lamenting the 'loss of meaning' in postmodernity boils down to mourning the fact that knowledge is no longer principally narrative."[20] If Lyotard is troubled by this loss of meaning or if he sees any way out of the meaningless state that purportedly characterizes postmodernity, he once again makes no mention. I must confess that I was simply not able to comprehend very much of Michel Foucault's writings and therefore am unable to comment on them directly.[21] However, a sympathetic interpreter writes that, according to Foucault, "history is *entirely* contingent. Things just happen. Intellectuals impose interpretations upon these happenings, but they are artificial."[22] An article by Richard Ashley and R. B. J. Walker, which helped introduce postmodernism into the mainstream of international relations theory, is replete with relativist statements, which are offered repetitiously and with little or no qualification: "*The very possibility of truth is put in doubt.* Every representation appears not as a copy or recovery of something really present in some other time or place but as a representation of other representations—*none* original, each *equally* arbitrary, and *none* able to exclude other representations."[23]

It is worth noting that relativism seems perfectly compatible with certain core features of postmodern thought. Terry Eagleton defines postmodernism as "a style of thought that is suspicious of classical notions of truth, reason, identity, and objectivity, of the idea of universal progress or emancipation, of single frameworks, grand narratives, or ultimate grounds of explanation."[24] It is only a small step to move from a suspicion of universals to outright rejection, all dismissed in the overall quest to deconstruct the grand narratives of modernity. In addition, postmodern epistemology is highly critical of positivist methodologies that purport to test various theories against evidence; alternative methodologies offered to test theories—when they are offered at all—tend to be extremely vague.[25] Again, such a standpoint is not synonymous with relativism, but it surely makes relativism easier to introduce.

The relativistic world described above is a disturbing one, for it does away altogether with the traditional distinction between scholarship and propaganda; any possibility of exposing error or falsehood must be abandoned as untenable, since analyses of propaganda would contain no greater "truth" value than the propaganda they purport to analyze. Even the most bizarre and ludicrous ideas—the political views of Timothy McVeigh or Lyndon LaRouche, for example—would merit equal consideration and respect with those of John Rawls or Jean Bethke Elshtain. Some may find this example overly polemical, but I do not think so. If one does away with all standards for evaluating the validity of ideas and establishes, moreover, that efforts to "marginalize" certain ideas are wrong, then on what basis should we marginalize McVeigh or LaRouche in scholarly discussion? On what basis should we "privilege" the views of Rawls or Elshtain? The "Timothy McVeigh problem," as I will term it, seems an intractable one for postmodernist versions of relativism (or any other kind of relativism). The problem is a long-standing and well recognized one, and it informed much of Orwell's writing on propaganda. Reflecting on the Spanish civil war, Orwell made the following observations: "I am willing to believe that history is for the most part inaccurate and biased but what is peculiar of our own age is the abandonment of the idea that history *could* be truthfully written. In the past people deliberately lied or they unconsciously colored what they wrote or they struggled after the truth, well knowing that they must make many mistakes; but in each case they believed that 'the facts' existed and were more or less discoverable."[26] The relativist ideas expressed by Derrida et al. would preclude any possibility that the facts even in principle can be discovered.

On reflection, it is unsurprising that, when pressed, postmodernists steadfastly deny that they are relativists since the position is such an obviously weak one. The main drawback of relativism is that it is boring.[27] If all perspectives are equally valid, then why bother to advance one's own perspective? If all facts are equally suspect, then why bother to gather facts? If any analysis that the researcher undertakes on these (already meaningless) facts can never be validated or falsified, even in the most preliminary sense, then why go through the trouble of analysis? And if social scientific theories, whether postmodern or otherwise, are based on facts and analyses that are and necessarily must be arbitrarily selected, what is the utility of theory? If all positions are equally flawed, then why debate? Relativism, if carried to its logical extreme, would end all research and scholarly activity, and it is very difficult to see how relativism could produce any other result.

Relativism Qualified

Now I will consider another possibility, one that I alluded to previously: Perhaps the quotes above are simple exaggerations intended to make a point and to elicit the reader's attention, a technique of calculated overstatement. Some readers, including a few who are generally critical of postmodernism, make precisely this point.[28] Pauline Rosenau, for example, writes of a category of "affirmative postmodernists," who do not seek to do away altogether with the possibility of objective knowledge but who only seek to "problematize" the issue to some extent.[29] It may be argued that the postmodernists are not really arguing for a complete relativism but rather for a social construction of knowledge—that what we call knowledge is socially and linguistically constructed *to some extent*; our understanding of the world results from a combination of rational and irrational factors. What constitutes "the facts" according to this perspective is potentially discoverable, but the process of establishing factual information is complicated by the predispositions, biases, uses of language, and social position of the observer.

All of the above quotes could at least potentially be reinterpreted as overstatements, employed in order to make the point that the process of knowledge acquisition is more complex than implied by traditional positivist methodologies. Let us now consider this possibility. Taken in its more moderate version, postmodernist accounts yield important insights, generally ignored by positivist approaches (or at least the more dogmatic versions of positivism). One such insight is the limitation of positivist methodology itself: Positivism emphasizes the central importance of empirical testing of theories in order to establish their truth or falsity and, hence, to enable scientific progress.[30] Postmodern analyses, in contrast, have demonstrated how *little* positivist approaches tell us about the real world of science. Consider Donald McCloskey's analysis of the economics profession, which demonstrated that the rise and fall of theoretical fixations, such as Keynesianism or monetarism, cannot always be explained according to traditional scientific criteria:

The Keynesian insights were not formulated as statistical propositions until the early 1950s, fifteen years after the bulk of younger economists had become persuaded they were true. By the early 1960s the Keynesian notions of liquidity traps and accelerator models of investment, despite repeated failures in their statistical implementations, were taught to students of economics as matters of scientific routine. Modernist methodology would have stopped all this cold in 1936: Where was the evidence of an objective, controlled, and statistical kind?

Nor was the monetarist counterrevolution a success in fact for modernist methodology . . . it was not modernist certitudes [regarding experimental confirmation of theories] that won the day for the view that money mattered. It was crude experiments and big books, by their crudeness and bigness, not the modernist rituals performed in the professional journals.

The Kennedy tax cut for example, raised their Keynesians to the peak of prestige; the inflation of the 1970s brought them down again, leaving the monetarists as temporary kings of the castle.[31]

McCloskey does not argue that economic doctrine is altogether arbitrary and uninfluenced by empirical facts: The inability of Keynesian thought to account for the inflation of the 1970s was a major factor in bringing discredit on the underlying theory and leading to the fall from popularity of Keynesian theory more generally.[32] However, McCloskey also emphasizes the nonscientific factors, ignored by positivism, that often do influence research. One could easily extend this analysis to the application of rational choice theory in political science, which has achieved immense popularity, despite the relative absence of empirical confirmation for its central predictions.[33] The main point is that positivistic methodologies may be fine and well in principle; however, they tell a very incomplete story of how social science progresses—or degenerates—in the real world, where research is influenced by political biases, social pressures, fads, and other nonscientific considerations.

At a more affirmative level, postmodernist approaches emphasize the way that social conditions and linguistic practices can influence both scholarly research and policy making. Much of the literature in this category furthers our understanding, without lapsing into the nihilistic mode discussed above. McCloskey, for example, has argued that the popularity of invisible hand analogies in economics cannot be separated from the ideological needs and social context of capitalism. Novick elucidated how the social context of the cold war influenced the course of American historiography and compromised its pretense of scientific objectivity.[34] The literature on "postcolonialism" underscores the salience of social construction with regard to conditions of colonialism and imperialism.[35] Similarly, postmodernist writers have placed great emphasis on the importance of language in shaping our understanding of political and social issues: Roxanne Doty has demonstrated the importance of racist language in U.S. counterinsurgency policies in the Philippines; Schneider and Ingram have shown how the language of "deserving" and "undeserving" groups has structured social policy; and Deborah Stone has elucidated how rhetorical presentation can affect public interpretations of political conflict across a broad range of issues.[36] And there is a vast literature, generally postmodern in orientation, that focuses on how gender influences knowledge.[37] Taken as a whole, this literature emphasizes that our understanding of reality must take into account the "standpoint" of the observer and consider the varied ways that individual circumstances, affected by varied social contexts, can slant the acquisition of knowledge.[38] Postmodern epistemology can be interpreted, in sum, as stating that "[a]ll understanding, in art, the human sciences, and the natural sciences is understanding that is contextual and historical, rooted in tradition and prejudice."[39]

Old Wine in New Bottles?

The studies cited above have an important drawback: They tend to ignore the fact that the social construction of knowledge was a very well established feature of social science long before the term *postmodern* was coined. It is difficult to understand what, if anything, is distinctively post-modernist or even new about this idea that social context can influence the acquisition of knowledge. Max Weber, generally considered an expo-nent of the "scientific" study of society, was well aware that research took place in a social context and that this context could and often did influence scholarly agendas. Weber wrote at length on the problem of ideological, political, and ethical biases among researchers, how these factors could influence the way that researchers selected questions for study, how biases could influence the empirical investigations that re-searchers undertook on these questions, and the serious impediments that the whole process posed for the objective social science that Weber favored. Weber readily understood that scientific considerations were not the only influences on research, and he warned against the potentially corrupting effect of external pressures: "The pseudo- 'ethically neutral' prophet who speaks for the dominant interests has, of course, better op-portunities for ascent due to the influence which these have on the politi-cal powers that be. I regard all this as very undesirable."[40] The salience of social context in research is very much a part of Weberian methodology. Similarly, Karl Mannheim, writing during the 1920s, coined the term "the sociology of knowledge" as the study of how social context can in-fluence the production of ideas, and how ideologies tend to be associated with and reflect the interests of specific groups.[41] And we have seen that George Orwell wrote at length about how language can affect human knowledge.

It was probably Karl Marx who first wrote at length on the social con-struction of knowledge, and he did so more than a century before Fou-cault rediscovered the concept. It is of course unfashionable to quote Marx at length at this late date, but no matter:

The ideas of the ruling class are in every epoch the ruling ideas: i.e. the class which is the ruling *material* force of society is at the same time its ruling *intellec-tual* force. The class which has the means of material production at its disposal has control at the same time over the means of mental production, so that thereby, generally speaking, the ideas of those who lack the means of mental pro-duction are subject to it. The ruling ideas are nothing more than the ideal expres-sion of the dominant material relationships, the dominant material relationships grasped as ideas.[42]

Weber, Mannheim, Orwell, and Marx are all generally classed as "mod-ernists," yet they clearly recognized the epistemological significance of social context, as well as the problems posed to scientific social inquiry.[43] It is thus very difficult to see what postmodernism offers with regard to epistemology that is not present in these four modernist writers. True, the above modernists viewed social context primarily in terms of social classes, political parties, or interest groups, whereas the postmodernists focus on gender, race, and sexual preference. The essential point, however—that social context influences the acquisition of knowledge—is not an insight that originated with postmodernism. Claims that postmodernism represents a sharp break with traditional epistemology or that it constitutes a "revolutionary approach to the study of society"[44] seem overwrought, to say the least.

Conclusion

At this point, it is useful to return to the point on which we began this discussion, that is, the question of language. At the outset, I should note that any analysis of postmodernism is rendered problematic, given the very complex language that is used in the genre. This is of course a common objection to postmodernism, recently restated with considerable force by Noam Chomsky:

As for the "deconstruction" that is carried out . . . I can't comment, because most of it seems to me gibberish . . . Since no one has succeeded in showing me what I'm missing, we're left with [this] option: I'm just incapable of understanding. I'm certainly willing to grant that it may be true, though I'm afraid I'll have to remain suspicious, for what seem good reasons. There are lots of things I don't understand—say the latest debates over whether neutrinos have mass or the way that Fermat's last theorem was (apparently) proven recently. But from 50 years in this game, I have learned two things: 1) I can ask friends who work in these areas to explain it to me at a level that I can understand, and they can do so, without particular difficulty; 2) if I'm interested, I can proceed to learn more so that I will come to understand it. Now Derrida, Lacan, Lyotard, Kristeva etc . . . write things that I also don't understand, but (1) and (2) don't hold: no one who says they do understand can explain it to me and I haven't a clue as to how to proceed to overcome my failures. That leaves one of two possibilities: a) some new advance in intellectual life has been made, perhaps some sudden genetic mutation, which has created a form of "theory" that is beyond quantum theory, topology etc in depth and profundity, or b) . . . I won't spell it out.[45]

This is unduly harsh in tone, but it does raise a simple question: Why is postmodern prose so difficult to understand? The fact that Chomsky, who has very extensive interdisciplinary interests and considerable accomplishments, cannot understand this literature must raise some doubts.

I will attempt to offer an explanation for this opacity of style: It reflects an intellectual dilemma faced by postmodernism, one that offers no reasonable prospect of resolution. Postmodernists are caught, in essence, between an untenable nihilism and an equally untenable lack of originality.

Once we remove the obscure verbiage, the technical language, the plays on words, the witticisms, and the other aspects of the packaging that gives postmodernism its distinctive quality, it is very difficult to see anything that is terribly new about the insights regarding the importance of socially constructed knowledge—*unless* one wishes to take them to the nihilistic extremes noted above. It is the tendency to take social construction to the point of absurdity that gives postmodernism its distinctiveness and generates ideas that clearly go beyond the modernist contributions of Weber, Mannheim, et al. If one wishes to argue that human perception of reality is the result of social context and *nothing but the result of social context*, so that the potential for objective analysis is lost completely— then postmodernism has a contribution (of sorts) to make. The problem with this "contribution" is that it renders meaningful research impossible. And if one wishes to moderate the idea and argue that human perception of reality is biased *to some extent* by social context, then we are back to the position advocated by the modernist classics.[46]

Postmodernism is thus faced with an unpleasant set of options: Either accept an absurd and nihilistic position or settle for a reasonable, moderate position that is unoriginal. Often, the result of this dilemma is a form of writing that can charitably be termed confusing. Opaque language enables the postmodernist to obscure the problem and avoid the task of resolving the ambiguity. Without any explicit effort to address this problem, we are left with a postmodernist universe that is caught between nihilism, on the one hand, and unoriginality on the other.

Notes

1. The author thanks Larry George, who, despite fundamental disagreements with my argument, offered some very useful criticisms. I have benefited immensely from our discussions. The essay is the revised version of a paper presented at the annual meeting of the International Studies Association, March 1998, Minneapolis.

2. The recent trend in "constructivist" interpretations, which have some affinities with postmodernism, emphasizes the mutual constitution of subject and object. In light of Orwell's quote above, it is important to note that this is *not* a very original insight. For an overview of constructivism, see Jeffrey Checkel, "The Constructivist Turn in International Relations Theory," *World Politics* 50, no. 2 (1998).

3. George Orwell, "Politics and the English Language," in *A Collection of Essays by George Orwell* (Garden City, NY: Doubleday, 1954), pp. 163, 172.

4. Alan Sokal, "Transgressing the Boundaries: Towards a Transformative Hermeneutics of Quantum Gravity," *Social Text*, nos. 46/47 (1996), available at <www.physics.nyu.edu/faculty/sokal>.

5. Sokal, *Transgressing the Boundaries*, pp. 1, 2. Emphasis added.

6. See Alan Sokal, "A Physicist Experiments with Cultural Studies," *Lingua Franca*, May/June 1996. Available at Sokal website, see n. 4, above. Emphasis in original.

7. See Stanley Fish, "Professor Sokal's Bad Joke," *New York Times*, May 21, 1996; Stanley Aronowitz and Sandra Harding are quoted in Liz McMillen, "Scholars Who Study the Lab Say Their Work Has Been Distorted," *Chronicle of Higher Education*, June 28, 1996.

8. Fish, "Professor Sokal's Bad Joke."

9. Richard Rorty, "Pragmatism, Relativism, and Irrationalism," in *Consequences of Pragmatism* (Minneapolis: University of Minnesota Press, 1982), pp. 166–67.

10. Jacques Derrida, *Of Grammatology* (Baltimore: Johns Hopkins University Press, 1976), pp. 158–59. Note that the first sentence was italicized in the original. The latter italicized phrases in the quotation were all my emphasis.

11. Jacques Derrida, *Spurs: Nietzsche's Styles* (Chicago: University of Chicago Press, 1979), p. 103. Emphasis added.

12. Jean Baudrillard, *The Gulf War Did Not Take Place* (Bloomington: Indiana University Press, 1995), p. 41. Emphasis added.

13. Ibid., p. 27. Emphasis added.

14. Jean Baudrillard, *Simulacra and Simulation* (Ann Arbor: University of Michigan Press, 1994), p. 160. Emphasis added.

15. Murray Edelman, *Constructing the Political Spectacle* (Chicago: University of Chicago Press, 1988), p. 5.

16. Ibid., p. 118.

17. Peter Novick, *That "Noble Dream": The "Objectivity Question" and the American Historical Profession* (Cambridge: Cambridge University Press, 1988), pp. 540, 543. Emphasis added.

18. Frederic Jameson, "Postmodernism, or the Cultural Logic of Late Capitalism," *New Left Review*, no. 146 (1984), p. 87.

19. Ibid., p. 71. Emphasis added.

20. Jean François Lyotard, *The Condition of Postmodernity* (Minneapolis: University of Minnesota Press, 1984), p. 26.

21. Michel Foucault, *The Archaeology of Knowledge* (New York: Pantheon, 1972).

22. Donald J. Puchala, "The Pragmatics of International History," *Mershon International Studies Review* 39 (1995), p. 9n. Emphasis added.

23. Richard K. Ashley and R. B. J. Walker, "Reading Dissidence/Writing the Discipline: Crisis and the Question of Sovereignty in International Studies," *International Studies Quarterly* 34, no. 3 (1990), pp. 378–79. Emphasis added.

24. Terry Eagleton, *The Illusions of Postmodernism* (Oxford: Blackwell, 1996), p. vii.

25. This is true, for example, in a recent postmodernist analysis of the Spanish-American War, by Larry George. George begins by evaluating and then dismissing various economic explanations of the U.S. role in the war, stressing the inadequacy of the theories' positivist assumptions; George argues instead for an explanation that emphasizes the symbolic benefits that the war provided for the American political system and for President William McKinley in particular. The paper offers many sharp insights into the symbolic uses of war. However, I was unable to discern any comprehensible methodology that could be used to establish the validity of George's preferred explanation or its superiority over competing

explanations. See Larry George, "The M(other) of Postmodern Wars: William McKinley, the Spanish-American War, and the Pharmacotic Presidency" (paper presented at the meeting of the International Studies Association, Minneapolis, March 1998).

26. George Orwell, "Looking Back on the Spanish War," in *A Collection of Essays by George Orwell* (Garden City, NY: Doubleday, 1954), p. 204. Emphasis in original.

27. I do not deal here with the obvious point that the relativist position is self-contradictory: If one affirms relativism of thought, then the *antirelativist* position must be considered equally valid. For more on this point, see Paul Boghossian, "What the Sokal Hoax Ought to Teach Us," *Times Literary Supplement*, December 13, 1996.

28. This is even true of Christopher Norris, who is highly critical of postmodernism but nevertheless defends Derrida against charges that he is a relativist. See Christopher Norris, *Reclaiming Truth: Contribution to a Critique of Cultural Relativism* (Durham, NC: Duke University Press, 1996).

29. Pauline Rosenau, *Postmodernism and the Social Sciences* (Princeton, NJ: Princeton University Press, 1992), pp. 82–84, 144–54.

30. For a classic statement on positivist methodology, see Carl G. Hempel, *Philosophy of Natural Science* (Englewood Cliffs, NJ: Prentice-Hall, 1966). It is sometimes unclear whether Hempel is arguing that science *should* proceed according to positivist standards that he advocates or that science *does* in fact achieve these standards in most cases. Postmodernists score points by noting the limitations of positivist accounts, such as Hempel's, in explaining the history of science. At this level the postmodernist critique has considerable merit.

31. Donald N. McCloskey, *The Rhetoric of Economics* (Madison: University of Wisconsin Press, 1985), pp. 17–18.

32. McCloskey may be faulted for failing to elucidate the specific social conditions that led to the rise and fall of Keynesianism. Others have argued that the popularity of Keynesian economics during the three decades following the Great Depression reflected the power of organized labor in the American political process, as well as support from certain segments of the business community. The subsequent decline in the fortunes of Keynesian thought correlates closely with the political decline of labor and a shift in priorities in elite business sectors. See Robert M. Collins, *The Business Response to Keynes, 1929–1964* (New York: Columbia University Press, 1981); and Thomas Ferguson and Joel Rogers, *Right Turn: The Decline of the Democrats and the Future of American Politics* (New York: Hill and Wang, 1986).
The vagaries of Keynesian economics nicely illustrate the salience of social context in scholarly analysis, as well as Mannheim's sociology of knowledge.

33. This is the central argument of Donald P. Green and Ian Shapiro, *Pathologies of Rational Choice Theory: A Critique of Applications in Political Science* (New Haven, CT: Yale University Press, 1994). Note that there is nothing to indicate that Green and Shapiro would accept the postmodernist label; certain of their conclusions do lend support, however, to the postmodern critique of positivism as a guide to understanding purportedly scientific disciplines.

34. McCloskey, *Rhetoric of Economics*, p. 82; Novick, *That "Noble Dream,"* chaps. 10–12.

35. Gayatri Chakravorty Spivak, *The Spivak Reader* (New York: Routledge, 1996). For a useful critique of Spivak and the postcolonial literature

more generally, see Russell Jacoby, "Marginal Returns: The Trouble with Post-colonial Theory," *Lingua Franca*, September/October 1995.

36. Roxanne Doty, "Foreign Policy as Social Construction: A Post-Positivist Analysis of U.S. Counterinsurgency Policy in the Philippines," *International Studies Quarterly* 37 (1993); Ann Schneider and Helen Ingram, "Social Construction of Target Populations: Implications for Politics and Policy," *American Political Science Review* 87, no. 2 (1993); and Deborah A. Stone, *Policy Paradox and Political Reason* (New York: HarperCollins, 1988). I should point out that many of the studies in this category, despite their merit, also tend to lapse into the same nihilism and obscurity that characterizes much of the other literature cited above.

37. See summary in Gregor McLennan, "Feminism, Epistemology, and Post-modernism: Reflections on Current Ambivalence," *Sociology* 29, no. 3 (1995). Regarding epistemological questions in the study of international relations, see the excellent study by V. Spike Peterson, "The Gender of Rhetoric, Reason, and Realism," in Francis A. Beer and Robert Hariman, eds., *Post-Realism: The Rhetorical Turn in International Relations* (East Lansing: Michigan State University Press, 1996).

38. Susan Hekman, *Gender and Knowledge* (Cambridge: Polity Press, 1990), p. 133.

39. Hans-Georg Gadamer, paraphrased in Hekman, *Gender and Knowledge*, p. 14.

40. Max Weber, "The Meaning of 'Ethical Neutrality' in Sociology and Economics," in *The Methodology of the Social Sciences* (New York: Free Press, 1949), p. 9.

41. Karl Mannheim, *Ideology and Utopia* (New York: Harcourt, Brace, and World, 1936). Even Anthony Downs, whose work epitomizes modernist social science, recognized at least some of the limitations to objectivity, due to the corrosive effects of ideological bias: "Ideologies are nearly always viewed partly as means to political power employed by social classes or other groups. . . . No *Weltanschauung* is accepted at face value, because it is seen as tainted with its espousers' desire to gain power." Evidently, Downs too was aware that knowledge is always influenced by social context, at least to some extent. Anthony Downs, *An Economic Theory of Democracy* (New York: Harper and Row, 1957, pp. 96–97).

42. Karl Marx, "The German Ideology," in Robert C. Tucker, ed., *The Marx-Engels Reader* (New York: Norton, 1978), pp. 172–73. Emphasis in original.

43. A recent updating of the social construction perspective (without the inconsistencies of postmodernism) can be found in John S. Dryzek, "The Progress of Political Science," *Journal of Politics* 48, no. 2 (1986); and Howard Zinn, *The Politics of History* (Boston: Beacon Press, 1970).

44. Quoted from the jacket cover of Rosenau, *Postmodernism and the Social Sciences*. Although Rosenau represents a viewpoint that is skeptical of postmodernism, similar claims are routinely advanced by defenders of the approach as well.

45. Noam Chomsky, "On Postmodernism, Theory, Fads, Etc," no date (probably 1996), at <http://199.172.47.21/lbbs/forums/ncpmlong.htm>. I thank John Sonnett for bringing this citation to my attention.

46. This is also true of Thomas Kuhn's (undeniably brilliant) work, which intermittently implies that the selection of paradigms by the scientific community is

based *partly* on how well they resolve previously unexplained anomalies and *partly* on nonscientific considerations such as aesthetics; at other points, Kuhn implies that the selection of paradigms is based *solely* on nonscientific considerations. The latter proposition is an entirely different—and less plausible—argument from the first. Thomas Kuhn, *The Structure of Scientific Revolutions* (Chicago: University of Chicago Press, 1970).

All the same, it cannot be denied that Kuhn's work offers a strikingly original perspective, one that differs from traditional positivist perspectives on the history of science, since it was the first major work to demonstrate that nonscientific factors do play a significant role in the progress of physics. Postmodernist critiques of *social science* methodology, in contrast, are not original, since the salience of nonscientific influences had been recognized by orthodox social scientists long before the age of Derrida.

MARGARET A. McKEAN

Rational Choice Analysis and Area Studies

Enemies or Partners?

TREMENDOUS MISPERCEPTION ABOUNDS about the basic ingredients of rational choice analysis, what it includes, what it implies, and what ideologies follow necessarily rather than coincidentally from its assumptions. The debate that has circulated within my own field of Japanese politics has been a particularly angry one (Johnson, 1997; Keehn and Johnson, 1994). Much of this anger is misplaced, and it exacerbates misunderstandings rather than correcting them. I was asked to write this chapter, explaining the strengths and weaknesses of rational choice theory, because I am both an early user (my reliance on rational choice theory began perhaps two decades ago, a full decade or more before the topic became a matter of angry debate in the social sciences) and a demure one (my publications dealing with rational choice foundations have appeared in comparative work on environmental problems and property rights but not in the Japan field). In this essay I have three objectives:

Editor's note: Margaret A. McKean is a member of the Political Science Department and Nicholas School of the Environment, Duke University. She advances the claim that a mainstay of economic analysis—that people know what they want and try to pursue those preferences—works as the basis of a useful methodology within her own discipline and as an approach to area studies. Her chapter, "Rational Choice Analysis and Area Studies: Enemies or Partners?" makes the case that there is nothing inherent in the methodology of rational choice that promotes the homogenization so feared by practitioners of in-depth area studies. McKean takes pains to assure her readers that the method does not always work, that she recognizes that people do not always behave rationally, that rational choice is not a creature of the political right but covers an ideological spectrum. Above all, she sees the method as a kind of insurance that research on cultures will take on an added dimension of depth.

1. to lay out what rational choice analysis and some of its subdomains and offshoots include;
2. to distinguish rational choice as an analytic paradigm from the full right-to-left range of ideological views, each of which begins with rational choice assumptions but then adds moral values and social norms to arrive at policy positions and comprehensive ideological worldviews; and
3. to build methodically on these distinctions to understand the implications of rational choice analysis for scholars in area studies who seek to understand particular societies.

The ideological views that I describe in the middle section of this essay run the full spectrum from right to left. It may surprise readers who are unfamiliar or uncomfortable with rational choice analysis that the ideological spectrum available to rational choice aficionados extends leftward at all. My purpose in spelling out the components and derivations of rational choice in some detail is to lay a good foundation for a discussion of this ideological spectrum. That will clear the air and enable us to examine the relationship among rational choice as a body of analysis, the ideological spectrum it supports, and the conduct of area studies.

Origins and Development of Rational Choice Analysis

There are *two cardinal assumptions* in rational choice theory, and really only these two:[1]

Individuals have *preferences* (know what they want).

They try to *pursue* those preferences.

This is quite an innocuous pair of assumptions, and the only way to take exception to them is to argue either that individuals do not have preferences (sometimes this is in fact true) or that individuals run away from their preferences rather than trying to pursue them (overt flight from one's preferences is probably rare, but very muddled or clumsy pursuit of them does occur). This pair of assumptions is equivalent to saying that individuals will consider the material and nonmaterial costs and benefits of a course of action in order to decide whether to pursue it. Choosing a course of action whose costs exceed the benefits or that produces less net benefit as the actor himself defines it, rather than some other course of action would be irrational. There are several additional and virtually unavoidable nonnormative derivations from these two assumptions (see chart after page 41).[2]

Rational individuals will not exert effort from which they gain no utility. As it stands, this is simply a matter-of-fact prediction: whatever allows people to capture the gains from their effort will promote effort, and whatever prevents people from capturing the gains from their effort will dampen such effort. The utilitarians, also known as classical liberals and ideological individualists—John Stuart Mill, Jeremy Bentham, and James Mill in particular—made these inferences but also combined them with their normative belief that the good society is one that maximizes the opportunity of individuals to pursue their preferences. Therefore, they articulated the policy proposition that the good society must define, award, and enforce individual property rights; otherwise, society hobbles people with uncertainty, prevents them from investing any effort in pursuing what they might want, and sentences them to dissatisfaction. Thus, the utilitarians went from a pair of matter-of-fact assumptions about human beings, to a vision of normative goals for the good society, to an ideology advocating certain social mechanisms that would, in their view, increase the likelihood that society might actually accomplish these goals. Although their views about property rights only assist individuals toward the pursuit of material utility, the utilitarians were also concerned about nonmaterial utility and actually predicted that most individuals would reach material satiation and become increasingly concerned with the pursuit of nonmaterial utility. Economic growth, which the utilitarians advocated as long as there were poor people with serious material wants in society, would slow down and perhaps even stop, as individuals felt no need to amass further wealth and would begin to spend their spare time on books, music, and conversation. One may still accept the nonnormative derivation articulated here—that rational individuals will not exert effort that gives them no utility—without sharing the ideology of the utilitarians and classical liberals or without regarding this ideology as a sufficient guide to social design.

Although the ancient philosophers usually assumed that individuals had preferences and that individuals pursued them, we usually see Thomas Hobbes as the first architect of rational choice because he dwelt on it at length in order to spell out its implications for social groups. Hobbes was convinced that no one would dare cooperate to generate social peace by refraining from violence, because of each person's utterly justifiable fear that others would not refrain from violence. However, just as with the utilitarians, a modern user of rational choice can accept the objective or nonnormative derivation (that this important problem exists) without agreeing with Hobbes's remedy, requiring that all individuals submit to a dictator! Twentieth-century political economists developed Thomas Hobbes's insight into collective action theory or the theory of public/collective goods, which I describe next.

Not all goods are alike. There are some (both material and nonmaterial, both tangible and abstract) goods that can be consumed rather easily, not only by those who contributed to their production (say, by buying access to them from the producer) but also by persons who did not contribute at all—*it is difficult to exclude noncontributors from consumption of collective goods.* For such goods—both depletable common-pool goods like air quality and nondepletable pure public goods like price stability or the level of nonviolence in society—one can benefit from the amount of the good that others produce without contributing oneself; and one incurs high costs from contributing to the good if others do not also contribute and thereby prevent the good from being produced at all, yielding no benefit for one's effort. Thus, rational individuals will often opt not to contribute to the production of goods they want, and such goods will be chronically underproduced compared to the degree to which people really want them (Buchanan, 1968). This collective goods problem applies to tangible goods, like a clean park, which require the joint effort of many, and also to intangible goods like political mobilization—whether to install or oppose street signals, establish a local labor union, protest corruption, or promote new legislation.

Examples from politics and environmental issues will illustrate this important derivation from rational choice assumptions. Think of workers who want safer working conditions, citizens who all want stricter gun control, or small farmers who would like to reduce their use of pesticides and herbicides. All of these objectives or goods (industrial safety, gun control and reduction of social violence, and environmentally safer methods of pest management) have two important features. First, they cannot be produced by individuals acting alone but are dependent for their production on the action of many of the people who want them *(joint production).* Second, once produced, the benefits will be available not only to persons who did invest in obtaining these goods but also to others who did not invest any time or money in the effort to obtain them *(nonexcludable benefits).* It will take joint protest, possibly unionization and strikes with other workers, to improve working conditions, but those benefits are then available to all the workers there whether they put time into the struggle or not. An individual citizen can keep guns out of her own household but needs similar action by others to reduce the total quantity of guns in the wider environment; and once the total level of guns has dropped, then all are safer even if they made no donations and attended no meetings. A farmer who shifts to organic methods needs neighboring farms to agree to do the same, because otherwise all the pests will simply move to the one farm in the area that is not using pesticides. However, each farm that switches to organic methods not only increases benefit (effectiveness) for the coalition of organic farmers but also helps the conventional farmers who continue to use pesticides, because every organic farm nearby becomes bait and reduces the need for conventional farmers to spend as much on pesticides as before.

If the benefits from joint production were available only to those who contributed (or to buyers willing to pay appropriate sums to those who contributed), then provision of jointly produced goods would be nonproblematic. Those who wanted them would know that they had to join in the effort of provision in order to get the benefits, they would volunteer their effort, and the goods would be produced in precise proportion to the effort that people would willingly invest. However, because the benefits are *non*excludable, there is a temptation, obvious to all at the outset, not to contribute and then to partake free of charge in whatever level of benefits the work of others has managed to produce. Each actor also knows that others may also decide not to contribute and that the benefits will not materialize at all. Someone who is very poor and who stands to gain tremendously if the collective good is actually achieved might be eager to invest if a good outcome could be guaranteed but cannot afford to invest real resources in obtaining benefits that may not materialize at all. For this class of jointly produced nonexcludable (collective) goods, then, individuals can pursue their long-term interest in producing the joint good only if they can trust others to cooperate and invest effort also. If they cannot trust others to contribute, they must then reduce their time horizons to short-term interests. This is the fundamental character of jointly produced or collective goods: the outcome for all depends on the choices of many interdependent individuals and cannot be secured through the actions of a single individual, no matter how devoted or energetic.

The person who opts not to contribute, either in the expectation that he will be able to benefit from the good produced by others anyway, because he anticipates that the good will not be produced and his contribution will simply be wasted, or because he cannot see how his truly infinitesimal contribution will have any overall impact on the outcome is also called a shirker, cheater, or a free-rider. Unfortunately, these labels imply that such people are immoral or antisocial, and that is not the case if there are no social norms or rules promoting cooperation and denouncing shirking in this situation. All too often, free-riders are desperately poor people who simply have no resources to spare and thus cannot take the risk involved in cooperating to produce collective goods, even collective goods that they desperately want. This miserable or tragic outcome, in which people who would like to cooperate to produce a jointly desired and mutually beneficial outcome do not, is called a collective action dilemma. We obviously need to examine a situation thoroughly before making moral judgments about people trapped in collective action dilemmas.

Thus, it is possible to proceed quite matter-of-factly from rational choice assumptions and the observation that some goods are nonexcludable to the collective action dilemma, which if left untreated will paralyze people and prevent them from obtaining the joint goods they actually want. Moreover, the obstacles to collective action are not randomly distributed across populations and groups. We have good reason to believe that small groups of persons who each have relatively large stakes in the outcome are more likely to overcome obstacles to cooperation than are large groups of persons who each have relatively small stakes in the outcome, even if the total amount at stake for the small and the many is far larger than the amount that the large and the few will mobilize to protect. Thus, the deck is stacked: just as groups of employers and owners are more likely to coalesce than groups of workers, so polluting firms will have a mobilizational advantage over pollution victims, political elites over the rank and file, manufacturers over individual consumers who want safe products, leagues of landlords over their many tenants, members of the priesthood over ordinary believers, members of the American Medical Association over the legions of medical patients who might be interested in universal health insurance. The uneven distribution of mobilizational potential comes simply from incentives, so it may compound the effect of uneven distribution of initial assets. This feature of distribution is an inescapable fact; whether one feels it is good or bad lies in the realm of normative judgments that we will discuss below.

The body of work that focuses on the collective consequences of individuals making individual but interdependent choices and especially on solving collective action dilemmas is *collective choice theory*.[3] Although this line of analysis leads to the depressing conclusion that it is difficult to produce collective goods, we also know it happens. We do have labor unions, popular campaigns to change legislation, some level of public peace, government, regulation of hazardous waste, protest movements, public radio, revolutions, and the International Red Cross. So somewhere in the human repertoire exists the ability to generate cooperation and collective goods. Collective choice theorists have taken on the task of figuring out how this happens, almost always out of their own normative commitment to improving our rate of success and enabling people to generate the collective goods they actually want in spite of collective action dilemmas (Buchanan, 1968; Buchanan and Tullock, 1962; Hardin, 1982; Laver, 1981, 1997; Olson, 1965, 1971, 1982; Ostrom, 1990, 1998; Taylor, 1987).

Game theory is a recent development (1940s), a particular formal method of diagramming the interactive choices that rational actors might make when they make individual but interdependent decisions (collective action problems). Game theory was invented by John von Neumann and Oskar Morgenstern (1944), who wanted to study nuclear war without killing anybody. In purely deductive game theory, one posits hypothetical actors, social constructs, and payoffs (quantified, but arbitrarily invented) and then figures out what will happen (see also Kreps, 1990; Luce and Raiffa, 1957; Ordeshook, 1986; Schelling, 1978; Weintraub, 1992). In addition to formal game theory on paper, there is experimental game theory, in which researchers design artificial (fabricated but real) social constructs, add real (small and nonthreatening) payoffs, and insert real actors (usually students or others pulled in off the street) and thus test the predictions drawn from deductive theory. Experimental game theory not only offers real-world confirmation and disconfirmation but builds a foundation of empirical findings from which inductive hypotheses can also be generated and further tested. Nobody imagines that experimental games are realistic or that they are a substitute for studying the real world, but they do provide settings in which particular modifications in the situation can be examined without changing anything else. Studying invented games like Prisoner's Dilemma, Chicken, Assurance, Deadlock, Harmony, and various bargaining games has helped us to identify the key features of particular situations and then to find those situations in the real world. It is often valuable to be able to look at a real bargaining situation, figure out if it resembles one of these archetypical games, and then test predictions about the outcome based on derivations from formal game theory or from experimental results.[4]

The collective action insight leads to another derivation from rational choice assumptions: *methodological individualism*. This is not a normative individualism arguing that, say, individuals' needs and wants are more important than society's needs but stipulates simply that the collective action insight demonstrates to us that we do not understand the behavior of a group until we understand the choices made by the individuals in it (see Tsebelis, 1990, 19–24). Once we understand collective action dilemmas and the importance of methodological individualism, we cannot say that inaction signifies satisfaction or complacence or that the social result a group gets is what its members wanted. We can no longer say that if people really wanted product safety, or independence from Russia, or an expanded court system, or legal protection for traditional small-scale farming, then they would have demanded it and gotten it, so if they don't have it, they didn't really want it very badly. Another crucial inference is the prediction that much group action that we do see is probably based on the preferences of a coordinated core group of interested individuals, possibly overriding the preferences of a much larger but unorganized group of interested individuals who could not overcome their collective action problems and thus remain unmobilized and unrepresented in the group's active leadership. A further inference from both of these findings is that much group action will be described by its proponents as action in the interest of an enormous latent group of deserving persons when in fact the group's action may actually be much more narrowly channeled to serve the (not necessarily identical) interests of the core group that did mobilize and act. These predictions are rich with moral implications that we will address later.

What I have itemized thus far consists of the two basic rational choice assumptions and some elementary (nearly automatic) derivations or inferences from them. Hobbes and Mill, who combined these assumptions with their contrasting normative beliefs about the appropriate goals for society, each built comprehensive prescriptions for the their vision of the good society on the foundation of these assumptions. There are additional nonnormative (empirical) observations that one may derive from rational choice assumptions and the collective action insight that have particular relevance to politics. I next describe some of these, along with ideological destinations on the left-to-right spectrum that can be built on these derivations in conjunction with still other normative beliefs about the goals and priorities that society should have.

Optional Nonnormative Derivations for Those Interested in Politics

The PRINCIPAL-AGENT PROBLEM *arises whenever two individuals have different (real) preferences and one of them is in some formal sense the boss ("principal"), trying to order the other one (the "agent") to do something.* The principal faces limits in her capacity to monitor and coerce or persuade the non-boss ("agent"). Depending on how well the principal persuades the agent to do voluntarily what the principal wants the agent to do (e.g., to create "incentive compatibility" between agent and principal), the agent may possess discretion, or "slack," and do what the agent wants to do rather than what the principal wants the agent to do. Thus, we should not be surprised to find that organizations do not necessarily do what their leaders ask, employees do not necessarily do what their managers hope for, bureaucrats do not necessarily do exactly what their superiors or their elected overseers intended, and so on. When agents do what their principals wanted them to do, either the principal and the agent really had very similar goals or else the principal has reduced agency slack by creating incentive-compatible mechanisms. Whether we see agency slack as good or bad depends on whether we think the right people or group have been put in charge as principals or whether we approve of the formal political structure. Small-*d* democrats in a totalitarian society would root for the agents rather than for the principals and would hope for all the agency slack they could possibly get. The same people, looking instead at a democratic society whose design they endorsed, would want to reduce agency slack in order to get decisions made and implemented the way citizens and their elected representatives wanted them to be.

In government regulation, REGULATORY CAPTURE, *in which the regulated captures the regulator, can arise when the principal has very few resources at her disposal to influence the agent, but the agent who is subject to regulation has vastly more resources than the principal does.* A cozy relationship between regulatory principal and regulated agent can also emerge, in which the regulatory principal gives up on forceful regulation in order to economize on effort, and the regulated agent may also share resources with the regulatory principal (pay bribes) in order to soften and routinize the nature of regulation.

RENT-SEEKING, *or diverting public policy from widely advertised public goals to private ones, can arise because of the principal-agent problem and the possibility of regulatory capture.* Accountability in hierarchies is imperfect even when it may be a normative goal, and it becomes possible for persons and organized groups to use the political process to divert public policy and public moneys toward their own ends. These distortions might be regulatory exemptions that lower costs—certain polluting sources are exempt from inspection, or retailers of a certain size do not need to collect and pay consumer sales tax to the government. They might also be direct transfers of public funds: growers of tobacco and nongrowers of corn receive direct handouts, and installers of active solar equipment receive tax credits equal to their expenses. The result is an effective transfer of wealth either from the general population, if general tax revenues are used, or from a specific subset of the population, perhaps air travelers, milk drinkers, displaced herders, or families with children. This transfer is called *rent,* and the activity that potential beneficiaries undertake through the political process to achieve these transfers is called rent seeking (Buchanan and Tullock, 1962; Krueger, 1974; Rowley, Tollison, and Tullock, 1988; Tullock, 1990). Moreover, the rents received are smaller than the resources taken—that is, the losers lose more than the winners win, and the difference is dissipated, not only a loss for the losers themselves but also a deadweight loss to society as a whole. *Thus, rent seeking causes net economic loss to society; it reduces economic and social efficiency.* Because of the collective action problem, the seekers and receivers of rents are most likely to succeed in transferring benefits toward themselves from an unorganized group that is paralyzed by collective action problems and will therefore not protest the loss.

At this point, we have encountered several objective conclusions about likely developments in society that will sound alarm bells for anyone with certain moral values, not just the classical liberals who hoped that clear property rights would fix everything. Collective action problems and principal-agent problems should alarm all small-*d* democrats who believe that every citizen should have an equal right and chance to participate in important decisions. Rent seeking will bother both those who do not want to see the disadvantaged made even worse off and those who value economic efficiency for society as a whole. We are now ready to lay out the ideological positions that have been adopted by persons concerned about the moral implications of the derivations above.

Ideological Prescriptions That Combine Normative Values with Rational Choice Derivations

Because individuals will not exert effort if they cannot derive utility from their effort, secure and clear property rights are a very good thing if one also believes, with the utilitarians, that society should be built around maximizing the utility of its members. But because of principal-agent problems, regulatory capture, and rent seeking, some people would argue that we cannot trust government to do anything that is desirable for society or for most individuals in it. If we can get government to do anything at all, they think it should be to protect the property rights of individuals and to protect their liberties (freedom to pursue utility) from government intrusion. Government's main job, then, is to protect citizens from itself and each other, and we should leave everything else to the marketplace. Because government cannot be trusted to intervene in markets with good results—the results will consist only of ham-fisted interference that diverts rents to rent seekers and imposes deadweight losses and reductions in social efficiency on society—we should not ask government to intervene at all. This is the reasoning underlying most ideological individualism and right-libertarianism. This ideological view is unconcerned with the production of desirable collective goods. Occasionally proponents of this view display awareness of collective action problems and methodological individualism, citing the difficulties in collective decision making and the orchestration of democratic social choice as reasons for avoiding social decisions altogether and for minimizing government in the extreme. The most right-wing view on this spectrum exhibits little concern for the needs and losses of the ordinary citizen and concentrates instead on preserving the privileges of the elite (which is sometimes a visible agenda item).

But not all persons who follow this line of logic are elitists. Some arrive at economically conservative (pro-market and antigovernment) views because of their concern with the welfare of ordinary citizens. Because of principal-agent problems, regulatory capture, and rent seeking, they conclude that it is virtually impossible for a society to produce collective goods through the political process that really benefit the majority of the members of that society. To prevent this virtually inevitable theft, which because of collective action dilemmas will almost always be a transfer from poor to rich and thus doubly offensive to them, they want to reduce the nonmarket provision of goods by shrinking the size and tasks of government. The collective goods forgone were never available anyway because they would have been converted into private goods for the already privileged. Variants of this reasoning (some more concerned about how the poor pay for these losses, others concerned only that society as a whole suffers from overall losses of efficiency) underlie the antigovernment views of many economic conservatives who do have a democratic concern with the life chances of the poorer segments of society.

The right-libertarians and the more moderate economic conservatives who remain antigovernment and pro-market are confident of the market's ability to produce private goods and highly dubious about government's ability to produce the collective goods that people really want, since these are shams, just private goods for rent seekers in the end. I share some of this skepticism and all of the implied moral concern over economic losses to society as well as additional distress if those losses are paid for by the poorest members of society. Nonetheless, I see profound flaws elsewhere in the logic. First, some of this view's advocates seem to slip into thinking that the market can produce the collective goods that government cannot, because they expect private citizens to mobilize to produce these things—environmental quality, for instance (Anderson and Leal, 1991). Although the collective action problem is part of the reasoning along the way, they dismiss it outright at this stage, and completely overlook the fact that the market does not produce nonexcludable collective goods. They therefore avoid confronting the possibility that society suffers other efficiency losses because of a failure to produce these collective goods. I am particularly concerned about environmental quality as a collective good, where it has been demonstrated to my satisfaction that the unfettered market does *not* produce the amount of environmental quality that citizens want.

The free-market environmentalists talk a great deal about markets, litigation as an enforcement method, and insurance as a market-supplied method of generating environmental quality. They call often upon the Coase theorem (Coase, 1960). This is the very credible deductive proposition that, in a world with zero transactions costs, people will be able to negotiate efficient solutions to externalities (the harm that one citizen does to another) on their own if property rights have been well defined and that converting just one of the possible solutions (say, a particular pollution-reducing technology or a particular level of acceptable emissions) into government policy might well reduce aggregate welfare. But they utterly neglect the second half of Coase's seminal article, in which he acknowledges that transactions costs are not zero in the real world. Moreover, since citizens do not always know that they are suffering harm, let alone who might be causing it, and because the burdens of mobilization and of proof are very heavy, it may actually increase social well-being for government to take the preventive measure of criminalizing outright the acts that generate such harm. The right-libertarians also forget that their scheme relies on some vital collective goods that governments alone can produce: smoothly functioning markets, a legal system large enough for ordinary citizens to have ample access to it, and government enforcement of property rights and contracts to make sure that both the market and insurance mechanisms operate as hoped. There is at least a glaring contradiction in assuming that government can do these things and believing that government can produce no other collective goods properly.

Finally, I think it very important to describe the left end of the ideological spectrum based on rational choice analysis. Because of collective action problems, we know that the poor and the small in any society are going to be systematically underrepresented in all arenas, in both the political process and even in mobilization to exert leverage in the marketplace. Those who find this reality intolerable believe that the most important functions of government (in addition to providing public goods like smoothly functioning markets and social peace) involve redressing this balance. Thus, even at the risk of allowing some degradation in public performance to occur as a result of principal-agent problems, regulatory capture, and rent seeking, this view holds that *we must work to have governments produce (also as public goods) full disclosure about government activities, freedom of information, and protection of all basic civil liberties.* We certainly want governments to provide a legal system and protection of property rights, but what is crucial about these public goods is that they be *widely and impartially offered*, to make sure that the little people also have access to them. In this view, democratic control and oversight, vulnerable as they are to the risk of capture by elites and to collective action problems that reduce citizen vigilance, is the only way one can imagine to have governments that ever, even occasionally, serve the interests of the ordinary citizen. Perhaps governments should provide services like legal aid or even subsidies and tax breaks for nonprofits, to reduce initial mobilization costs for the underrepresented so that they may participate more, not less, in democratic politics. We may even want to adopt certain society-wide policies that transfer income, enhance quality of life, provide environmental protection, and otherwise raise the baseline so that the underprivileged need not mobilize over and over again—to protect their interests and to prevent the diversion of rents to other mobilized groups—over every single issue, since we already know that they cannot and will not mobilize most of the time, even when they want to and need to. This view relies in part on the second and generally ignored half of the Coase theorem: the real world is full of substantial transactions costs. One of the most morally repugnant of such costs is the built-in disadvantage to mobilization faced by the poor and the many, so it is both morally superior and socially more efficient in the long run to prevent harm (externalities) outright in these cases than to let it occur and rely on citizens to mobilize to complain about it afterward. This is the reasoned justification of views of many left-libertarians, whether they are aware of its rational choice foundations or not.

Basically, the right-libertarians and many economic conservatives fear politics enough to give up on it and are willing to sacrifice the production of collective goods and the interests and needs of the underrepresented, since they believe these things are lost anyway. The left-libertarians are aware of the potential for distortion but are willing to use the political process and invest in extra vigilance in order to generate the collective goods that benefit the underrepresented, because they have more faith in the power of their own vigilance to correct rent seeking and improve accountability in politics. The right-libertarians and economic conservatives have tremendous faith in government to produce ordered markets, protection of property rights, and a legal system to enforce contracts, but no faith in government to do anything else. Rational choice provides a foundation that leads all three groups to an identificiation of all of these risks, but it is their normative priors that guide each group to the tradeoffs they prefer. As for me, the right-libertarians strike me as unacceptably indifferent to externalities and the socially desirable qualities of certain very important collective goods (not just environmental quality but also social tranquillity). My normative concerns lead me to hold out the hope that if we can make minimalist governments operate adequately, then we can use the same methods to make governments produce additional public goods that are truly public, reduce the burden of externalities on citizens by preventing the predictable ones before they occur, and

Combining Rational Choice Assumptions with Personal Normative Values to Arrive at Ideological Prescriptions

Assumptions of Rational Choice and their derivations (these assumptions are stipulations about the way the world works whether we like it or not)	*Normative values and priorities* that one may choose to add to basic assumptions about the way the world works (a person's normative values are stipulations about what is good and bad and how people and society ought to work)	*Ideological prescriptions for society* based on a combination of one's normative values with basic assumptions about the world (these ideological packages produce policy prescriptions as methods to achieve one's normative goals, given the way the world works)
Rational Choice assumptions —Individuals have preferences. —Individuals pursue their preferences as best they can.		
Collective Choice derivations from these assumptions —Rational individuals will invest no effort in something from which they can reap no utility; clear and specific property rights will raise levels of individual effort to pursue utility. —Not all goods are alike; individuals who want non-excludable or collective goods will not often risk investing in such goods, which are therefore chronically underprovided; when collective outcomes depend on interdependent individual choice, individuals are not always able to get what they want, and may not even try to get what they want. Game theory is one approach available to study interdependent decisions by multiple individuals. —Any understanding of collective consequences or social decisions must be built on microfoundations (understanding the individual decisions that make up the social decision): methodological individualism.	*Two points on the classical Left-Right spectrum of the enlightenment* War is the most horrible collective bad imaginable. Thus cooperation among individuals to refrain from violence and to produce peace is what society must aim for. But it is very risky for any individual to become the first pacifist—each needs assurance from the others that the others will also refrain from violence. Society should be devoted to helping individuals pursue their utility (material and non-material); individuals should have free choice of the utilities they want to pursue.	*Hobbes' Leviathan:* The only way to produce this social cooperation is for all individuals to bind themselves and each other equally in a covenant with a dictator who has a monopoly of coercive force. Liberty will lead to war and social disintegration. *Utilitarians and Classical Liberals, and Democrats:* Society needs to protect individual liberty in order to give individuals opportunity to pursue their preferences. Society needs to establish property rights that channel material utility toward those who exert effort, to insure that this effort is made (no recommendations on how to channel non-material utility to people, which one hopes they can obtain anyway).

Political implications and applications of collective choice

—Principals want to get agents to obey them, but when agents and principals have different preferences, agents will not want to obey principals; principals will try to reduce agency slack; agents will try to enlarge agency slack.

—Regulatory capture (agents controlling principals, or the regulated capturing their regulators) can occur when agents have more resources/power than principals.

—Rent-seeking occurs when those with an advantage in solving their collective action problems successfully mobilize and divert public goods and moneys to goals and transfers to their group from others; rent-seeking causes net economic loss to society.

Three ideological points on the Left-Right spectrum today

Agency slack, regulatory capture, and rent-seeking are so bad that we cannot ever expect government to do what we want. They are more dangerous threats to liberty and happiness, even for the poor and the many, than any other collective goods we might want to have. Individual liberty has higher priority than any other social goal.

Agency slack, regulatory capture, and rent-seeking are so bad that we cannot expect government to do what we want. Indeed, government action might actually harm the poor and the many even more than the status quo does, which would be worse. Since our hearts bleed slightly, keeping the poor from mobilizing for revolution is a goal to be weighed against individual liberty and minimalist government.

Agency slack, regulatory capture, and rent-seeking are bad, but the disproportional disadvantage in collective action suffered by the poor and the many is worse. Providing collective goods that many people want only as sporadically and intermittently as they manage to mobilize to ask for them is not good enough. Real transaction costs are high, so society should provide these goods routinely.

Right-Libertarians: We must shrink government to the size that we can monitor effectively, limiting it to the task of protecting liberty, protecting property rights, providing a court system for enforcement, and leaving the marketplace as unfettered as possible. If the consequence serves to protect the privileged, and to underproduce collective goods that might benefit the poor and the many, then so be it.

Economic conservatives: We should keep government small and ask it to protect liberty, protect property rights, provide courts for enforcement, and intervene in the market only occasionally to deal with the most egregious market failures. However, when citizens are angry enough to mobilize to demand collective goods, we favor some interventions to serve the interests of the poor and the many.

Left-Libertarians: Government must (1) protect liberty, property rights, smoothly-functioning markets, and courts, just as any classical liberal would insist upon, but also (2) insure that all of these things are widely available and (3) provide collective goods that will help to compensate for the disadvantage in mobilization suffered by the poor and the many. The task of citizens, in turn, is to watch closely and scream loudly and often.

thus give citizens the collective goods they want and deserve to have. Although I recognize as valid virtually every concern and worry of the economic conservatives, I have strong small-d democratic and small-p populist sympathies with the left-libertarian camp. The trade-off I prefer is to try, rather than to give up, on desirable collective goods.

It should now be clear that rational choice does not lead one inexorably to right-wing views or to ideological individualism, and that the full ideological spectrum is available to practitioners of rational choice analysis, who will choose their politics on the basis of their own values and normative priorities, as do people who have no interest in rational choice analysis. Ideological determinism is not one of the faults of rational choice analysis. But there is still a perception among those hostile to rational choice that most of its adherents actually end up as right-wingers. We should not equate a set of innocuous assumptions with a very extreme ideology that is, admittedly, built on those assumptions but relies on much else that is more controversial. I am not familiar with any careful survey of ideological variety among rational choice users so can speak only from my own idiosyncratic experience, but here is my own sense of the distribution:

I would say that economists scatter all over the spectrum from slightly left, to center, to very right, but only perhaps one fourth would really settle on the right-wing and conservative views that I have described here. Many of the others are Keynesians who advocate government intervention for macro-economic management anyway. Many believe that although markets should be present, to do what markets do best, that still leaves a vast region of market failure that requires the attention of governments with the duty to enhance social well-being. Many remember that markets only behave well under the assumption of competition and know that many capitalists would like to eliminate competition if they could, so they believe that it is government's job to be an antitrust crusader. Many believe that big labor is another vital antidote to big capital, although then both big capital and big labor have to be watched closely for possible misbehavior and collusion. Among noneconomists who have adopted rational choice assumptions in order to exploit the collective action insight and do sensitive and careful research on institutions, right-wingers and economic conservatives are a very small minority. Most of us agree with right-wingers that property rights and markets are wonderful inventions, but, that said, we prefer to concentrate on "more important" problems that markets do not take care of. Most, after all, are interested in the collective choice problem because we find its antidemocratic implications very troubling, and we find the right-wing response to it logically flawed and inadequate.

It remains now to examine the weaknesses and the strengths of what rational choice, as defined above, really is and then to explore what role a rational choice analysis with these strengths and weaknesses might play in area studies.

Criticisms of Rational Choice Analysis

Rational choice comes in for many criticisms that are thoroughly undeserved.[5] First, it does not eliminate the possibility that people try to operate on the basis of long-term interests rather than short-term interests. As we have seen, the entire subfield of collective choice theory is devoted to understanding how people can be enabled to pursue their long-term interests. Second, it does not rule out the possibility of cooperative action or trust among individuals. Again, the entire subfield of collective choice theory sees mutual trust as one of the most important collective goods of all and is devoted to learning how people can be enabled to cooperate in the pursuit of joint goals rather than be trapped forever in a suboptimal world. Third, some people seem to think that rational choice requires or dictates the use of mathematical tools and criticize it for this. This is simply baloney. Even game theory, which *can* become quite mathematical, can be explained and successfully used up to a point without mathematics. This criticism is a bit like asserting that all monotheists wear pointy hats and use gold chalices in their services. In fact, some do and most don't. A great deal of wasted antimathematical foaming at the mouth results from this mysterious misunderstanding.

Rational choice can be fairly criticized for assuming that people have clear preference orderings before choosing the behavior they will use to pursue those preferences. Similarly, it can be criticized for overlooking the possibility that people develop and cultivate their preferences through behavior, that they sometimes have to act in the absence of clear preferences. But this simply means that there will be behaviors that rational choice cannot explain. This is only disappointing to those who expected it to have universal applicability to all times, places, and decisions. George Tsebelis (1990, 18–39) and Jon Elster (1989b), major advocates and users of rational choice theory, readily admit that the theory does not explain all behavior and that irrational behavior exists.

Rational choice is often criticized for failing to explain where preferences (values) come from, although this is not something that rational choice claims to do. Rational choice takes over after the preferences exist and says that people will then pursue them. It does not deny that preferences have to come from somewhere and that finding out where they come from is a worthy research goal. Rational choice does assume that preferences are prior to action, so if we ever find situations in which behavior or action causes preferences (e.g., causes someone to develop new preferences), then rational choice clearly does not work in that situation.

Rational choice can be criticized quite justifiably for being mechanically inept at explaining situations where people must choose between conflicting preferences or between packages that combine valued and hated consequences in different ways. We can easily conceive of choice situations so complicated that there is no way to diagram the options in a tidy fashion, let alone to choose among them. The problem here is not the rational choice approach but the fact that the world is a messy and troubled place, a reality that any attempt to analyze decisions must contend with. This constraint, too, is only disappointing to those who wanted rational choice to be an all-purpose tool without limitations. This problem seems to me to be a call for further refinement and development of rational choice, not for abandoning it. I would still rather attempt analysis of decisions than give up entirely.

Rational choice is often criticized for assuming that people spend all kinds of time acquiring costly information about their options, checking *Consumer Reports* before every decision, struggling and agonizing constantly. But Anthony Downs (1957) pointed out "information costs," and Herbert Simon (1982) developed the notion of "bounded rationality," noting that it would be silly (irrational!) to invest more effort in researching a decision than the benefit to be yielded by a decision one way or another on the matter (see also March, 1986). Rationality only involves calculating or collecting information ahead of time when that information is easily acquired. Otherwise, rational people should actually be willing to settle for less than the perfect solution rather than to maximize, even to stumble through a decision rather than exert themselves a great deal to make the "right" decision. Rational choice is often criticized for assuming that people really calculate their options, but this is not necessary: rational choice still holds up as a predictor of behavior if people really do behave *as if* they had calculated. Although Newtonian physics has turned out to be based on incorrect assumptions, it works wonderfully as a predictor of events on the surface of the earth because its incorrect assumptions are indeed excellent surrogates for the more correct and general Einsteinian assumptions in certain situations. It is therefore a shorthand with high predictive power that we use in appropriate conditions. The fact that rational choice may be bad psychology (because people don't examine their payoffs all the time or because people have poor information and conflicting preferences) does not mean it cannot help us understand what's going on, and conversely the fact that it is a powerful predictor where collective action problems are involved does not mean that the persons involved are hypercalculators.

Rational choice is often criticized for being *tautological* in that many rational choice theorists are willing to infer an actor's preferences from the behavior adopted: thus, the preferences lead to the behavior, and the behavior is the indicator of the preferences.[6] This flaw—the fact that practitioners do too often use behavior as the indicator of initial preferences—is the principal pathology that Green and Shapiro (1994) attack,[7] but it is also criticized by Tsebelis (1990), one of rational choice's most vocal defenders. To use the consequence as the indicator of the cause and thus to guarantee a powerful correlation between suspected cause and the consequence is simply bad science, whether one is using rational choice or studying bacteria in petri dishes, and it is the practitioners rather than the theory that should be blamed. There should always be independent indicators for the two things whose relationship we are trying to examine: we therefore need to learn what actors' preferences are from some source other than the behavior they pursue.[8] We might consider asking them, a task best performed by none other than area specialists with language training.

Rational choice analysis is often criticized for assuming that *people are materialistic and greedy or that all of their preferences can be quantified.* It is true, of course that many economists slip quickly into thinking of their actors as materialistic automatons, and there is much work that deserves this criticism. But the faithful user of rational choice assumptions will remember that preferences are exogenous to the model, and actors are entitled to begin with *any* set of preferences to pursue. The honest user of mathematical game theory should be quick to acknowledge that the numerical payoffs in the game matrix are simply heuristic illustrations. This is perhaps the best place to explain that because actors are entitled to any set of preferences or values, rational choice analysis is not supposed to assume that actors are *sane* in the clinical sense or that they have socially respectable preferences or that their values are the same as the researcher's values!

First, we need to remember that what rational actors maximize is utility measured in little imaginary "utils," not material wealth more easily measured in money, so rational actors do not lose their rationality or their self-interest when they pursue nonmaterial utility. Rationality has to do with the behavior adopted in pursuit of preferences and should not be confused with the sanity or social attractiveness of the actor's preferences. Thus, someone we all would agree is insane (hears things, imagines things) is a rational actor if, for instance, he firmly believes that gremlins will reward him with gold doubloons (or free tickets to the movies or internal peace, whatever the person in question values highly as a reward) for making very tall stacks of bottlecaps, and he therefore goes out to collect the necessary bottlecaps. And similarly, someone we all would agree is sane and socially acceptable (never hallucinates, has values we like) can be nonrational: to be able to state clear, intense, and mutually contradictory preferences perhaps and thus to resort to a random selection device like tossing a coin in order to choose a course of action.

Second, the "self-interest" that rational actors pursue has been picked apart to include altruistic values (Monroe, 1996). Thus, it is argued that someone who highly values pleasing others, who receives tremendous emotional rewards from do-gooding, is actually serving his self-interest at the same time he does good for others and is in that sense rational. Giving blood has attracted tremendous attention in this regard. Michael Taylor (1987) has written about *pure* negative altruists (people who get personal rewards from reducing the rewards that others receive) and *pure* positive altruists (people who get personal rewards from raising the rewards that others receive). He has also examined the transformations in games played by people who seek *relative* "superiority," whose secondary rewards grow by increasing the degree to which their primary rewards exceed the primary rewards earned by others. Most of us would define such people as antisocial monsters. He also considers players who seek *relative* "inferiority," whose secondary rewards grow when the primary rewards that others receive exceed the primary rewards they themselves take in. These would be rational ascetics, including Mother Theresa. This infinitely expanding definition of self-interest does come in for criticism, of course. If every goal that people might pursue can be defined as part of their self-interest, then nothing falls outside the realm of self-interest, and nearly all behavior becomes self-interested, by definition. But this effort at expanding what is properly "rational" is not an attempt to rescue an approach but an attempt to incorporate the variety in human beings that is real and thus to make rational choice analysis more useful rather than ridiculously irrelevant. It seems to me that in extending self-interest to include altruistic behavior from which we derive nonmaterial utility, all we lose is a unit of vocabulary—the term *self-interest* ceases to be meaningful. Along the way, we have gained rich specifications for many different conditions that we can then explore. What outcomes emerge from the interplay of negative altruists with positive altruists or of negative altruists with each other? Under what circumstances do people engage in extraordinary acts of heroism and self-sacrifice, throwing themselves on a hand grenade that is about to explode or protecting Jews during the Holocaust? What circumstances embolden people who have cowered in the face of totalitarian controls to take to the streets and go public with their discontent? This leads me now to explore the strengths of rational choice.

Strengths of Rational Choice Analysis

First, we can actually treat the initial assumptions of rational choice as temporary and testable if we like. Rational choice can actually be regarded as a gigantic hypothesis: let's pretend people are rational, see what they do, and see if what they do can be explained without abandoning the assumption of rationality. It is not critical to rational choice that people *are* rational. Rational choice theory is just an experiment to find out how people would behave if they *were* rational, and whether the way people do behave is consistent with the possibility that they are rational. If their behavior remains inexplicable, rational choice theory must be willing to say "not applicable here." Rational choice *does not* assume universal preferences (e.g., everybody wants cars and hamburgers, or even everybody wants material wealth). It does not even assume that everybody wants to satisfy basic human needs for food, shelter, and clothing before they move on to wants less crucial for survival, though I suspect most of us, including opponents of rational choice, really would be willing to make that assumption about 99 percent of the world's population. When we use rational choice assumptions as hypotheses for testing and find that our predictions are disconfirmed, we then have to decide if the flaw was with the rational choice assumptions, with the information we had about the actors' preferences, or with the hypotheses about how such an actor would have to pursue those preferences. Generally speaking, disconfirmation of predictions is an invitation to go back and figure out what we got wrong, and thus it is an opportunity to examine the real world once again with greater care than before. This is a call for more, but directed, "soaking and poking" aimed at the mystery exposed by our initial bad predictions.

Second, for me the truly powerful feature of rational choice analysis is the collective action insight. The fact that real people really do have these problems convinces me that the assumptions are right a lot of the time. The fact that the remedies one can dream up deductively actually turn out to have been employed in real societies is an additional confirmation of the assumptions (see the work on solving collective action problems on natural resources or within the firm by Bromley et al. [1992], McKean [1992b], Miller [1992], and Ostrom [1990]. Finally, the fact that there is no way to develop the collective action insight without using rational choice assumptions is for me the most important selling point of rational choice: a dire problem that people have to face all the time cannot be understood without this foundation. The collective action insight makes great sense out of environmental politics by explaining why we have environmental (and other social) problems and why we fail to correct them. It also provides a theoretical checklist that can be used to examine real situations where people did manage to overcome environmental and other collective action problems. Did they find a way to monitor free-riders? Did they invent additional side payments to reward cooperators and punish noncooperators? What social mechanisms provided the foundations for enforcement and any redistributive mechanisms? What social institutions and values were used to create mutual trust? Since problems of collective choice range across almost all human behavior—joining committees, launching a social movement, deciding whether to clap or stand up after a concert, running a political party, organizing a shrine festival, preserving a dying language, protesting government malfeasance, managing environmental resources—I see vital applications of rational choice analysis and its extensions everywhere. Finally, the normative derivations based on the collective action insight (outlined above), though driven by my normative priors and not rational choice per se, provide powerful personal motivation for my research into these problems as well.

Rational Choice and Area Studies

Another strength of rational choice, in my view, is that rational choice impels one to deeper studies of societies other than one's own. I say this in the face of notorious, widely circulated criticism that devout users of rational choice think they do not need to study anything real since they already "know" the answers—they know what they would find on the ground if they looked, and they know how they would explain it too, so need not bother with either the investigation or the interpretation. Chalmers Johnson (1997) has said that the rational choice approach leads people to think they know what all other people in the world want and leaves no room for ideology or culture. This is simply incorrect. It might be true that extreme ideologues on both right and left alike do this (Johnson actually has right-wing libertarians and economic conservatives in mind), but their ideological bias and intrinsic ethnocentrism are responsible for this, not their rational choice foundations. In fact, we do *not* know what an actor's preferences are and must do some very serious investigating to discover them. People in the same society have different preferences, and presumably the fact that cultures really are different also means that people in different societies will have different profiles of preferences. It is often noted that the material and emotional costs of pursuing a socially disapproved but individually preferred course of action (say, challenging an after-dinner speaker, wearing flashy clothing at the office, or filing a lawsuit against one's neighbor) are much higher for a Japanese than for an American. That is, Japanese are more likely to have a greater preference for social conformity than Americans are. Similarly, Muslims would probably have to be a lot hungrier than Catholics before they become willing to eat pork to fend off starvation. The rational choice approach does not prevent us from seeing this—if anything, it alerts us to look carefully for the material and nonmaterial costs and benefits associated with an action in both settings.

Nor does rational choice theory justify neglect of hypothesis testing and empirical research. The sort of ascientific nonfalsifiable arrogance that Johnson and others attribute to the rational choice approach is available to any user of any research approach. When we see something we do not understand (possible in our own society but quite likely when we study other societies), rational choice theory does not allow us to conclude "Well, those people are just crazy, or stupid, or uninformed." We should never grant legitimacy to a conclusion that simply gives up on the effort to understand with such a condescending dismissal. Rational choice challenges us to try a little harder to grant these people rationality to start with, to look for perverse incentives or systems of rewards and punishments we have heretofore overlooked, and to continue to investigate until the outcome makes sense. In fact, the feature of rational choice that is legitimately labeled universalistic (assuming that all people have preferences and try to pursue them) allows for tremendous variety among people, their values and preferences, and their social institutions, and it is more compatible with cultural relativism than with ethnocentrism.

Indeed, Ostrom (1998) calls for empirical grounding of all theory, particularly rational choice theories of collective action, because they actually predict lower levels of cooperation than real individuals and real groups achieve. The explosion of unstable results in formal predictions when uncertainty is introduced is not replicated in real-life experiments, where outcomes continue to be more stable and closer to optimal. Real people take greater risks to launch conditional cooperation, achieve greater mutual trust, and cement it together with norms of reciprocity more often than the artificial beings in game-theoretic exercises do. Rational choice theory is in this sense a living, evolving theory that can only help us further, insofar as empiricists and thoroughly grounded area specialists test it.

Indeed, in my view the rational choice approach and good area studies work are not incompatible at all but can be a very productive partnership. As I outlined above, the rational choice assumptions will cause the researcher to be troubled when she sees behavioral patterns that look at first glance as if people might not be doing what they "should" want to do. The response, though, should be to look more closely, to draw upon her area studies tools to deepen her knowledge of the values these people have and the institutions they face—their own perceptions of their costs, benefits, opportunities, constraints, and long-term options. To do this well, to do the sensitive and delicate kind of probing to make sure the researcher is really finding out about how these people perceive the world, substantial language training and lengthy intensive fieldwork—no quick flyovers—are obviously necessary. This is why Robert Bates (1996), who is an outspoken fan of rational choice too often misrepresented by his opponents, is also a strong advocate of long language training and extensive "soak-and-poke" fieldwork.

A real-world illustration might show how a rational choice approach can propel greater efforts to understand local society, local needs, and local circumstances. Enter the external observer-researcher, an agronomist who is pretty sure that all people should be interested in increasing food production and perhaps also in increasing cash income. (Dangerous materialistic assumptions, these, though correct in the particular instance I offer below; however, the researcher doesn't stick around long enough to find out what he was right and wrong about!) Our researcher arrives in rural Tanzania and points out to a community of farmers that their crops and local water resources would improve tremendously if they planted trees on the hillside to retain water and retard soil erosion. The farmers nod agreeably but do nothing, and our agronomist concludes that there is something hopelessly wrong with them, or perhaps they just nodded to make him go away but didn't really understand. They're probably just crazy, stupid, trapped in archaic cultural rituals, or doggedly uninformed.

However, a rational-choice area specialist will realize that the farmers' surprising reaction means that the researcher needs to ask more about what the farmers really thought about this proposal. Now our researcher finds out that the farmers are refusing to plant trees in the locations that would help them the most, not out of bullheaded stupidity or a strange fondness for barren landscapes, but because they know that they do not own the hillsides; and if they went through the tremendous effort of planting trees and protecting them through maturity, the local landlord would simply cut the trees for sale as fuel or timber without any regard for those farmers or their years of effort. Indeed, they have ignored several government programs to encourage tree planting already, because they were unsure about how the benefits would be divided and simply assumed, on the basis of past experience, that the government would take the proceeds. Still further study exposes the fact that although they say they would indeed be better off with the trees and a more abundant source of fuelwood and local water, they need water daily and spend much of their time collecting water. Thus, even if they could be sure that the benefits of tree planting could be theirs and would alleviate all sorts of problems they now have and even if the tree seedlings were free, they do not currently have a spare hour out of twenty-four to devote to a new tree project. Without trustworthy rural credit or assistance to get through the waiting period until long-term efforts finally yield benefits, they have to think in the short term. Only someone who spends enough time in this and nearby villages (same tribe and culture but with trees), speaking the local language to people about their needs and options, interpersonal relationships, livelihood strategies, experience with local elites and government, and property rights arrangements, will learn which features of the local context provide the crucial distinctions between our village and more successful ones (Timberlake, 1986, 120–23).

Most good area-studies work, even what is written by people who think they're opposed to rational choice, does not violate rational choice assumptions—the characters are really assumed to be rational, pursuing their goals under constraints. The field of area studies includes some superb research that relies on rational choice foundations, sometimes without the author's realizing it, simply because the author questioned appearances and prevailing explanations and inquired further into individual motivations rather than treating groups as unproblematic wholes. The contribution that implicit or explicit rational choice foundations makes to the findings in these works is to break collectivities down into constituent parts and reveal subgroups with conflicting interests or goals, to highlight particular difficulties or accomplishments in cooperation to overcome collective action dilemmas, or to provide a plausible explanation for a phenomenon that we did not understand before. In the bodies of work I am familiar with, materially based explanations give way to those based on nonmaterial cultural values only in rich societies or groups that simply do not need to worry about material needs.[9] Far more often, we find that nonmaterial cultural values complement or reinforce material values and/or subsistence needs, either of the society as a whole or of a particular group within it.

The best-known dispute over rational choice in Asian area studies is the debate between James Scott (1976) and Samuel Popkin (1979) over whether Southeast Asian farmers are rational actors. Are they driven by communitarian norms, as Scott says, or by individualistic egoism that prevents cooperative effort, as Popkin says? Daniel Little (1989), who uses the definition of rational choice and its correlates described here, concludes that both are really right and that their disagreements vaporize once we incorporate the important advances in the theory of collective action and cooperation that have been published since they wrote. These advances tell us that cooperation is individually rational if you tackle the problem of cheating, it can evolve spontaneously, and it is reinforced when social norms develop to promote it (Axelrod 1984, 1986; Elster 1986, 1989a, 1989b; Hardin, 1982; Ostrom, 1990, 1998; Taylor, 1987). Thus, Scott described communities containing individual egoists who have overcome their collective action dilemmas to reap the net benefits of cooperation and who reinforce this cooperation with communitarian norms, which in turn survive because they serve individuals and community well. In contrast, Popkin described villages that have not solved their collective action problems or have lost this ability due to social and economic changes surrounding the village that offered attractive alternatives to individual villagers. Once cooperation is broken, it is arduous indeed to restore it. In fact, cooperation is more rational than Scott realized and more possible than Popkin realized.

Other works by scholars with area expertise have incorporated rational choice microfoundations in their explanations of community and cooperation. Robert Netting studied mountain communities of Switzerland to learn why they held the alp in common and how they managed it. I (1992a) have examined how Japanese communities cooperated to keep their mountains under forest cover. Robert Wade (1988) studied villages in India to learn why some have robust cooperative arrangements for irrigation and grazing while others do not. Fikret Berkes (1987, 1992) uses repeated participant observation over many years to learn about successes and failures in cooperative resource management in Turkish fishing villages and Canadian Cree fishing and hunting territories. The study of cooperation in managing environmentally pressed natural resources has grown rapidly because it is increasingly a life-and-death matter. Though an interdisciplinary field that includes generalists without area training— the best known being Elinor Ostrom, whose prize-winning work (1990) in this field is as careful as any specialist's would be—it is also heavily populated with area specialists who are well schooled in rational choice microfoundations and collective choice theory.[10]

Since rational choice advocates argue that their approach is essential to understanding collective behavior, it has also played an important part in the work of area specialists who study rebellion and revolution. The rational choice analyst must ask how a rebel movement trying to attract rational citizens to the cause solves its own collective action dilemma. It will presumably have to reduce the risks and increase the benefits for participants so that they do not free-ride on the contributions of others, leading the movement to collapse. In her study of rebellion in China, Elizabeth Perry (1980) noted that successful rebel organizations formed local militias to offer protection against bandits and charged nonmembers of these militias extra fees. In his study of protest in Tokugawa Japan, James White (1995) found that because the regime tended to punish leaders harshly but to go very lightly on the rank-and-file, rebellions in Japan developed a "leaderless" format to reduce risk. Individuals with strong grievances mobilized under an initial leadership, possibly of quirky Robin Hood types; the group grew almost spontaneously because of the mild consequences for large groups; and the leaders then dissolved into safe anonymity. Stephen Vlastos (1986) found that Tokugawa tax policy actually favored local tax revolts by demanding collective payment of taxes from villages. Because the rich members of a village would have to make up for any taxes that the poor could not pay, they readily joined the poor in making a united stand against local tax collectors in petitioning for relief. Obviously, such studies do not resolve all questions about how rebellions begin and continue, but rational choice microfoundations enable us to start.

Area studies specialists who combine rich knowledge of the historical and cultural context with rational choice microfoundations have produced important explanations of social practices that have defied comprehension or elicited confused debate. Bina Agarwal's prize-winning work (1994) analyzes the socially dysfunctional constraints that stymie the best efforts of rural Indian women to provide for themselves and their families and locates the most serious of these in property rights to land. Jean Ensminger (1991) examines the strategies used by rich and poor households among the Galole Orma of Kenya to survive during a period of great economic pressure and resource scarcity, particularly the breakdown of collective action and the decision to shift from nomadic to settled pastoralism. Arun Agrawal (1998) carefully examines why the Raikas of northwest India opt for pastoralism rather than settled agriculture, why they migrate across state and national boundaries rather than limiting their tour to a smaller geographic area, and above all why they engage in this migration collectively rather than in household or extended family units. He learns how their cultural values complement their economic needs, how they select and get rid of community leaders, how they interact with the settled villagers in their communities of origin and along their variable routes, and how caste divisions in the communities they traverse affect their options. Along the way, he defeats the view that the

Raikas are nomads simply because they are culturally conservative or squeezed into this economic niche by other groups.

Finally, sometimes rational choice microfoundations can simply be the launchpad for probing whether a situation that looks like one thing is really the result of something else, a set of individually rational choices that produces an unintended social consequence or a social consequence to which individual choosers are indifferent. Robert Bates's work (1981) on agricultural marketing boards in African states grew out of an effort to ask whether there was any room for rational actors (or plausible preference sets) that could possibly explain why so many African countries were hell-bent on economic decline. He drew upon his thorough grounding in African area studies to question whether the farmers in these countries could really be as stupid or unimaginative, even in response to government and international efforts to encourage them, as plummeting agricultural production would indicate. Instead, he found that politicians' dependence on the support of urban populations who wanted subsidized food caused them to adopt policies so unfavorable to farmers that the farmers increasingly abandoned production for state-owned monopsonies and moved instead toward subsistence production and black market trade. The absolutely devastating and self-perpetuating social consequence was a result of calculated action by politicians and farmers in response to truly perverse incentives.

John Haley (1978), a specialist in Japanese history and law, wondered whether the much-touted Japanese avoidance of the courts was simply a result of long-held cultural aversion for open conflict or was a choice made on other criteria. He found that, just a few decades ago, Japanese people used the courts much more often than they do now. After investigating the material costs of going to court and the likely verdicts handed down then and now, he concluded that Japanese people avoid the courts today because of high material costs (including prohibitive delays) and the expectation of poor outcomes. He believes that the legal system has been refashioned by elites who do not want the inconvenience, cost, or threat of having it used. It is very important to note here that either finding—cultural aversion to conflict or material calculation—would have been consistent with rational choice and that this inquiry was really devoted to exploring whether material or nonmaterial concerns were the larger or more enduring components in individual preferences. The overall social result—low social expenditure on a legal system and legal disputes, protection from the foolish extremes to which legal conflict has taken America, and considerable individual injustice going uncorrected—is not one that Japanese people as a whole have chosen (though they might actually choose it if asked).

Because they have been challenged in recent years by the controversy over rational choice, some area specialists who find this approach useful have decided to test it in the analysis of struggles in which people are highly emotional: language preference and ethnic conflict. David Laitin (1992, 1994, 1998) has done very creative work, drawing upon Schelling's notion of "tipping points," to analyze battles over which language of which ethnic group will be adopted by the larger society and how individuals caught in that struggle choose which language to use and support. James Fearon and David Laitin (1996) together have experimented to see if they could fabricate a game that could explain why some Indian communities with both Hindus and Muslims experience violent conflict and others seem to control it. They hypothesized a situation in which elites of both religious groups agree to punish their own transgressors in order not to start a cycle of mutual retaliation, successfully building a climate of trust and peace. Where elites do not arrive at this pact, the level of violence would, theoretically, escalate. It remains, of course, to see if such pacts actually exist in India's peaceful multiethnic communities. Robert Bates, Rui de Figueiredo Jr., and Barry Weingast (1998) have similarly tried to fabricate a game in which they could understand why an aspiring political leader like Slobodan Milosovic might be able to use hate mongering to recruit followers from a population whose individuals do not actually feel ethnic hatred and thus to foment ethnic suspicion and violence on top of a foundation of high rates of ethnic intermarriage and peace. Again, they were able to hypothesize a situation in which decent, risk-averse people might opt to follow a monstrous leader, but they have not yet compared this game to Milosovic's methods and the choices actually made by individual Serbs. These are only thought experiments, but they force us to question assumptions and causal statements that we might otherwise accept too handily.

Rational choice might appear to be a perspective that would be attractive to generalists seeking universal laws of human behavior, but its universal claims are quite innocuous in assuming only that people have preferences of some kind and try to pursue them. James Fallows once asked me if the rational choice that I explain and defend is any more than common sense, and if that's all it is, why do we need it? My answer was simple: it is only a bit more than common sense, it is innocuous, it is not worth being offended by, it is not worth attacking. But just as we would not want to discard common sense, we would not want to discard rational choice either, and be left with the view that people are irrational utility minimizers. Rational choice also leads to a vital idea that is not easily derived from common sense, and that is the collective action insight.

The additional derivations and inferences that can be developed from this pair of assumptions, without adding any normative components, are quite profound and valuable. Secure and clear property rights reduce uncertainty, extend time horizons, and stimulate effort. These rights need not, by the way, be vested in individuals or in the individuals who have them now, so defending property rights does not amount to defending the status quo or the rights of property-owning elites over others. Individuals have enormous trouble getting what they want when they face collective action problems, and thus groups and societies often fail to produce the collective goods that their citizens or members really want. Sometimes agents have lots of slack that can undermine what principals want to do. Regulatory capture is a perpetual hazard in government regulation. Rent seeking that drains social wealth is a constant curse. But rational choice should *not* be confused with various ideological prescriptions that its users may also hold: ideological individualism, right-libertarianism, economic conservatism, left-libertarianism, or something in between.

For me, then, rational choice is a simple but useful tool that forces me to ask one more round of questions when I think I have begun to understand something and thus leads me to discover variety in cultural values and institutions along with other generalities in the human condition. This book talks about the contrast between researchers who focus on a single society and those who want to find general "laws" that operate in all or most societies. The research described here should put to rest the rather arrogant view that there is a natural division of labor between area studies specialists, as the drones of the scholarly world who should gather empirical data, and the brilliant theoreticians who should analyze the data. With some additional effort and intense collaboration, both specialists and generalists can and probably should do both. Otherwise, the wrong information will be gathered mindlessly by people who don't know what it's for and misused stupidly by people who don't know what it means.

Notes

1. I distinguish here between rational choice and "public choice," which is a narrower offshoot or derivation from rational choice as I use the term. Clinically speaking, public choice is the application of rational choice to politics (and not to the choice of detergent or highway speed). But in fact, many of those who identify their field as public choice also think of individuals as primarily materialistic and narrowly selfish and often end up on the right end of the ideological spectrum to be outlined below.

2. "Normative" beliefs concern norms, or what one believes should be: people ought to be kind to each other, individuals should have freedom to pursue

their own goals, all citizens should be required to perform two years of national service, murder is wrong, adult females should all have facial tattoos to indicate their social status, men should wear head coverings during religious services. Nonnormative or empirical beliefs or views are free of normative content and are assertions about the way the world really works: ants live in the dirt, water runs downhill, murder occasionally happens, automobiles use more fuel than bicycles do, the earth exists inside a large bowl with stars painted on it, all frogs are really princes.

3. By contrast, social choice theory concerns the aggregation of independent choices to produce a collective decision, as opposed to an inadvertent social outcome. See Arrow, 1963.

4. I have encountered the claim that game theory does not require rational choice assumptions, but this is dead wrong. The imaginary actors in game theory are all rational actors trying to maximize their payoffs or avoid minimum payoffs. If we did not require our imaginary game players to be rational (pursuers of their preferences), we would have no way to guess which courses of action they would choose, and game theory would end before it could begin.

5. For a wonderful catalog of criticisms, defenses, and limitations of rational choice theory, see Cook and Levi (1990).

6. Tsebelis (1990) argues that rational choice is actually tautological for another reason: its predictions derive solely from its assumptions and are always as true as the assumptions are, and this is what actually permits falsifiability and generates close inquiry! If what happens in the real world does not match one's rational choice predictions, then something is profoundly wrong about the assumptions one started with, and very close inspection of the real world is necessary before one can start again with better assumptions and the hope of a more accurate prediction. (pp. 42–43).

7. The assault by Green and Shapiro (1994) on rational choice is controversial. When their argument is distilled down to its basic elements, Green and Shapiro praise the desire of rational choice scholars to be systematic but say these scholars have done an inadequate job of testing their predictions in the real world. Thus, their criticisms focus on poor execution (they praise examples by Fiorina and Aldrich where they believe the tests were performed well and yield robust findings), not really on fundamental flaws in the approach. For responses to Green and Shapiro, see the many essays in Friedman (1996).

8. This is not quite as serious a problem when we are doing research over time. That is, if we can't actually ask people what their preferences were but have behavior over time to go from, we can pretend that behavior at time 1 reveals preferences at time 1 and then examine behavior at times 2 and 3. Here we are not assuming what we want to test (we would only be doing that if we then "tested" the relationships between preferences at time 1 and behavior at time 1) but testing the relationship between two separately measurable items: preferences/behavior at time 1 and behavior at *later* times. However, two other problems, multicollinearity and path dependence, remain and plague most inference about causation over time, simply because behavior and events at later times are probably quite constrained by behavior and events at earlier times.

9. Rational choice acknowledges the existence of nonmaterial preferences alongside material preferences and tremendous variety in definitions of material adequacy. Some individuals may, of course, place some moral values above survival itself, though obviously no society can do this collectively and last very long.

But tremendous variety exists among societies in any case. The Jains go to great lengths to avoid harming even insects, and certain Jain monks will eat only fruits and vegetables that have already fallen from the plant. Hutterites, who are well fed, comfortably housed, and sometimes collectively quite wealthy, see no need for personal possession of that wealth or additional material goods, like belt buckles, which lead to vanity. At the other end of the spectrum, some Americans seem to think that their families are materially deprived unless they have a telephone for each hand and a television for each eyeball.

10. For the history of this field and voluminous bibliographic and other references, see the web site of the International Association for the Study of Common Property (IASCP) at <www.indiana.edu/~iascp> and the quarterly newsletter, *Common Property Resource Digest*.

References

Agrawal, Arun. 1998. *Greener Pastures: Politics, Markets, and Community among a Migrant Pastoral People*. Durham, NC: Duke University Press.

Agarwal, Bina. 1994. *A Field of One's Own: Gender and Land Rights in South Asia*. Cambridge: Cambridge University Press, 1994.

Anderson, Terry, and Donald R. Leal. 1991. *Free Market Environmentalism*. Boulder, CO: Westview Press, for the Pacific Research Institute for Public Policy.

Arrow, Kenneth J. 1963. *Social Choice and Individual Values*. New Haven, CT: Yale University Press, 1951, 1963.

Axelrod, Robert. 1984. *The Evolution of Cooperation*. New York: Basic Books.

———. 1986. "An Evolutionary Approach to Norms." *American Political Science Review* 80:4 (December):1095–1111.

Bates, Robert. 1981. *Markets and States in Tropical Africa*. Berkeley: University of California Press.

———. 1996. "Letter from the President: Area Studies and the Discipline." *APSA-CP: Newsletter of the APSA Organized Section in Comparative Politics* 7:1 (Winter).

Bates, Robert H., Rui J. P. De Figueiredo Jr., and Barry R. Weingast. 1998. "The Politics of Interpretation: Rationality, Culture, and Transition." *Politics and Society* 26:2 (June): 221–57.

Berkes, Fikret. 1987. "Common-Property Resource Management and Cree Indian Fisheries in Subarctic Canada." Pp. 66–91 in *The Question of the Commons: The Culture and Ecology of Communal Resources*, ed. Bonnie M. McCay and James M. Acheson. Tucson: University of Arizona.

———. 1992. "Success and Failure in Marine Coastal Fisheries of Turkey." Pp. 161–82 in *Making the Commons Work: Theory, Practice, and Policy*, ed. Daniel Bromley, David Feeny, Margaret A. McKean, Pauline Peters, Jere Gilles, Ronald Oakerson, C. Ford Runge, and James Thomson. San Francisco: Institute of Contemporary Studies.

Bromley, Daniel, David Feeny, Margaret A. McKean, Pauline Peters, Jere Gilles, Ronald Oakerson, C. Ford Runge, and James Thomson, eds. 1992. *Making the Commons Work: Theory, Practice, and Policy*. San Francisco: Institute of Contemporary Studies.

Buchanan, James M. 1968. *The Demand and Supply of Public Goods*. Chicago: Rand McNally.

Buchanan, James M., and Gordon Tullock. 1962. *Calculus of Consent: Logical Foundations of Constitutional Democracy*. (Ann Arbor: University of Michigan Press.

Coase, Ronald. 1960. "The Problem of Social Cost." *Journal of Law and Economics* 3 (October), 1–44.

Cook, Karen, and Margaret Levi, eds. 1990. *The Limits of Rationality*. Chicago: University of Chicago Press.

Downs, Anthony. 1957. *An Economic Theory of Democracy*. New York: Harper.

Duara, Prasenjit. 1988. *Culture, Power, and the State: Rural North China, 1900–1942*. Stanford, CA: Stanford University Press.

Elster, Jon, ed. 1986. *Rational Choice*. Oxford: Basil Blackwell.

———. 1989b. *Solomonic Judgements: Studies in the Limitations of rationality*. Paris: Cambridge University Press.

———. 1989a. *The cement of society: A study of social order*. New York: Cambridge University Press.

Ensminger, Jean. 1991. *Making a Market: The Institutional Transformation of an African Society*. Cambridge: Cambridge University Press.

Fearon, James D., and David D. Laitin. 1996. "Explaining Interethnic Cooperation." *American Political Science Review* 90:4 (December):715–35.

Friedman, Jeffrey, ed. 1996. *The Rational Choice Controversy: Economic Models of Politics Reconsidered*. New Haven, CT: Yale University Press.

Green, Donald P., and Ian Shapiro. 1994. *Pathologies of Rational Choice Theory: A Critique of Applications in Political Science*. (New Haven, CT: Yale University Press.

Haley, John. 1978. "The Myth of the Reluctant Litigant." *Journal of Japanese Studies* 4:2 (Summer), 359–90.

Hardin, Russell. 1982. *Collective Action*. (Baltimore: Johns Hopkins University Press for Resources for the Future.

Hobbes, Thomas. 1651/1962. *Leviathan: On the Matter, Forme, and Power of a Commonwealth Ecclesiasticall and Civil*. New York: Collier Books.

Johnson, Chalmers. 1997. "Preconception vs. Observation, or the Contributions of Rational Choice Theory and Area Studies to Contemporary Political Science," 22 March, posted on Dead Fukuzawa Society listserve.

Keehn, Barry, and Chalmers Johnson. 1994. "A Disaster in the Making: Rational Choice and Asian Studies." *The National Interest* (Summer), 14–22.

Kreps, David M. 1990. *Game Theory and Economic Modelling*. Oxford: Clarendon/Oxford University Press.

Krueger, Anne O. 1974. "The Political Economy of the Rent-Seeking Society." *American Economic Review* 64:3 (June):291–303.

Laitin, David D. 1992. *Language Repertoires and State Construction in Africa*. Cambridge: Cambridge University Press.

———. 1994. "The Tower of Babel as a Coordination Game: Political Linguistics in Ghana." *American Political Science Review* 88:3 (September):622–34.

———. 1998. *Identity in Formation: The Russian-speaking Population in the Near Abroad*. Ithaca, NY: Cornell University Press.

Laver, Michael. 1997. *Private Desires, Political Action*. Beverly Hills, CA: Sage Publications.

———. 1981. *The Politics of Private Desires: The Guide to the Politics of Rational Choice*. New York: Penguin.

Little, Daniel. 1989. *Understanding Peasant China: Case Studies in the Philosophy of Social Science.* New Haven, CT: Yale University Press.

Luce, R. Duncan, and Howard Raiffa. 1957. *Games and Decisions.* New York: Wiley.

March, James G. 1986. "Bounded Rationality, Ambiguity, and the Engineering of Choice." pp. 142–70 in *Rational Choice*, ed Jon Elster. Oxford: Basil Blackwell.

McKean, Margaret. 1992a. "Management of Traditional Common Lands [Iriaichi] in Japan." Pp. 63–98 in *Making the Commons Work: Theory, Practice, and Policy*, ed. Daniel Bromley, David Feeny, Margaret A. McKean, Pauline Peters, Jere Gilles, Ronald Oakerson, C. Ford Runge, and James Thomson. San Francisco: Institute of Contemporary Studies.

———. 1992b. "Success on the Commons: A Comparative Examination of Institutions for Common Property Resource Management." *Journal of Theoretical Politics* 4:3 (July):247–81.

Miller, Gary. 1992. *Managerial Dilemmas: The Political Economy of Hierarchy.* Cambridge: Cambridge University Press.

Monroe, Kristen Renwick. 1996. *The Heart of Altruism: Perception of a Common Humanity.* Princeton, NJ: Princeton University Press.

Olson, Mancur. 1965, 1971. *The Logic of Collective Action: Public Goods and the Theory of Groups.* Cambridge, MA: Harvard University Press.

———. 1982. *The Rise and Decline of Nations: Economic Growth, Stagflation, and Social Rigidities.* New Haven, CT: Yale University Press.

Ordeshook, Peter C. 1986. *Game Theory and Political Theory.* Cambridge: Cambridge University Press.

Ostrom, Elinor. 1990. *Governing the Commons: The Evolution of Institutions for Collective* Action. New York: Cambridge University Press.

———. 1998. "A Behavioral Approach to the Rational Choice Theory of Political Action: Presidential Address, 1997." *American Political Science Review* 92:1, 1–22.

Perry, Elizabeth. 1980. *Rebels and Revolutionaries in North China, 1945–1945.* Stanford, CA: Stanford University Press.

Popkin, Samuel. 1979. *The Rational Peasant: The Political Economy of Rural Society in Vietnam.* Berkeley: Los Angeles, and London: University of California Press.

Rowley, Charles K., Robert D. Tollison, and Gordon Tullock, eds. 1988. *The Political Economy of Rent-Seeking.* Boston: Kluwer Academic Publishers, for the Center for the Study of Public Choice at George Mason University.

Schelling, Thomas C. 1978. *Micromotives and Macrobehavior.* New York: W. W. Norton.

Scott, James C. 1976. *The Moral Economy of the Peasant: Rebellion and Subsistence in Southeast Asia.* New Haven, CT: Yale University Press.

Simon, Herbert 1982. *Models of Bounded Rationality.* Cambridge, MA: MIT Press.

Taylor, Michael. 1987. *The Possibility of Cooperation.* Cambridge: Cambridge University Press.

Timberlake, Lloyd. 1986. *Africa in Crisis: The Causes, the Cures of Environmental Bankruptcy.* Philadelphia: New Society Publishers, for the International Institute for Environment and Development.

Tsebelis, George. 1990. *Nested Games: Rational Choice in Comparative Politics.* Berkeley: University of California Press.

Tullock, Gordon. 1990. "The Costs of Special Privilege." Chapt. 8 in *Perspectives on Positive Political Economy* ed. James E. Alt and Kenneth A. Shepsle. Cambridge: Cambridge University Press.

Vlastos, Stephen. 1986. *Peasant Protests and Uprisings in Tokugawa Japan.* Berkeley: University of California Press.

von Neumann, John, and Oskar Morgenstern. 1944. *Theory of Games and Economic Behavior.* Princeton, NJ: Princeton University Press.

Wade, Robert. 1988. *Village Republics: Economic Conditions for Collective Action in South India.* Cambridge: Cambridge University Press.

Weintraub, E. Roy. 1992. *Toward a History of Game Theory.* Durham, NC: Duke University Press.

White, James W. 1995. *IKKI: Social Conflict and Political Protest in Early Modern Japan.* Ithaca, NY: Cornell University Press.

RAVI ARVIND PALAT

Fragmented Visions

Excavating the Future of Area Studies in a Post-American World

⌒○⌒

> There are many maps of one place, and many histories of one time.
> —Julie Fredrickse, *None but Ourselves*

THOUGH THE INSTITUTIONALIZATION of area studies in professional associations, scholarly journals, and academic programs since the end of the Second World War has had a transformative impact on comparative studies of societies and histories outside the privileged arena of Europe and North America, there has been little, if any, questioning of its conceptual underpinnings and continuing relevance as we stand at

Editor's Note: Ravi Arvind Palat is Associate Professor of Sociology, SUNY Binghamton. His essay, "Fragmented Visions: Excavating the Future of Area Studies in a Post-American World," appeared originally in the journal of the Fernand Braudel Center, *Review* (vol. 19, no. 3 [summer 1996]) and is the only essay in this volume that has been published elsewhere. Palat takes a much stronger stance than do other writers against the segmentation of the globe in the wake of World War II into "area studies" units. He sees the partitioning as "a consequence of the reconstitution of the world market under the leadership of the United States," and he proceeds to roundly condemn the distorting effects of U.S. hegemony on area studies and global scholarship. For Palat, areas should be defined by activity of humans, not by cartographic features. To do otherwise, he argues, "imposes a unity on peoples who were never unified this way before. At the same time, it fractures the unities of pre-existing social relations." Much of Palat's criticism is derived in part from postmodernist perspectives, yet he takes postmodernism to task for ironically reinforcing the concept of "advanced" over "unadvanced" hierarchies. Palat applauds the 1994 decision by the Mellon Foundation to stop funding area studies in favor of themes, such as nationalism and the shaping of national identities. Yet he does not abandon the local entirely. He lauds the "dual insistence on locating phenomena within their historically specific contexts and on the singularity of large-scale, long-term processes of capitalist expansion."

the threshold of the twenty-first century.[1] Even the occasional survey of particular areas of study habitually seeks only to identify topics that are underrepresented in order to target these fields for future growth or to plead for greater resources claiming the actual or potential strategic significance of a particular segment of the globe. The most penetrating of such surveys have merely bemoaned the lack of inclusion of the findings of area specialists in the received canon of disciplinary departments, especially in economics (Johnson, 1988; Amsden, 1992), or the decline in linguistic competence among contemporary practitioners when compared to pioneer scholars (Anderson, 1992). None have questioned or even examined the continuing relevance of the segmentation of the globe enshrined in the various programs of area studies in the context of the enormous sociopolitical and economic changes of the last decade. Moreover, given the geographical focus and disciplinary orientation of most practitioners, it is hardly surprising that the only surveys of the development of area studies as an academic enterprise over the last four decades have been those commissioned by private foundations and the U.S. Departments of Defense and of Education.[2] The very terms of reference of these reports, and their methods of investigation precluded an examination of the intellectual foundations of area studies programs. Hence, apart from making pious declarations on the need for greater global awareness they are silent on the *type* of awareness that is required as we stand at the cusp of the twenty-first century.

If it is true that every piece of knowledge, every work of human creation, is heavily tinged by the conditions of its production, then a refusal to submit the intellectual enterprise represented by the area studies project to the protocols of a rigorous scrutiny is doubly egregious, since its constitution as a field of study was directly related to the rise of the United States to a hegemonic position in the capitalist world economy in the aftermath of the Second World War. Originating in specialized military training programs devised to train soldiers and civilians assigned to administer occupied territories in Europe and the "Far East,"[3] area studies was constituted as a field of inquiry on the U.S. ascension to a position of global hegemony.[4]

Born in the throes of the most widespread and destructive war ever known to this planet, I shall argue, area studies is thoroughly impregnated with the geopolitical conditions of its conception. My concern here is neither with a depiction of the nature of U.S. hegemony nor with a detailed inventory of the evolution of programs of area studies in the last forty-odd years, though I will have occasion to touch on aspects of both these issues. Rather, my focus is on how the geopolitical imperatives of U.S. hegemony conditioned the institutional underpinnings and substantive content of area studies programs. I seek, in particular, to excavate the unexamined intellectual assumptions underlying these programs and to assess their validity.

In this endeavor, the first section of this essay locates the emergence of area studies programs in the context of the bipolar rivalry between the United States and the USSR and the restructuring of the global flows of trade and investments after the Second World War. I argue that these processes involved a shift from colonial control to monopoly control over peripheral raw materials and labor, which was reflected in a new geopolitical segmentation of the globe, and to a consequent redefinition of the units of analyses, institutionalized in universities as area studies programs. Moreover, though these programs were envisaged as multidisciplinary assemblages of scholars to study broad geocultural areas—"to breed a new kind of academic amphibian," as an enthusiastic proponent once put it, "the scholar whose habitat is in one medium but who is fully at home in another" (Gibb, 1963: 14)—the mode of their insertion within universities has meant that despite pretensions to catholicity, area studies scholarship has tended toward microlevel analyses. Hence, though area studies scholarship has considerably increased the pool of empirical information on the peoples of Africa, Asia, Latin America, the Middle East, and the Pacific, it has not contributed to an assimilation of their distinct historical experiences and contemporary realities into our theoretical categories, which continue to remain mired in their narrow Euro–North American referential bases.

The unraveling of the geopolitical ecology of U.S. hegemony—due to an increase in competitive pressures in the core with the reconstruction of the economies of Western Europe and Japan, the exhaustion of import-substituting industrialization policies in most low- and middle-income states, and the structural crises of centrally planned economies—undermined the partitioning of the globe on which area studies programs had been based. Consequently, the second section examines the implications of the continued segregation of programs of area studies from studies of "postindustrial," postmodern economies in an era when material and cultural production have become increasingly globalized. It is argued that, despite the explicit repudiation of post–European Enlightenment rationality by several new academic specializations, area studies continue to perpetuate and reinforce the series of binary oppositions between an essentialized and totalized West and its equally essentialized and totalized other(s).

If the units of analysis in comparative studies are framed by the structures of hegemonic control over peripheral material and human resources—colonial control during the era of British hegemony, monopoly control during U.S. hegemony, transnational control in the contemporary period of capitalist restructuring—the final section suggests that the onset of an era of transnational integration of networks of finance, production, and trade makes a reformulation of our inherited categories of analysis imperative. In particular such a reformulation must seek to integrate the distinctive experiences of non-Western peoples into the conceptual frameworks of the humanities and the social sciences, rather than blithely assume that Euro–North American patterns of capitalist development and state formation will be diffused across the globe. This implies a fundamental excavation of the theoretical categories framing the various disciplines and hence entails the forging and deployment of procedures of conceptualization that are resolutely *antidisciplinary* in orientation.

Despite scattered references to area studies in other parts of the world and to the work of scholars from a variety of 'areas,' the focus of this essay will be on the institutionalization of area studies in universities in the United States. While it is true that the development of area studies elsewhere—particularly in the former European colonial powers—was not identical to the U.S. pattern, a reorganization of the academic universe denoted by the institutionalization of area studies in the hegemonic power has had a profound impact everywhere. This is primarily because, as we shall see, the contemporary partitioning of the globe into several distinct areas was a consequence of the reconstitution of the world market under the leadership of the United States. The acceptance of these divisions as adequate units for analysis, debate, and research has had an inordinate influence on the study of non-Western societies, even in those states with a long tradition of such scholarship. Finally, as the organization of knowledge in Western universities has been replicated in institutions of higher learning elsewhere on the planet, the ethnocentric biases inherent in the basic organizing principles of the Western academy has had and continues to have a pervasive influence.

Imaginative Geographies of U.S. Hegemony

Prophecy now involves a geographical rather than historical projection;
it is space not time that hides consequences from us.
—John Berger, *The Look of Things*

The end of the Second World War marked a radical shift in the global balance of power. The devastation of the industrial economies of Western Europe and Japan had made the United States unquestionably the first industrial power on earth; the occupation of Eastern Europe by the Red Army signaled the rise of the Soviet Union as a world power and foreshadowed the Cold War; the initial Japanese defeat of colonial forces in Asia had stoked fires of national and liberation movements all across Africa and Asia that European colonizing powers were increasingly unable to restrain. These geopolitical conditions, particularly the haunting fiction of the spread of communism on a world scale, provided the substantive and ideological justifications for a reconstitution of the capitalist world market under U.S. hegemony (Wallerstein, 1992).

A key element in the U.S. strategy to reintegrate the world market under its auspices was the restructuring of global flows of trade and investment (see Arrighi, 1982; 1990; 1994; Palat, 1993a, 1996). The exponential increase in the productive capacities and technological capabilities of U.S. industries during the war had created a demand for new sources of minerals and other industrial raw materials. Simultaneously, as peripheral exports of raw materials to the United States grew at a lower rate than their imports of manufactured goods from the hegemonic power, it created inflationary pressures and thereby threatened U.S. industrial expansion. These pressures could only be resolved by expanding U.S. access to peripheral resources at a pace greater than the rate at which markets for its industrial products was growing. However, the acquisition of peripheral resources was constrained by colonial structures of control—restrictions on trade, patterns of land tenure, metropolitan state ownership of mineral rights, control over foreign exchange, regulations on investment, and so on. The United States was successfully able to break down these barriers by threatening to withhold reconstruction assistance to European colonial powers and by manipulating the nationalist aspirations of peripheral states, eager for foreign investment (Bunker and O'Hearn, 1993). In contrast to the era of British hegemony, when core capitalists had sought access to peripheral raw materials through colonial controls, access to these materials was now being increasingly sought through monopoly control—patents, exclusive contracts between resource-rich peripheral states and large, vertically-integrated corporations domiciled in the core. On the other side of the ideological divide, the establishment of Soviet dominance over Eastern Europe led to a parallel, though more spatially circumscribed, reconstitution of relational networks orchestrated by Moscow. The consequent reorientation in the flows of trade and investments remapped the political geography of the world.

The origins of area studies as a field of academic inquiry can be traced to this vast expansion in the scale and scope of the activities of the U.S. state and business corporations and the outbreak of the Cold War.[5] As the acute dearth of expertise on the peoples and institutions of most parts of the world had been made painfully evident during the Second World War, a series of reports commissioned by learned societies to study the wartime programs[6]—most notably the Committee on World Area Research set up by the Social Science Research Council (Hall, 1947) and the Commission on Implications of Armed Services Educational Programs of the American Council of Education (Fenton, 1947)—advocated the creation of multidisciplinary assemblages of scholars specializing in specific geocultural regions to provide accurate information useful to policy makers. Corporate interests were particularly involved in this project, and private foundations were the main underwriters of area studies programs in universities until 1958, when the U.S. federal government, shaken by the Soviet launch of the Sputnik, assumed primary responsibility.[7]

While this project promised to transcend the disciplinary partitioning of knowledge and to provide an integrated and holistic perspective on the peoples and institutions of the world, its integral link with the foreign policy objectives of the hegemonic power and the rise of contract research pervade every aspect of area studies as currently constituted. It infects, violates, and contaminates all area studies scholarship, not only in the social sciences but also in the humanities, not only economics and political science but also the performing arts and philosophy. Most important, U.S. hegemony impresses upon and pervades all area studies scholarship by redefining the units of analysis and then by reifying them. By thus projecting the strategic geopolitical ecology of the immediate postwar period into the past, I shall argue, it distorts our comprehension of long historical processes and inhibits our projections of future possibilities.

Respatializing Comparative Studies

After forty-odd years of area studies scholarship, we are so accustomed to the segmentation of the globe into several regions—Western Europe, Soviet Union (now the Commonwealth of Independent States, Georgia, and the Baltic republics) and Eastern Europe, the Middle East and North Africa, sub-Saharan Africa, South Asia, Southeast Asia, East Asia, Australasia, the Pacific, North America, Latin and Central America, the Caribbean—that we noddingly accept this divisioning of the world as obvious and natural. When few terms appear as self-evident as these, it is instructive to wonder why "East Asia" and "Southeast Asia" are not called "West Pacific" and "Southwest Pacific" (Emmerson, 1984: 4; Issacs, 1980). Once we pose such questions, it immediately becomes obvious that the contemporary designations, for all their apparent normality, are historical constructions, that there is nothing natural or self-evident about the segmentation of the globe on which area studies scholarship is based, that it is not the inert physical features of cartography but the activity of human beings that structure regions as coherent units of analysis (Dirlik, 1992).

The sheer arbitrariness of the geopolitical segmentation of the globe institutionalized by the development of area studies programs can easily be illustrated by a few examples. The term "Southeast Asia," for instance, gained widespread currency only during the Second World War, when Lord Mountbatten's command of the Allied forces in that theater was designated as such in 1943 (Emmerson, 1984: 7). Prior to that time, while it may have been convenient to describe the zone between India and China as Southeast Asia, it seldom occurred to anyone to view the peoples living between Assam and the Philippines and between Indonesia and China—professing a number of different faiths, speaking a multiplicity of languages, and administered by several colonial powers—as inhabiting a cohesive geocultural region. Indeed, the fact that there were no roads or communication links connecting Burma, Thailand, Malaya, the Netherlands East Indies, French Indo-China, or the American Philippines should caution us not to assume that locational proximity necessarily engenders the growth of relational linkages between politico-juridical units. Instead, reflecting colonial control over raw materials and peripheral markets, these territories were linked directly to the colonial metropoles or, in the case of Thailand, to the then hegemonic power, the United Kingdom (Dixon, 1991: 86–121).[8]

Though forged in war, the current demarcation of Southeast Asia as a distinct region was equally shaped by the strategic concerns of the Cold War and the restructuring of the patterns of trade and investment under U.S. hegemony. U.S. plans to stem the tide of communism in Asia were rooted in an attempt to reconstruct Japan as a second-rank economic power. This policy entailed a reorientation of preexisting patterns of trade and investment because a resource-poor Japan could act as a U.S. surrogate only if assured supplies of raw materials, particularly since its earlier sources in Manchuria and North Korea were inaccessible. Thus, using its reconstruction assistance as a leverage against European colonial powers, the United States compelled them to loosen their controls over trade and investment in their remaining colonies in Asia (Cumings, 1987, 61–62).

These strategic imperatives led to the extension of the term "Southeast Asia" to French Indo-China and the Philippines, which were never part of Mountbatten's command. At the same time, the partitioning of the British Indian empire into several independent states gave currency to the term "South Asia," which included Sri Lanka, where Mountbatten's headquarters had been located. These changes are reflected not only in the contemporary demarcation of Southeast Asia as a distinct geocultural zone but also in the change in nomenclature from the "Far East" to "East Asia" and in the subsequent reorganization of the Far Eastern Association as the Association for Asian Studies.

Similarly, the occupation of Eastern Europe by the Red Army and the onset of the Cold War determined the creation of the Soviet Union and Eastern Europe as a region separate from and opposed to Western Europe. It was, after all, this redivisioning of Europe that led to the (perhaps temporary) political obsolescence of the designation "Central Europe." Before this extension of the Soviet "sphere of influence," as Milan Kundera (1981: 230) once remarked, Bohemia, Poland, and Hungary had historically been a part of Western culture and the fount of some of the greatest "impulses" of "modern culture," including "psychoanalysis, dodecaphony, Bartók's music, Kafka's and Musil's new esthetics of the novel." Likewise, the decolonization of Africa and the "Near East" was paralleled by the creation of the "Middle East and North Africa," and "sub-Saharan Africa" as distinct regions. These geopolitical imperatives also led to the demise of "Central Asia" as a cartographical designation. Only the geopolitical partitioning of the Americas, where the Second World War had not been waged, remained unchanged.

This redivisioning of the world represented a significant reorganization in the study of the peoples and institutions of the globe. Prior to the end of the Second World War—with the exception of some investigations in anthropology, comparative philology, and linguistics—comparative studies of non-European peoples tended to be examinations of similarities and contrasts between different colonial structures of control: examining the differences between French and British colonies in Africa, or between the British Indian empire and the Netherlands East Indies, or between the British colonies in Africa and India. Significantly, this tradition of scholarship—traces of which still linger on in journals like the *Journal of Imperial and Commonwealth History*—had little correspondence to the contemporary segmentation of the world because it reflected the colonial control over peripheral resources that was superseded by the geopolitical conditions of U.S. hegemony.

The redefinition of the units of analysis under U.S. hegemony also denoted a major change in the substantive nature of studies on the non-Western world since boundaries exclude as much as they include. As units of analysis determine the framework of research, defining the range of significant relational networks, the arbitrary projection of current regional designations to the past circumscribes the historical imagination and distorts the internal structuring of these areas. It imposes a unity on peoples who were never unified in this way before. At the same time, it fractures the unities of preexisting networks of social relations.

Once we begin to constitute courses on the history of "South Asia" or "Southeast Asia" from the mists of antiquity to the present day, for instance, we begin to posit these entities as enduring realities when they were in fact creations of the post–Second World War era. Relationships falling outside the boundaries of these areas are treated as inessential and inconsequential to the formation and re-formation of their internal structuring. At best, there is an acknowledgment of the transmission of religious beliefs, political institutions, writing systems, and trade across the Bay of Bengal in the first millennium A.D. Even if the importance of such relationships is recognized, the eastern coasts of India figure only in the background, while the Philippines, which had no similar pattern of linkages, is considered an integral part of Southeast Asian history. By what logic is an area which had a formative influence on the peoples and institutions of the eastern Indian Ocean archipelago considered an inessential aspect of its history while another area, which was marginal at best, is considered a constitutive element of the region? Similarly, the separation of "Asian" studies from "Middle Eastern" and "African" studies marginalized the historical and contemporary relationships between the peoples inhabiting these regions.

Triumph of Microperspectives

Even if the areas of study derived from the post–Second World War divisioning of the world are accepted as adequate units of analysis, the enormous diversity of languages within each geocultural zone quickly put to rest any pretensions to comprehensive scholarship. In fact, quite paradoxically, the creation of area studies programs in universities has accentuated the difficulties of acquiring the linguistic competence and research skills necessary to produce in-depth analyses integrating the various disciplinary competencies and synthesizing trends within broad cultural regions by shifting the locus of work away from the areas of study to metropolitan centers of instruction. Bereft of the institutional support that academics now take for granted, it was inevitable that the bulk of scholarly work on the non-Western world prior to the end of the Second World War be produced by colonial bureaucrats and missionaries.[9] These pioneer scholars were able to produce exemplary works in the absence of large libraries, research assistants, and grants, primarily because their lifelong association with particular locales familiarized them with local customs and reflected a mastery of at least the current vernaculars, while their insertion within the colonial enterprise ensured easy access to research materials, native informants, and archival sources (Anderson, 1992: 25–27).

In contrast, the requirement that scholars spend much of their time teaching and publishing has meant that they no longer command either the linguistic competence or the familiarity with indigenous sources that their predecessors once did. After all, a field trip or a year or two at the beginning of their academic careers, collecting material for their dissertations, and the odd sabbatical is no substitute to residing in the area of study for the entire course of their professional careers. The consequences of this are nicely captured by Benedict Anderson's (1992) interesting observation that though sexual relations between area specialists and peoples from their locales of study have persisted, the implications of these relationships have been reversed from those of the colonial era. Thus, "[r]ather than the scholar-bureaucrat being creolized by these relationships, out there in the colony, it is the spouse or significant other, moved to California or Massachusetts who is likely to be Americanized" (28). As a result, though the intellectual project that led to the creation of area studies programs promised integrative scholarship on broad cultural regions, the highly diversified linguistic environment and the institutionalization of area studies programs in universities has produced a rapidly accumulating collection of country-specific studies rather than analyses integrating trends spanning jurisdictional frontiers within geo-cultural regions.

Of course, the trend toward country-specific studies cannot merely be attributed to the institutional structures of metropolitan academies. It was reinforced by the strategies deployed by state bureaucracies and dominant élites in the former European colonies in Africa and Asia to promote national integration.[10] Formal independence inevitably led to a vigorous involvement of the state apparatus in curricular matters, ostensibly to correct the distortions of colonial education but designed as well to assimilate ethnic minorities by obliterating their distinct identities and to obscure the *comprador* role played by indigenous élites in the colonial enterprise. Thus, attempts to create a national culture and a national history inevitably entailed a series of selections, annotations, displacements, and silences to serve the interests of dominant élites.

Yet, in many former European colonies in Africa, Asia, and the Middle East, jurisdictional frontiers provided unviable units of analysis since the arbitrary determination of jurisdictional boundaries by colonial powers split ethnic and linguistic groups between different colonial possessions or between the equally arbitrarily formed internal administrative units within colonies. The familiarity and ready acceptance of jurisdictional entities like "India" and "Nigeria," and their depiction in distinct colors on world maps obscures that their constitution as states involved a violent reorganization of preexisting patternings of social relationships;[11] that maps are, in essence, the very symbols of possession and instruments of plunder (McClintock, 1988: 151). Indeed, the etymological derivation of terms associated with cartography—region, province, field—from the vocabulary of aggression should alert us that mapmaking, far from being an inert politically neutral scientific exercise, is an integral element of colonialism (editors of the journal *Hérodote* in Foucault, 1980: 69; see also Mudimbe, 1988).

A recognition of this fact neither implies that no social systems existed in these spaces before they were incorporated into the capitalist world economy nor that the agencies of capitalism were free to reshape the global map at will. Rather, it is to insist that, while peoples have interacted with one another for millennia, their consciousness of these relationships differed from the nomenclatures that now dominate maps of the world. Indeed, Arthur Whitaker's perceptive observation about the Americas, has equal validity for all areas outside Europe: "The idea that America possessed a unity of any kind . . . was one which, before the arrival of the Europeans had never occurred to anyone in all the agglomeration of atomistic societies that inhabited America from Alaska to the Tierra del Fuego" (quoted in Dirlik, 1992: 64). Moreover, even when the continent was named after Amerigo Vespucci, the set of relational networks we currently associate with the term—Canada being the single largest trading partner of the United States, Central and Latin America being insultingly labeled its "backyard," and even the existence of the states of the Americas as currently constituted—did not exist. The thirteen colonies that were to become the nucleus of the United States were more closely connected to England than to the Pacific coasts on the west, and the colonial possessions of Spain and Portugal were more tightly integrated with the European metropoles than with their northern neighbors. The same can clearly be said about Asia—a term unknown to any indigenous language of that quarter of the globe—and Africa, while the limits of the Pacific were only traced by Europeans and their transplants in the Americas (see Spate, 1979; Dirlik, 1992). Finally, even a cursory glance at historical maps will reveal that the boundaries of the various empires of China fluctuated widely.

The trend toward compartmentalized, micro-level studies rather than country-specific analysis was reinforced by the diversity of source material within multilingual and multiethnic states. These sources ranged from oral traditions and lithic inscriptions to palm-leaf manuscripts and printed texts which were organized by categories, orders of concepts, and discourses rooted in a multiplicity of indigenous systems of knowledge (see Vansina, 1961; Dirks, 1987; Errington, 1989). Since the acquisition of the skills required to recover the cultural contexts that invested specific symbols, classes of events, and particular juxtapositions of episodes with meaning in multilingual, multiethnic states varied widely according to the linguistic and ethnic configurations of each locality, studies were largely of particular localities rather than of the country as a whole—studies of the Punjab or Bengal rather than of India or of Bali or Java rather than of Indonesia. In the absence of a broad theoretical framework synthesizing the various micro-level investigations, these analyses either tended to inappropriately generalize their findings on a state-wide or area-wide scale or to emphasize the unique particularities of their region of expertise to the detriment of a broader comparative framework (Munck, 1993: 481).

In this context, the arbitrary encapsulation of each geocultural area of study as a closed, self-validating arena of research and debate has meant that area studies specialists are largely unaffected by the disputes and theoretical approaches employed by scholars investigating similar themes in other segments of the world, apart from occasional one-off references. This is particularly true of Asian studies scholarship. Though other programs of area studies frequently divide their region of study into smaller segments—"Anglophone" and "Francophone" states in Africa and in the Caribbean, or the "southern cone" and the Andean regions of Latin America, for instance—the marginalization, decimation, and sometimes even the total annihilation of indigenous peoples (particularly in Australasia and the Americas) has meant that records, at least since European contact, are almost exclusively maintained in a handful of metropolitan languages.[12] Similarly, though the Levant and northern Africa have had a long history of contact with the peoples of the northern Mediterranean, the spread of Islam and its universal language, Arabic, as well as the political hegemony long exercised by the Ottoman empire has contributed to create a relatively unified research environment for studies on the Middle East. In all these cases, the relative homogeneity of a linguistic environment for research has promoted a certain degree of genuinely comparative approaches, as witnessed, for instance, by the influence of the *dependencia* tradition or the bureaucratic-authoritarian model in Latin American studies. Whatever errors of archaeology-like misconstructions these paradigms may contain, they have nevertheless stimulated widespread debate and discussion and have left an indelible imprint on country-specific analyses conducted within the rubric of area studies scholarship on these regions.

That no similar paradigm pervades Asian studies scholarship, that it remains a constellation of country-specific and microregional studies isolated in relatively impermeable, compartmentalized bodies of research and debate, is a function of the significant historical differences in the encounters between the peoples of Europe and Asia. Even more than Islam, Asia was constitutively constructed as Europe's "other"—its chief cultural contestant, its exemplar in the arts, sciences, and even in practical craftsmanship. Even after the reversal of the positional superiority between Asian and European states from the mid-eighteenth to the mid-nineteenth centuries, there could be no question of marginalizing, decimating, or exterminating the peoples of Asia. The very magnitude of populations in that cartographic space ensured that the European presence would be confined to a few insertions along the coasts and at administrative seats. These factors entailed a qualitatively different research environment—the diversity of source materials and languages, value systems and artistic styles all contributed to an almost exclusive concentration on country-specific or microregional studies, loosely grouped together by the geopolitical divisions of the post–Second World War era (e.g., China, Japan, Southeast Asia). As a result, they have remained stubbornly resistant to a variety of theoretical approaches that have fundamentally transformed the study of, say, Latin America or sub-Saharan Africa over the last few decades. This is perhaps best illustrated by noting that, though the work of the Subaltern studies group, influential in modern Indian history, shares convergences, similarities, and parallels with the work of scholars investigating "everyday forms of resistance" in Southeast Asia, there has been little or no cross-fertilization of ideas, concepts, and research strategies between the two schools.

Imperialism of Departments

If the diversity of languages, ethnic groups, value systems, and sociohistorical conditions in the broad geocultural divisions of the post–Second World War era frustrated the promise of integrated macro-regional investigations, the institutionalization of area studies programs in universities has also meant that the promise of an integrated, multidisciplinary perspective, a new synthesis of knowledge, on the peoples of the various segments of the globe has remained largely unfulfilled, as William Nelson Fenton foresaw in his prescient 1947 report. Such programs faced fierce resistance from the "imperialism of departments" since they challenged the fragmentation of the human sciences by disciplinary departments, each endowed with a particular methodology and a specific intellectual subject matter (26, 81). Responding to this departmental imperialism, university administrations ensured that most area studies programs had a weak institutional base and that most, if not all, of their faculty depended on disciplinary departments for tenure and promotion. As a result, in contrast to pioneer scholars who ranged freely across several fields of study, most "areaists" (to use Fenton's felicitous term) work within disciplinary boundaries and interdisciplinarity in area studies, which merely denotes the marriage of a modicum of linguistic competence with the policy sciences (Said, 1985: 106–7, 290).

In a sense, the continued fragmentation of knowledge by arbitrary departmental and jurisdictional boundaries admirably suited the interests of the two communities of scholars involved: disciplinary and area studies specialists. This arrangement absolved disciplinary specialists from the responsibility of testing their theories against the experiences of the vast majority of humanity and of familiarizing themselves with the work of their colleagues in cognate academic specialties. Disciplinary specialists also tend to believe that their colleagues in area studies programs are not equipped to provide insights relevant for the nomothetic social sciences as they spend inordinate amounts of time in particularistic investigations which detract them from the study of "theory." This abrupt refusal to attend to the findings of area studies scholarship has thwarted attempts to develop a genuinely comparative approach (Pletsch, 1981: 582–83, 586). Mainstream economists, politicians, and journalists, for instance, routinely ignore detailed investigations of the Japanese, South Korean, and Taiwanese economies, which reveal the central role of the bureaucratic apparatus in their strategies for upward mobility in the global divisioning of labor (e.g., Johnson, 1982; Amsden, 1989; Wade, 1990), and attribute the remarkable rates of growth registered by these states over the last few decades to their firm adherence to laissez-faire policies. Similarly, those who attribute the problems of political integration/fragmentation in contemporary Africa to the tenacious resilience of primordial tribal allegiances ignore the findings of historians that the "tribal concept was in fact an expression of the first stage of amalgamation resulting from colonial rule" (Oliver, 1991: 185).[13]

Conversely, "areaists" faced with the awesome task of learning a difficult language and alien culture were absolved from simultaneously mastering a vast theoretical literature (Hough, 1977:2; Pletsch, 1981: 587).[14] The strong idiographic thrust of these programs is evident in a basic postulate shared by most practitioners: linguistic homogeneity creates an enduring field of analysis, immune to geopolitical and epistemological shifts. Or, as Pierre Ryckmans (1984) was to assert in a hostile response to Edward Said's *Orientalism*:

The sinological field is defined linguistically . . . no specialist, whatever his area of expertise, can expect to contribute significantly to our knowledge of China without first mastering the Chinese literary language. In order to be able to read classical and modern Chinese, it is necessary to undergo a fairly long and demanding training that can seldom be combined with the acquisition and cultivation of another discipline. For this reason, sinology is bound to survive in fact, if not necessarily in name, as one global multidisciplinary humanistic undertaking, solely based upon a specific language prerequisite. (20)

The insularity which flows from such a conceptualization ensures that most areaists are unaffected by the theoretical and epistemological debates being conducted in the disciplines. This is amply evident from another hostile response to Said—this time from David Kopf (1980) who, in accusing Said of "distorting historical reality" and of shirking from "the hard work of discovering and ordering the data of past human experience" goes on to state his own epistemological premise: "that a primary responsibility of the historian is to allow the past to speak for itself" (499). That the premier U.S. journal on Asian studies could even publish a piece based on so anachronistic a premise—one that ignores practically *all* the important theoretical work done in this century, from Marc Bloch and Fernand Braudel to Thomas Kuhn and Michel Foucault—is testimony enough to the wide chasm that separates areaists from their colleagues in the disciplinary departments.

Consequently, despite an exponential increase in information about non-Western peoples, the persistent fragmentation of knowledge into discrete disciplinary tributaries has continued to exoticize the peoples of the various geocultural regions of the globe. The emphatic idiographic nature of area studies programs has permitted a reductionism of the "cultures and civilizations" of the inhabitants of these regions—particularly of Africa, Asia, and the Middle East—to a few simplistic axioms which, with what Said (1985) terms "the restorative citation of antecedent authority" (176), have acquired the status of unquestionable truth. Thus, Confucianism is said to represent the "essence" of Chinese culture; the caste-system, of Indian culture; tribalism, of African culture, and so on. This reductionism, biased toward patriarchy and the élites, has no vocabulary to encompass the vibrant belief systems of women, subordinate social groups, and ethnic minorities. Heterodox challenges to the orthodoxy in each geocultural area are simply dismissed as unruly, discontented, noisy voices, not meriting the attention of metropolitan scholars.

This reductionism of the cultures of non-Western peoples to a few simple axioms was reinforced by the institutionalization of comparative studies of the peoples and institutions of the world in area studies programs, set off against each other in hermetically quarantined politico-jurisdictional and disciplinary compartments. Whereas most disciplinary specialists in America and Europe are acquainted with another metropolitan language besides their own, few among them would know a single non-European language. Additionally, the very frequency of translations back and forth between European languages ensures that even those with a limited command of languages other than their own are at least familiar with the broad patterns of socio-historical conditions in the West. Conversely, though most scholars working in Asia and Africa are comfortable in at least one European language, only a few would know another non-European language besides his or her own; and translations to and from these languages are extremely limited and woefully inadequate (Ahmad, 1992: 97). In the absence of a complex grid of scholarly exchanges—translations, comparative analyses, collaborative research—the enclosed, self-referential character of area studies has reinforced Japanese, Zulu, Islamic, Tamil, and other exceptionalisms rather than produce a unified and coherent body of knowledge about each presumed geocultural macro-region.

In these conditions, comparative historical studies tend to compare and contrast developments in a particular segment or subsegment of the globe with the Western European experience, examining the causes for the periodic withering away of the emerging "sprouts of capitalism" in China (Balazs, 1960; Grove & Esherick, 1980), the "potentialities of capitalistic development in Mughal India" (Habib, 1969), or whether there was an "Indian feudalism" (Mukhia, 1981). All these exercises, implicitly or explicitly accept the Western European pattern of socio-historical transformation as the norm, against which the "Chinese" or "Indian" experiences are cast as deformed, travestied, and imperfect models, failing to evolve autonomously toward the universal goal of capitalist development due to a variety of structural impediments. By generalizing a model of long-term, large-scale social change derived from the particular experience of northwestern Europe, these studies are unable either to perceive the possibility of alternate trajectories of historical transformation or to recover the specific socio-historical dynamics of different historical social systems before capitalism englobed the world. Or, as Francesca Bray (1983) persuasively argues: "[I]if the dynamics of change differ from those we have identified as operating in European history, then it is not surprising that our traditional models fail adequately to interpret change in non-European societies, or even acknowledge its existence" (4). Since reigning procedures of comparative inquiry do not involve an examination of the patterns of socio-historical evolution in different parts of the globe—of social systems in peninsular India and southern China or patterns of urbanization in the "Middle East" and the Indo-Gangetic plain—without reference to the West European experience, they inhibit our comprehension of long-term, large-scale processes of change, both within these antiseptically sealed compartments and in Europe and North America as well.

Perhaps the best indication that the creation of area studies programs has not resulted in a new synthesis of knowledge transcending the partitioning of intellectual labor by disciplinary enclosures, and has not led to a truly holistic and interdisciplinary project,[15] is that, despite four generations of training in area studies, the content of such programs remains embarrassingly fluid. This is most tellingly illustrated in the curricula of area studies programs which have *never* sought to validate, theoretically or methodologically, their field of study—justifications for the creation of new academic programs in area studies or for enhanced funding of existing ones being typically couched in terms of their potential utility for the formulation of policies (see Gourevitch, 1989: 9). Indeed, the very claim to comprehensive study of large geocultural areas inherently precludes the development of a common set of methodological tools or theoretical perspectives. After all, what do students of Sanskrit poetry, fifteenth-century Khmer statecraft, and the impact of economic liberalization in contemporary Guangdong province share in common except an interest in the same cartographic sector of the globe?

Contract Research and the Link with Policy Objectives

Since area studies programs were constituted to provide information on the peoples and institutions of the world useful to corporate managers and political leaders, the overriding importance of the link between scholarship and policy concerns pervades every aspect of area studies as currently constituted. As a result, unlike pioneer scholars, who had primarily been concerned with precolonial history, epigraphy, archaeology, and philology, in keeping with the strategic political and economic interests of the United States, area studies research has been concentrated in the fields of modern history and contemporary political, social, and economic conditions.[16]

The structural dependence of area studies programs on corporate foundations, and increasingly on the U.S. federal government, for funding transformed the study of non-Western peoples in two additional respects. First, the rise of contract research in the social sciences has meant that the level of funding for each segment of the globe is determined by its perceived strategic or potential importance for the United States. Consequently, the distribution of resources between areas of study was allocated unevenly and tended to vary enormously over time, reflecting changing geopolitical imperatives. In the field of Asian studies, for instance, reflecting the Cold War opposition between a "democratic" India and a "communist" China, there was a disproportionate allocation of resources to the study of these two Asian giants in the fifties and sixties. The increasing involvement of the United States in the Vietnam War spurred an equally dramatic rise in the allocation of funds for Southeast Asian studies. However, the U.S. withdrawal from Vietnam and the onset of détente, as well as the sluggish rates of growth registered by the Indian economy, have led to a precipitous decline in resource allocations to these regions. Simultaneously, the economic resurgence of Japan and the "four dragons" (Hong Kong, Singapore, South Korea, and Taiwan) has witnessed an equally disproportionate allocation of resources to the study of states strung along the Pacific perimeters of Asia since the late seventies and early eighties. Similarly, though the implementation of market reforms and the possibility of tapping the enormous markets of the People's Republic of China have ensured continued high levels of funding for Chinese studies, détente and a thawing of the Cold War have resulted in a rapidly falling interest in Sovietology.[17]

The intimate relationship between policy considerations and area studies scholarship has also had a more invidious ideological influence, though an examination of this second characteristic must necessarily remain more speculative, given the impossibility of any one scholar examining the burgeoning corpus of work conducted under the rubric of area studies in its entirety. On the one hand, where large domestic constituencies deeply concerned with the implications of U.S. foreign policy exist, a tradition of scholarship has emerged that is strongly critical of American policy objectives and has sometimes successfully challenged its orientations and the foreign policy establishment's definitions of 'national interest.' Thus, for instance, the civil rights movement and the struggle against apartheid contributed to a radicalization of African studies and to the imposition of sanctions against South Africa, while the increasing presence of migrants and refugees from (and their compelling testimony regarding oppression in) Central and Latin America eventually forced the U.S. government to withdraw support from its client-dictators like Anastasio Somoza and Augusto Pinochet. On the other hand, where no similar constituency exists, a critical tradition of scholarship has rarely emerged. This is true not only of South Asian studies but of studies on the Soviet Union as well. Indeed, as Michael Burawoy (1992) has recently noted, "Western Marxists . . . were often much more critical of state socialism than Sovietologists" (774). Equally significantly, despite the ascendance of Japan as an economic powerhouse, a radical critique of the Japanese state and society is conspicuous only by its absence within mainstream currents of area studies scholarship.

In short, the creation of area studies programs was a reflection of the changed patterning of relational networks caused by the reintegration of the world market under the leadership of the United States in the context of the Cold War. Since the resultant configuration of economic and political linkages was profoundly different from those prevalent during the epoch of British hegemony, area studies programs were envisaged to provide a broad, catholic perspective on the peoples and institutions of the world organized by the segmentation of the post–Second World War globe. However, in the context of a highly diversified linguistic and research environment, rather than the promised integrative analyses of broad geocultural regions, area studies scholarship has produced a rapidly accumulating collection of narrow, localized studies. At the same time, since the institutionalization of these programs in universities did not challenge the disciplinary partitioning of intellectual subject matter, they perpetuated the fragmentation of knowledge within departmental enclosures. Finally, the policy-driven allocation of resources between the different areas of study has meant that serious imbalances in intellectual foci and ideological orientation exist among the various areas of study.

And yet, despite its failure to deliver the promised multidisciplinarity, despite the flawed intellectual assumptions informing it, despite its failure to understand the Euro–North American "other," area studies is not simply a monument of lies. It reflected the very real reorientation of commodity trade, investment flows, and labor migrations forged during the period of U.S. hegemony in the context of the Cold War—the creation of new core-periphery relations in previously incorporated zones of the world, in Pacific-Asia, in southern Africa, in the Soviet Union and Eastern Europe, and in Western Europe.[18] For a hegemonic power with extremely limited prior experiences of relationships with peoples outside its own hemisphere and Europe, the pronounced idiographic thrust of these programs served to cognitively map constellations of local pressure groups, factional alliances and animosities, and cultural sensitivities in strategically important arenas. The importance of this delineation of the diverse patternings of economic arrangements, political institutions, and value systems in the several regions of the planet can hardly be overestimated as they, at least theoretically, enabled policy makers to deploy their resources more optimally by adopting strategies adapted to local conditions to better manipulate peripheral élites, and thereby to further the objectives of the United States in an era of bipolar rivalry.

However, as I shall endeavor to show in the next section, these relational linkages have been rendered anachronistic with the transnational integration of production and the consequent decline in the regulative capacities of states. Additionally, while the abysmal state of education in most colonies (with educational institutions designed primarily to train clerks, apothecaries, and subordinate staff required for the colonial enterprise and their curriculum rarely reflecting social realities within the colonies) provided a certain rationale for area studies as a corrective measure, this has been undermined with the creation of impressive educational infrastructures in many former colonies. The rapid development of an intelligentsia among formerly colonized peoples, as well as their deep immersion in local cultures, their greater familiarity with local languages, and their easier access to source materials, precisely when metropolitan scholars of Africa, Asia, Latin America, and the Middle East are increasingly distanced from their locales of study, has radically transformed the terrain of scholarship. In these conditions, the work of indigenous scholars is often superior to those being produced in metropolitan academies, even if they remain trapped by theoretical categories developed for the study of Euro–North American societies. Consequently, the current segmentation of the globe is increasingly unable to provide an understanding of contemporary conditions and future possibilities, and we may plausibly expect that chairs in area studies will progressively become as anachronistic as chairs in colonial studies and imperial history became after the end of the Second World War.

Conceptualizing a Post-American World

All social sciences suffer from the notion that
to have named something is to have understood it.
—Clifford Geertz

As we have seen, area studies programs derived their legitimacy in large part from the reconstitution of the world market under the Bretton Woods system and the bipolar rivalry between the United States and the Soviet Union. The Bretton Woods system had created a mechanism for the international settlement of the balance of payments while preserving the autonomy of each state to maintain a social policy responsive to its particular needs. At the same time, the installation of a "free enterprise" system enabled large U.S. corporations to expand their operations across national borders to exploit wage and cost differentials within different territorial jurisdictions, particularly in the Americas and Western Europe. The collapse of this system due to the reconstruction of West European and Japanese economies and the consequent diminution of the industrial and financial lead of the United States, the growth of a supranational money market which could not be policed by state-centered regulatory mechanisms, and the increasing prominence of transnational corporations (TNCs), with the growing fragmentation and dispersal of manufacturing operations, has considerably eroded, though not eliminated, the ability of states to set social policy within their jurisdictions.[19] This is evident by the deregulation of economic activities in the core, the "structural adjustments" imposed on severely indebted low- and middle-income states by the International Monetary Fund and the World Bank, and the recent ratification of a wide-ranging agreement on world trade at the conclusion of the Uruguay Round of negotiations. The escalating transnational integration of production in fact required a progressive dismantling of state-centered regulatory mechanisms, since the task of coordinating a vast web of manufacturing and service operations, spread over an increasing number of jurisdictions, made the TNCs extremely vulnerable to political interventions from a variety of actors, ranging from recalcitrant officials to militant trade unions, holding diverse ideologies and responding to a wide array of local pressures (Picciotto, 1990: 38).

On the other side of the ideological divide, the exhaustion of an extensive model of economic growth in the Soviet Union, Eastern Europe, and the People's Republic of China led to an erosion of the hitherto impermeable walls between the two competing ideological blocs. In both cases, given the decline of state-centered regulatory mechanisms, the unique characteristics of particular configurations of socio-historical forces in jurisdictional entities are accorded less significance. This was most visible in the field of Soviet studies, where the numbers of students enrolled in Russian language classes in the United States were almost halved during the seventies and were fewer than those studying Latin![20] While other area studies programs—with the notable exception of South Asian studies—did not suffer declines of similar magnitudes, their rates of growth have slowed dramatically.[21]

Though the bipolar rivalry between the two superpowers postponed a recognition of the emergence of a "new world order" until the collapse of the Berlin Wall in 1989, the increasing transnational integration of global networks of production, trade, and investment by huge conglomerates, facilitated by the exhaustion of import-substituting industrialization strategies in many low- and middle-income states, has led to an increasing homogenization of the conditions of accumulation. In addition, the availability of vast pools of highly trained, relatively cheap, and politically docile labor with the end of "actually existing socialism" in the former Soviet Union, Eastern Europe, and China presents the TNCs with an unprecedented opportunity to expand the scale of their operations. Simultaneously, the implementation of a series of innovations—the automation, computerization, and robotization of production; the lowering of freight costs through containerization; and the development of satellite communications systems—has freed production from resource constraints to such an extent that there is a virtual denial of the validity of alternate patternings of economic arrangements, political institutions, and social relationships—a denial, in short, of the very rationale on which area studies programs were based. Finally, the "footloose" character of contemporary production also implies that areas where the infrastructure has been so devastated that local networks can no longer be reconstituted under the aegis of the TNCs and the coterie of global institutions led by the World Bank—as is the case over large swathes of sub-Saharan Africa, for instance—are being marginalized, simply declared redundant to the processes of capital accumulation and left to sink into chaos as their infrastructures are relentlessly destroyed by internecine warfare.

Old Wine in New Bottles

These fractures in the geopolitical partitioning of the globe on which area studies programs had been based have been accompanied by the creation of new regional designations. Reflecting the high rates of growth registered by economies along the Pacific perimeters of Asia and the eclipse of transatlantic trade by that across the Pacific, the term "Asia-Pacific" is gaining wide currency. The very catholicity of this term and the ease with which we can locate the dynamic economies and plot their complex economic and political relationships on maps endow it with an aura of obviousness. However, its popularity masks a profound redefinition of both "Asia" and the "Pacific": that discussions habitually exclude most of "peasant" Asia (Afghanistan, interior regions of China, India, Myanmar, etc.), as well as Australia, New Zealand, the Pacific islands, and all of Central and Latin America (e.g., Drakakis-Smith, 1992; Borthwick et al., 1992; Gibney, 1992).

Surprisingly, this redrawing of the boundaries of Asia has been fiercely contested, not by states that had previously been included within that designation but by states in Australasia and in Latin America. Denied their preferential access to markets in the United Kingdom since the seventies, Australia and New Zealand have been compelled to shed their identities as European outposts in the South Pacific and pose as the "white tribes" of Asia due to the changed geopolitical ecology of the contemporary world. Similarly, Latin American countries—even Brazil, which fronts the Atlantic—attempting to attract investments from the "miracle" economies of East Asia, are seeking to be included in a "Pacific" region that excludes the islands in its center. Finally, the dissolution of the Soviet Union has prompted calls for the reconstitution of "Central Asia" as a distinct unit of analysis encompassing the breakaway Muslim republics of that once awesome behemoth, particularly since the totalitarian monolithicity ascribed to the former superpower concealed the abysmal ignorance among U.S. scholars and policy makers of a raft of minority nationalities—such as the Abkhazis, Azeris, Chechens, Kirgizis, Ossetians, Tajiks—which are becoming increasingly assertive.

These attempts to reconstitute geopolitical units of analysis in the aftermath of the Cold War on the basis of the area studies paradigm ignore the hallmarks of the current phase of capitalist restructuring. The globalization of the circuits of exchange and investment and the fragmentation of production has undermined the regulatory competencies of nation-states to such an extent that states can no longer be taken as self-evident units of analysis. This is indicated by the progressive shift of macro-economic policy making to interstate negotiations and the consequent diminution in the political influence of domestic factions and alliances in all states. From these optics, any attempt to create new programs of study based on the contemporary spatialization of socio-political and economic relations—as, for instance, on "Asia-Pacific," the European Union, "Central Asia"—would be futile. Linguistic diversity within each of these regional units would once again lead to a proliferation of micro-level studies, while the continued fragmentation of knowledge by disciplinary boundaries ensures that the promise of interdisciplinary studies will remain unfulfilled.

Additionally, in the context of the large-scale diasporic movement of peoples, particularly the tremendous increase of Asian and Hispanic immigrants to the United States after the removal of discriminatory immigration restrictions in 1965,[22] the intellectual segregation of the study of non-Western peoples from the study of ethnic minorities in the West, denoted by the institutional separation of area studies from ethnic studies, fails to provide an adequate understanding of race relations in the core. This bifurcation, as Kristin Ross (1993) notes, tends to promote "a form of American exceptionalism . . . by leading students to conceive of issues like ethnicity, race, or gender, in a merely parochial or local way, as uniquely American experiences" (675) and serves to disempower them by obscuring connections between their conditions of existence and those of peoples elsewhere on the globe. At the same time, the ghettoization of socially disadvantaged minorities in programs of ethnic studies perpetuates their marginalization within the university. Similarly, the cultures of indigenous peoples are conceptually refrigerated as narratives of authenticity, as repositories "for some more genuine or organic lived experience" (Ross, 1993: 673), once again denying them agency and history. In all these cases, the resultant exoticization of non-Western cultures inhibits a study of these experiences as essentially contested, historically contingent processes. Instead, classic texts of the East, such as the *Analects of Confucius* and the *Bhagavad Gita*, are accorded a monumental status that severs them from their historical contexts and reifies them as timeless "truths" about the Chinese and the Indians.

Consequently, the cultural legacies of newer groups of migrants to the United States, especially of Asians, are reified, essentialized, and exoticized. Thus, for instance, Confucianism and the caste system are often caricatured as the irreducible essences of the Chinese and the Indians, respectively, rather than as cultural resolutions of historical processes of change and conflict, including colonialism. Moreover, the reification and exoticization of these cultural legacies tends to accept the weltanschauung of dominant, patriarchal élites and neglects the voices of women, subaltern classes, and ethnic and religious minorities in these states. These considerations are particularly significant as the riots following the verdict in the Rodney King case have made the continued framing of race relations within a Black/White dichotomy patently untenable (see Gooding-Williams, 1993).

While area studies scholars, eddying in self-referential ghettos, seek to constitute new programs of study on "Central Asia," and "Asia-Pacific," the inability of these paradigms to explain emerging socio-political and economic trends is becoming increasingly apparent to corporate sponsors. An early, if striking, indication of their recognition of the untenability of the partitioning of the globe into several antiseptically sealed compartments is provided by the Andrew W. Mellon Foundation's decision in February 1994 to replace its "support for area studies as they are traditionally defined" with seminar programs

on such themes as nationalism and the shaping of national identities, the resurgence of ethnic and religious rivalries, new varieties of democratization, the role of violence in settling—or exacerbating—disagreements, the spread of mass culture and Western economic values as well as countermovements emphasizing tradition, fundamentalism, and desecularization. (Quoted in Heginbotham, 1994: 36–37)

This decision indicates that the insularity of area studies programs renders them unable to analyze the consequences of the globalization of networks of material and cultural production just when such information is vital for the policy makers and corporate managers. Precisely when distances are being reduced on a variety of scales—physical distances through the development of satellite communications, containerized transportation, and long-haul aircraft; cultural distances through the globalization of American mass culture through satellite television broadcasts and the circulation of audio- and videocassettes—the continued acceptance of the post–Second World War geopolitical divisions as autonomous units of analysis precludes the study of the consequences of these phenomena. If the area studies paradigm is increasingly seen to be inadequate to provide politicians and "captains of industry" with the information they require to formulate national policies and investment decisions, can it be any more serviceable for those subject to the punishing rigors of "structural adjustments" imposed by the World Bank or subject to the wave of micro-nationalisms and the resurgence of ethnic conflict?

Globalization, Multipolarity, and the Postmodern Angst

The implications of the changed geopolitical ecology of the contemporary world have been equally ominous for the nomothetic social sciences though their seriousness has been partly camouflaged by the rhetorical triumph of laissez-faire economics and the installation of elected governments in many low- and middle-income states. The failure of enfranchised modes of inquiry to adequately analyze the seismic transformations in the material conditions of life occasioned by the transnationalization of the circuits of capital—including the erosion of state sovereignty, an apparent decline in the salience of social class as a political category, and the rapidly changing configurations of ethnic identity—is evident in the progressive corrosion of disciplinary boundaries, in the creation of a host of new academic specialties which de-center subject positions to highlight the multiple, complex, fluid character of identities, and in the postmodernist "incredulity towards metanarratives" (Lyotard, 1989: xxiv).

Since the pronounced idiographic, self-referential character of area studies programs have largely insulated them from the winds of change sweeping across the disciplinary departments, I will not attempt any detailed dissection of these trends here. Instead, I seek to explore some of the implications of the continued segregation of area studies programs in the context of the broader socio-economic and political changes during the current phase of capitalist restructuring and the epistemic changes they have occasioned in the disciplines.

Reflecting the determining influence of their link to policy objectives and their deeply entrenched insularity from contemporary theoretical and epistemological debates in the humanities and the social sciences, areaists have responded to the challenges posed by geopolitical changes in recent decades by reasserting their unique abilities to understand and interpret the region of their expertise. This instrumentalist advocacy of the utility of their training ignores a considerable body of work and argument that demonstrates the untenability of separating the "knower" from the "known," of "objective" knowledge (see Dutton & Jeffreys, 1993). It is also historically myopic, since those who attribute the economic dynamism of states strung along Asia's Pacific perimeters to their Confucian heritage (Morishima, 1982; Berger & Hsiao, 1988) conveniently forget that, at least until the sixties, this very tradition was castigated for the stagnation of the Qing Empire.

A secondary strand in the response of area specialists to changes in the geopolitical ecology of the contemporary world and the greater diversity and increasing assertiveness of ethnic minorities in the core has been to advocate the inclusion of their voices within the disciplinary curricula. Under the banner of "multiculturalism," this approach to "mainstreaming" the experiences of subaltern classes, women, indigenous peoples, and ethnic and religious minorities typically involves the introduction of texts by non-Western authors and women into the canon. However, since these attempts rarely entail a fundamental questioning of the epistemological status and theoretical categories of the different disciplines, they often tend to perpetuate the exoticization and essentialization of women and the non-Western "other(s)," particularly since the chrestomatic procedures which present *certain* texts and not others as the authentic voices of these diverse constituencies are rarely specified.

In this context, while the impetus toward the constitution of multicultural curriculums stems from the increasing presence of migrants from Africa, Asia, the Caribbean, Latin America, and the Middle East in Europe and North America, the continued isolation of the study of their regions of origin from the conditions of life faced by ethnic minorities in the core forecloses at the very outset the possibility of teaching texts by non-White authors, as well as by "women of color," in a nonexoticized manner. Cultural forms and genres then emerge, not as symbolic resolutions to historically contingent political and social contradictions but as the invariant characteristics of essentialized, exotic cultures: the patriarchal value system as an intrinsic ingredient of the Confucian heritage of East Asians, the hierarchical caste system of the Hindus, the religious fanaticism of the Muslims, and so on.

The idiographic, self-referential character of area studies programs and their continued anchoring in an anachronistic, postitivist epistemology has also had an adverse impact on the humanities and social science disciplines. The fragmentation and widespread dispersal of manufacturing operations by the TNCs, the emergence of major nodes of capitalist accumulation along the Asian perimeters of the Pacific, and the globalization of even the networks of cultural production render analytical categories of the several disciplines increasingly inadequate as they embody the theoretical encapsulation of West European and North American patterns of large-scale social transformation. A widespread recognition of these inadequacies, evident in Jean-Francois Lyotard's "incredulity towards metanarratives," has spawned a variety of new academic specialties and perspectives privileging of local, plural, and heterogeneous identities and interactions over global, monolithic, and homogeneous structures and practices.

However important this recuperation of a politics of location and difference may be from other points of view, as far as comparative studies are concerned, the postmodernist movement has reinforced the watertight separation between a postmodernist West and a modernizing postcolonial non-West (Said, 1989: 222; Anderson, 1992: 34).[23] Thus, despite the differences that otherwise divide them, both Lyotard and Fredric Jameson agree that they seek to investigate the "conditions of knowledge in the most highly developed societies" (Lyotard, 1989: xxiii; Jameson, 1991: x). Similarly, in his magisterial survey of the "condition of postmodernity," David Harvey (1989) pointedly ignores what used to be called the "second" and "third worlds." This segregation of "highly developed societies" from "developing" ones ignores a very considerable body of work stemming from the *dependencia* tradition—if not from Marx, given his well-known account of "primitive accumulation"—in the social sciences, which demonstrates that metropolitan socio-economic structures are so integrally linked to their peripheral opposites that it is impossible to study either one as an internally coherent, bounded whole. Even for those who have a particular antipathy to economic and political analysis, how is it possible to ignore the influence of the projection of racial hierarchies in the United States (particularly the negative depictions of African Americans in films and television programs, the distorted caricature of America as a meritocratic "land of opportunity," and the deliberate silence on the history of oppression and exploitation of Native Americans and other peoples of color, through Hollywood films, videocassettes, and satellite television broadcasts) on the waves of new migrants, as well as their implications for race relations, an influence so pervasive that travelers to remote villages in the Himalayas record children pestering them for tapes of Michael Jackson and Madonna?

The postmodern emphasis on ephemeral, multiple, de-centered identities and subjectivities, in fact, may be taken to reflect the changes in the forms of industrial organization and social life being implemented in the current phase of capitalist restructuring. The transformation of industrial production occasioned by the integration of the most backward forms of industrial organization with most advanced forms of capitalist organization—the integration of patriarchal, family-based sweatshops through extensive subcontracting networks and small-batch, "just-in-time," production processes to large TNCs—has spawned a variety of positions of subordination to capital while cutting the ground from under class-based organizations. In this context the postmodern discursive emphasis on multiple subject positions can be read as a bourgeois metaphor for contemporary industrial relations, that is, as the metaphor of the dominant class rather than the combative metaphor of the dispossessed masses, indeed as "the fetishization of alienation" (Dirlik, 1994b: 111–12).

Viewed in this light, it is striking that the positive revaluation of the Confucian tradition corresponds to the reappearance of family-based sweatshops, both in the newly industrializing regions and in the older industrial heartlands in Western Europe and North America. While the Protestant work ethic was the ideological expression of production relations in an earlier era, the Confucian ethic corresponds more closely to the relations of production in an era when capitalism has transcended its origins in Europe to become "an authentically global abstraction . . . [as] non-European capitalist societies now make their own claims on the history of capitalism" (Dirlik, 1994a: 350). It is hence quite appropriate that the most vocal advocates of Confucianism as a modernizing, developmentalist ideology are mainstream establishment intellectuals in and of East Asia.

To recapitulate, an increase of competitive pressures in the core with the rebuilding of the Japanese and West European economies, the limits imposed on import-substituting industrialization strategies by narrow domestic markets, and the realization of the limits of extensive growth in centrally planned economies all combined to dissolve the post–Second World War geopolitical segmentation of the globe into three worlds. The consequent expansion of the networks of production, exchange, and investment, along with associated changes in the patterns of labor migration have severely undermined the regulatory competence of nation-states. Simultaneously, the collapse of "actually existing socialism" in the Soviet Union and Eastern Europe and the installation of market-oriented reforms in the People's Republic of China have signified the irrelevance of an earlier orthodoxy that stressed the central role of the state in economic affairs. Given the apparently increasing homogeneity of the conditions for investment and production, area studies programs are progressively becoming irrelevant as the Cold War partitioning of the globe rapidly unravels as a consequence of the current phase of capitalist restructuring. The inability of currently enfranchised modes of inquiry to account for the seismic changes in the material conditions of life caused by the current phase of capitalist restructuring has spawned a host of new academic specialties which, despite their explicit claims to challenge the Eurocentricity of dominant conceptions of knowledge, have tended to reinforce and perpetuate the axiomatic distinction between Europe and its others.

Antidisciplinarity as Praxis

Can one divide human reality, as indeed human reality seems to be genuinely divided,
into clearly different cultures, histories, traditions, societies, even races,
and survive the consequences humanly?
—Edward Said, *Orientalism*

If the massive dislocations caused during the "long" nineteenth century by the French and industrial revolutions and the spectacular expansion of the capitalist world economy to englobe the planet led to the current institutional partitioning of knowledge into discrete disciplinary tributaries, the emergence of major nodes of accumulation in Asia and the simultaneity of the globalization of circuits of material and cultural production in the contemporary era with the implosion of a variety of ethnic and religious particularisms call for an equally sweeping reorganization of the academic universe. Put differently, the terminal crisis of area studies programs indicates a far deeper malaise: the fundamental untenability of the nineteenth-century institutionalization of knowledge as non-European societies make their own distinctive contributions to the history of capitalism.

Though there is a widespread acknowledgment of the inadequacy of enfranchised modes of inquiry, manifested by the progressive corrosion of disciplinary boundaries and the postmodern repudiation of post-European Enlightenment rationality, the conceptual and analytical categories forged over the last century have rarely been excavated or challenged. By way of illustration, consider reigning conceptions of economic development. Since the industrial revolution transformed England into the "workshop of the world," industrialization has been so inextricably linked to development that most studies take the form of tracing the rise of urban-industrial complexes in individual states and ranking them by the extent of industrial activities within their jurisdictions. Correspondingly, the growth of an industrial proletariat is charted and conceptually distinguished from the mass of rural workers, often termed "traditional peasants" (cf. Bergquist, 1986; Ward, 1990; Martin, 1994).

The fundamental premise underlying these inquiries is the assumption that the European narrative of capitalist development and state formation will gradually be diffused across the globe, the very modernist assumption that present-day peripheral societies represent the past of core states. Yet, the evidence against this foundational premise of the modern social sciences is compelling. A rapidly accumulating collection of studies has shown that the expansion of capitalism and consolidation of state structures in Europe was predicated on the economic underdevelopment—"the development of underdevelopment" in André Gunder Frank's marvelously adequate phrase—and the unraveling of state structures elsewhere; that much of what are commonly perceived as "traditional" structures in Asia and Africa are, in fact, the results of European expansion and colonial structures of rule rather than pristine survivals from a precapitalist past; that capital accumulation in sixteenth-century northwestern Europe resulted in an intensification of "feudal" ties in Eastern Europe and the creation of slave plantations in the "New World;" that the industrialization of England caused the forced deindustrialization of India in the nineteenth century; that the decolonization and creation of nation-states in nineteenth-century Europe was paralleled by the colonization and violent rupturing of governance structures in Asia and Africa.

The virtual identity between industrialization and development is, however, so tenaciously ingrained in contemporary conceptual frameworks that even the *dependencistas* who forcefully refute the axiomatic distinction between "modern" and "traditional" sectors in a comparative context often recuperate this binary opposition within peripheral societies. Thus, by positing that a de-linking from metropolitan structures of accumulation could lead to the creation of autonomous urban-industrial structures within peripheral areas, they continue to operate within the framework of a "dual economy" thesis that they otherwise reject. However, as feminist scholars have demonstrated, the dichotomous opposition between a "modern industrial proletariat" and a "traditional" sector merely reinforces the gendered biases of "productive" waged work even in the core by divorcing wage labor from the wider social networks of reproduction (Scott, 1988: see also Ward, 1990). If the distinction between "productive," waged work, and "unproductive," unwaged work provided an inadequate understanding of the heartlands of industrial capitalism itself, it is increasingly evident that it produces grotesque caricatures when blithely applied to other regions where substantial populations remain outside the waged sector altogether.

The synonymity between industrialization and development is especially invidious in the current phase of capitalist restructuring as the progressive fragmentation of production into part-processes implies that the benefits that had accrued during earlier historical phases of industrialization no longer accrue to the "newly industrializing" states. The implementation of selective labor recruitment policies—manifested by the femininization of the workforce, particularly in the low-skilled assembly-line processes in a number of industries, ranging from garments and foot-wear to consumer electronics—as well as the pervasive growth of a variety of subcontracting arrangements not only led to a progressive shift of the costs of reproduction to households and to the "subsistence" sector but also transformed the terrain of class struggle. Thus, as Harvey (1989: 153) observes, "struggling against a father or uncle who organizes family labour into a highly disciplined and competitive sweatshop that works to order for multinational capital" is very different from struggling against managers of large, vertically integrated corporations. To put it another way, the transformation of the family into a highly disciplined, low-wage labor force working to order for multinational capital in farms and small subcontracting units

operates against the tendency toward empowerment of workers in advanced sectors of capital and, at the limit, neutralizes the politico-economic consequences that Marx associated with the generalized increase in capital intensity of production and that more recent analysts have associated with large, vertically integrated firms. (Sassen, 1991: 31–32)

Approaching the issue from another angle, studies on proletarianization are dominated by a set of assumptions derived from the European experience, which typically endows the working class with "a (potentially) uniform, homogenized, extrahistorical subjectivity" (Chakrabarty, 1989: 223). Built into this central, "extrahistorical," theoretical category are the cultural legacies of the "free-born Englishman"—"the remembered village rights, of notions of equality before the law, of craft traditions" (Thompson, 1966: 194)—where the worker appears in "dot-like isolation," as Marx (1973: 472) once put it. The mechanical transfer of the set of expectations that flow from this extrahistorical conceptualization of the working class to places marked by inegalitarian, hierarchical structures of power and community, as in the case of India, where identities based on language, religion, and place of origin habitually override class solidarities, has been shown to be seriously flawed (Chakrabarty, 1989). Similarly, in the case of South Korea, though there was an extraordinary degree of ethnic homogeneity, a mere application of a dehistoricized notion of a working class has proved to be grossly inadequate, since there was an absence of the artisanal traditions which were so important in the formation of class consciousness in the paradigmatic case of England (Koo, 1990).

In the context of the contemporary globalization of the networks of material and cultural production, it is also clear that these anomalies cannot be addressed by simply adding the history of the "peoples without history" to the narrative of Euro-American history. Eric Wolf's (1982) survey of the global circuits of commodities, labor exchanges, and capital flows illustrates, for example, the limitations of such attempts, as it does not forge any new theoretical categories to integrate the distinctive experiences of non-Western peoples into the conceptual arsenal of the modern social sciences (Martin, 1994: 151). Similarly, the inadequacies of the conventional comparative-historical method are shown by Charles Tilly's (1990) contention that it is "not utterly stupid to suppose that non-Western states would undergo some of the same experiences as their Western counterparts and end up looking much more like them" (92), a contention that is all the more startling as it comes precisely when we witness a consolidation of structures of governance in the core (European Union, greater intergovernmental coordination through the G-7 meetings, etc.) and the unraveling of state structures in much of sub-Saharan Africa. Moreover, even when the "nation" is presented, not as a "natural" development of a universal human rationality but as an "imagined community" (Anderson, 1991), the historical experiences of non-European peoples continue to be denied, since they are still condemned to follow the trails blazed by Europeans and their transplants in the Americas (Chatterjee, 1993: 5).

These observations indicate that the consequences of the expansion of capitalism cannot be tracked by uncritically employing the conceptual tools forged by a century of core-centric social science but require a radical reconceptualization of our analytical frameworks. Indeed, if we are right in seeing the postmodern disenchantment with metanarratives, despite its explicit repudiation of post-European Enlightenment rationality, as reinforcing the binary opposition between the "highly developed societies" of the core, where the "modernization process is complete" (Jameson, 1991: x), and the non-Western peripheries, a strategy to transcend this dichotomy must perforce begin not with the fragmentation of social life but with the underlying singularity of the historical processes of capitalism.

The insistence on the fundamental unity of continual capitalist (re)structurings of the world does not license a recuperation of reigning metahistorical analytical categories and the current institutional partitioning of intellectual subject matter by a theoretical sleight of hand. Rather, as suggested by the preceding sketches illustrating the inadequacy of applying categories of analysis encapsulating a false understanding of the Euro-American experience to other regions, the challenge is to contextualize dense narratives of local processes within larger global forces of transformation. For instance, instead of unproblematically transposing the trajectories of the rise and fall of labor movements in the core to the "newly industrializing countries" on the Pacific perimeters of Asia or in Latin America, these procedures of inquiry will seek to locate workers in export-processing zones within local structures of labor control and networks of social reproduction which are integral elements of a global divisioning of labor (Ward, 1990; Martin, 1994: 171–74).

Proceeding from both ends of the nomothetic-idiographic spectrum, as the rubric of programs called world-systems analysis and "world literature and cultural studies" (Ross, 1993) indicate, the dual insistence on locating phenomena within their historically specific contexts and on the singularity of large-scale, long-term processes of capitalist expansion implies a transcendence of the binary Western/non-Western, postmodern/modern(izing) oppositions inscribed in our inherited theoretical categories. An essential aspect of such forms of inquiry is a repudiation of a synecdochical model of knowledge, whereby parts represent the whole. Instead of transhistorical, metatheoretical categories, the emphasis on the relational nature of historical processes dictates that analytical categories represent theoretical encapsulations of temporally and spatially specific processes to conceptually encompass the local processing of global forces, to investigate the consequences of the interpenetration of world-relational processes of accumulation and commodification with local structures of power and community.

In both cases, the word *world* signifies a stubborn refusal to delineate in advance the object of inquiry. Since the complacent acceptance of units of analysis that are given to the analyst rather than being constructed during the course of inquiry reduces relationships which transcend the boundaries of these units to the status of epiphenomena and thereby distorts causal explanations within these units themselves, this strategy offers a means to locate our analyses within the widest informational range. A refusal to accept a priori units and tools of analysis implies an erasure of these hermetically sealed partitionings of knowledge, while the contextualization of relational processes within the widest possible frame of reference endows analysis with a deeper time-and-space specificity than more narrowly focused, spatially and temporally circumscribed modes of inquiry.

Immanuel Wallerstein's (1974: 67–129) creative reconceptualization of the so-called second serfdom in Poland, for example, indicates how local processes of change can be integrated within a wider relational matrix. By situating different forms of labor exploitation within a larger organizational nexus, this analysis is able to provide a more precise conceptual context without diluting their concrete historical specificity. Similarly, as Said (1993) and others have insisted, we cannot study the blossoming of cultural production in the core without studying the conditions in the periphery; wider relational processes were deeply imbricated in the production of that which the nineteenth-century institutionalization of knowledge had cast as decidedly local and particular.

The emphasis on embedding richly textured historical narratives within wider relational networks entails two further propositions. First, the coincidence of the emergence of critiques of Eurocentric diffusionist models with the unraveling of U.S. hegemony indicates that conceptual categories are determined by the geopolitical location of researchers. Thus, the diffusionist model provided a workable framework during the fifties and sixties as decolonization and the global spread of industrialization proceeded apace. Its inadequacies were revealed only during the phase of global economic contraction beginning in the late sixties, a contraction that was marked by the corrosion of disciplinary boundaries and the emergence of radical critiques to post–European Enlightenment rationality. The critique of metahistorical theoretical categories also entails that conceptual tools be forged in relation to the object of inquiry, that analytical procedures for the study of forms of labor control during the "long" sixteenth century may be quite inadequate to investigate the global divisioning of labor during the current phase of capitalist restructuring, marked by the fragmentation of production into part-processes and the revival of patriarchal family-based sweatshops even in the core (see Martin, 1994: 170–71). Or, as George Marcus and Michael Fischer (1986) note, "rather than hardening into dogma or a 1950s-style paradigm, the so-called world-systems theory survives today primarily as a general orientation" (81).

Second, the construction of new theoretical and conceptual tools and of genuine world-scale sets of data poses formidable challenges. Constrained as individual researchers are by their abilities, resources, and training, much of the most important work has involved densely structured local or regional studies that attempt to place these developments as moments within wider relational processes (e.g., Bergquist, 1986; Tomich, 1990). The more challenging task of devising truly world-relational data sets, as indicated by the work of the Research Working Group on World Labor (1986) at the Fernand Braudel Center at SUNY-Binghamton, involves a quite different procedure. While it is increasingly being recognized that states are inadequate as units of analysis, they remain units of observation. However, since national data sets are decidedly not world-relational in their construction, the creation of world-relational data sets necessitates the combination of individual research with the efforts of collective teams of researchers, merging their different competencies to tackle large, collaborative projects, as is increasingly the case in the natural and physical sciences and in the entrepreneurial world. This again implies that scholars in the humanities and the social sciences repudiate the long tradition of individual research and begin to participate in truly cross-disciplinary, collaborative investigations.

The creation of such cross-disciplinary—or better yet, *antidisciplinary* —clusters of knowledge will, of course, face the "imperialism of departments" that area studies programs faced, as we have seen. However, in the present conjuncture, the very proliferation of a multiplicity of fragmented bodies of knowledge and the increasing erosion of disciplinary boundaries perhaps provide an opportune moment to create new paradigms of knowledge. Such paradigms must, initially at least, emerge from the initiative of small groups of faculty and graduate students spread across several disciplinary departments and/or area studies programs facing similar intellectual concerns and frustrations at having to devise ad hoc solutions in isolation and fighting a series of separate curricular battles. Indeed, since the current phase of capitalist restructuring—with the emergence of major nodes of accumulation in East Asia, the diasporic movement of peoples, and the downgrading of industrial production in the global divisioning of labor—represents a climacteric at least as profound as the nineteenth-century "age of revolutions," it is imperative that such groups spearhead a move to break the shackles imposed by the nineteenth-century partitioning of knowledge production as we forge toward a brave new world.

Briefly put, despite its claims to provide a holistic analysis of the peoples and institutions of the non-Western world by transcending the disciplinary divisioning of knowledge, the area studies project has reinforced the axiomatic distinction between Europe and the "peoples without history." The inability of areaists to challenge the disciplinary partitioning of knowledge has meant that the conceptual categories of the various disciplinary departments continue to remain theoretical encapsulations of the Euro–North American narrative of capitalist development, state formation, and social change. The inadequacies of these inherited conceptual categories have been cast in stark relief with the globalization of the networks of material and cultural production, the declining salience of states, and the downgrading of industrialization in the global divisioning of labor. These limitations can only be overcome if we can transcend the nineteenth-century fragmentation of knowledge into discrete disciplinary tributaries and reconceptualize our analytical categories in world-relational terms. Finally, in the context of the widening disparities in income and wealth between the core and the periphery and the resultant imbalances in library facilities, computer facilities, and the like, scholars located in the core have a special responsibility to aid their colleagues in less-favored locales resist the deepening commodification of everyday life by providing them the information to locate particular configurations of social relations within larger contextual frameworks.

Notes

Earlier versions of this article were presented at conferences at the University of Hawaii at Manoa and at the University of Wisconsin at Madison. I am grateful to participants at these conferences, and to Giovanni Arrighi, Cristina Bacchilega, Charles Crothers, Arif Dirlik, Mike Forman, Patricia Lane, Peter Manicas, John Rieder, Faruk Tabak, and Rob Wilson for detailed comments, some of which I have incorporated, others I have recklessly ignored, and yet others I am still pondering over.

1. While the debates surrounding Edward Said's *Orientalism* underscore the Eurocentric biases of area studies discourse, they do not address the broader issues involved in the geopolitical segmentation of the world. Though world-historical studies, in contrast, provide the most sustained and comprehensive critiques of the current partitioning of the globe (see Pletsch, 1981; Wolf, 1982; Wallerstein, 1974, 1991c), they are primarily concerned with the fragmentation of the social sciences within arbitrary disciplinary enclosures, or with the division of the globe into "three worlds." Hence, they impinge only tangentially upon the intellectual underpinnings of the area studies project.

2. The most comprehensive survey to date is the one commissioned by the Department of Defense, see Lambert et al (1984). The 1991 study by the National Council of Area Studies Associations commissioned by the Department of Education focuses solely on the prospects for hiring new faculty within the area studies programs and not on the substantive intellectual content of the programs, National Council of Area Studies Associations (hereafter NCASA, 1991). Represented on this council are the Association for Asian Studies (AAS), the American Association for the Advancement of Slavic Studies (AAASS), the African Studies Association (ASA), the Latin American Studies Association (LASA), and the Middle East Studies Association (MESA).

3. Recognizing that the United States was ill-equipped to administer occupied territories in the two major theaters of the Second World War—the "Far East" and Europe—due to the relative ignorance about the peoples living in these areas, the Provost Marshal General established the Army Specialized Training Program in 1943 to train officers and enlisted men of the occupying forces in the cultures of the regions they were assigned to administer. Supplemented by other programs, such as the Foreign Area Language Study and the Civil Affairs Training Schools, these programs were eventually instituted in 227 universities and colleges and had a peak enrollment of 13,185 by December 1943. For an overview, see Fenton (1947); Angiolillo (1947: 29–34); Lambert et al. (1984: 5–6).

4. There were, of course, some exceptions to this generalization. By the turn of the twentieth century, Yale and Columbia Universities had begun to lay the foundations for their programs in East Asian Studies, and the Oriental Institute for the study of the Middle East and South Asia was established at the University of Chicago in 1923. The mid-1930s saw the creation of several programs. Among the more prominent of these were the University of Michigan's programs in Oriental Civilizations (dealing primarily with China and Japan) and in Latin American studies; the Latin American Studies programs at the Universities of California at Berkeley and Los Angeles; and the Far Eastern Department at the

University of Washington (Hall, 1947: 17, 55; Lambert, et al. 1984: 3). Most of these pre–Second World War programs, however, had no autonomous status within the universities and depended on individual faculty members volunteering their time in addition to their normal assignments.

5. The first national 'area studies' association to be formed in the United States was the Far Eastern Association in 1943, subsequently reorganized as the AAS in 1956. This was followed by the creation of the AAASS in 1948; the ASA in 1957; and MESA in 1966 (NCASA, 1991). It is emblematic of the marginal significance of Australasia and the Pacific Islands to the strategic concerns of the United States that there is no professional association to foster the study of these societies as yet.

6. Though the experience of training military and civilian personnel in the languages and cultures of the areas they were assigned to administer provided a model for the creation of integrated area studies programs, it was recognized that the urgencies of war had meant that the courses of instruction had very limited objectives. Or, as William Fenton (1947) wryly puts it, "Although general education admits of varying views, training demands the right answer" (p. 5; see also Hall, 1947: 18).

7. The Rockefeller Foundation had helped create the Oriental Institute at the University of Chicago in the 1920s. Additionally, in 1946, the foundation provided substantial assistance for the creation of the program in Far Eastern and Russian Studies at Yale, the Far Eastern Institute at the University of Washington, and the Russian Institute at Columbia. The Carnegie Corporation's grant of $740,000 to Harvard University in 1948 for the establishment of its Russian Research Center was the largest endowment of its kind at that time. To enable their state universities to compete with private East Coast institutions, the state legislatures of Michigan and California also appropriated substantial grants for international and area studies in the late forties and early fifties. Between 1953 and 1966, the principal private funding agency for area and language studies was the Ford Foundation, which disbursed over $270 million to 34 universities for this express purpose (Hall, 1947: 52, 55–56, 60; Lambert, et al., 1984: 8–9).

8. In fact, taking cognizance of these geopolitical realities, Mountbatten's command was originally designated the American-British-Dutch-Australian (ABDA) Command (Emmerson, 1984: 7).

9. In the United States, studies on the Soviet Union, between the Bolshevik Revolution and the outbreak of the Second World War, were largely confined to the works of journalists, missionaries, and fellow-travelers, see Filene (1967).

10. These points are conveyed telegraphically here since their full elaboration falls beyond the purview of this article.

11. Roland Oliver (1991) notes that it "was quite normal for a single one of the newly defined [European] colonies [in Africa] to comprise two or three hundred earlier political groupings, even after discounting those societies which recognized no authority wider than that of the extended family" (185).

12. This is particularly important since many of the indigenous inhabitants of these areas had nonliterate cultures prior to the arrival of European "discoverers"—indeed, in many cases it was the European missionaries who devised alphabets and compiled dictionaries for the indigenous languages in these regions as a part of their evangelizing endeavors. Hence, the source material for the reconstruction of their histories are almost exclusively compiled in metropolitan

languages (e.g., travelogues, accounts of explorers, missionaries, colonial administrators, and journalists).

13. Or, as John Iliffe observed of colonial Tanganyika: "Africans wanted effective units of action just as officials wanted effective units of government. . . . Europeans believed Africans belonged to tribes; Africans built tribes to belong to" (quoted in Ranger, 1983: 252).

14. While Hough and Pletsch were primarily concerned with the impact of this divisioning of intellectual labor for the nomothetic social sciences, it had an equally significant impact on the idiographic humanities, as evident, for example, by the fact that "philosophy" typically refers to the traditions of knowledge and inquiry derived from Graeco-Roman antiquity, while other ways of thinking and knowing are *always* qualified by an adjective (e.g., "African," "Chinese," or "Indian" philosophy (see Mudimbe, 1988).

15. "To do something interdisciplinary," as Roland Barthes once put it, " it's not enough to choose a 'subject' (a theme) and gather around it two or three sciences. Interdisciplinarity consists in creating a new object that belongs to no one" (quoted in Clifford, 1986: 1).

16. It should be noted that one important reason for the pioneer scholars to neglect contemporary issues was the fact that such research would inevitably have highlighted their location within the colonial enterprise.

17. For an indication of the fluctuating distribution of resources between the different areas of study, compare Bennett (1951) with Lambert (1973), Lambert et al. (1984), and NCASA (1991).

18. I have developed these arguments at greater length elsewhere (see Palat, 1993a, 1996); for southern Africa, see Martin (1986; 1991); for the Soviet Union and Eastern Europe, see Wallerstein (1991a, 1991b: 90).

19. Since I have discussed the geopolitical conditions that led to the unraveling of the relational networks constituted under U.S. hegemony and their consequences at length elsewhere (see Palat, 1993a, 1993b, 1994), I repeat them here only in order to make the present argument intelligible.

20. By the beginning of the seventies, 40,000 students were enrolled in Russian language classes in the United States, while only 24,000 were enrolled by the early eighties (Atkinson, 1991: 20–21).

21. Though the incompatible methods of estimation utilized by different area studies associations make an accurate assessment impossible, an indication of the declining interest in such programs is provided by projections of anticipated loss of area studies faculty in the nineties. NCASA (1991), for instance, estimates that the AAASS will lose 42.7 percent of its faculty; AAS, 41.2 percent; MESA, 36.7 percent; LASA, 34.5 percent; and the ASA, 33.7 percent (79). For an assessment of the changing patterns of funding for Fulbright programs, see Koppel (1995).

22. While Europeans had accounted for over 50 percent of immigrants to the United States as recently as 1960, migrants from Europe accounted for only 11 percent of all legal immigrants in 1985. Correspondingly, Asian migrants rose from 9 percent in 1960 to 47 percent in 1985 (Sassen, 1990: 62–63). Other core locations experienced a similar pattern in the influx of migrants from low- and middle-income states—from Africa, the Middle East, and Eastern Europe to Western Europe, from East and Southeast Asia and the Pacific Islands to Australasia, from continental Asia and the Philippines to Japan—though the magnitudes of these inflows were much smaller.

23. Studies on Japan prove a rare exception to this generalization; but then, Japan is considered a modernized economy, and it does not challenge the ethnocentricity of the postmodern project. For Japan, see Miyoshi & Harootunian (1989).

References

Ahmad, Aijaz. 1992. *In Theory: Classes, Nations, Literatures.* London: Verso.

Amsden, Alice. 1989. *Asia's Next Giant: South Korea and Late Industrialization.* New York: Oxford University Press.

———. 1992. "Otiose Economics." *Social Research* 59, no. 4 (Winter): 781–97.

Anderson, Benedict R. O'G. 1991. *Imagined Communities: Reflections on the Origin and Spread of Nationalism.* London: Verso.

———. 1992. "The Changing Ecology of Southeast Asian Studies in the United States, 1950–1990." Pp. 25–40 in *Southeast Asian Studies in the Balance: Reflections from America,* ed. Charles Hirschman, Charles F. Keyes, & Karl Hutterer. Ann Arbor, MI: Association for Asian Studies.

Angiolillo, Paul F. 1947. *Armed Forces' Foreign Language Teaching: Critical Evaluation and Implications.* New York: S. F. Vanni.

Arrighi, Giovanni. 1982. "A Crisis of Hegemony." Pp. 55–108 in *Dynamics of Global Crisis,* ed. Samir Amin et al. New York: Monthly Review Press.

———. 1990. "The Three Hegemonies of Historical Capitalism." *Review* 13, no. 3 (Summer):365–408.

———. 1994.*The Long Twentieth Century: Money, Power, and the Origins of Our Time.* London: Verso.

Atkinson, Dorothy. 1991. "Soviet and European Studies." Pp. 19–34 in *Prospects for Faculty in Area Studies: A Report from the National Council of Area Studies Associations,* ed. National Council of Area Studies Associations. Stanford, CA: American Association for the Advancement of Slavic Studies.

Balazs, Etienne. 1960. "The Birth of Capitalism in China." *Journal of the Economic and Social History of the Orient.* 3, no. 2 (June): 196–216.

Bennett, Wendell C. 1951. *Area Studies in American Universities.* New York: Social Science Research Council.

Berger, Peter L. & H.-H. Michael Hsiao, eds. 1988. *In Search of an East Asian Developmental Model.* New Brunswick, NJ: Transaction Books.

Bergquist, Charles. 1986. *Labor in Latin America: Comparative Essays on Chile, Argentina, Venezuela, and Columbia.* Stanford, CA: Stanford University Press.

Borthwick, Mark, et al. 1992. *Pacific Century: The Emergence of Modern Pacific Asia.* Boulder, CO: Westview.

Bray, Francesca. 1983. "Patterns of Evolution in Rice-Growing Societies." *Journal of Peasant Studies* 11, no. 1 (October):3–33.

Bunker, Stephen G., & Denis O'Hearn. 1993. "Strategies of Economic Ascendants for Access to Raw Materials: A Comparison of the United States and Japan." Pp. 83–102 in *Pacific-Asia and the Future of the World-System,* ed. Ravi Arvind Palat. Westport, CT: Greenwood Press.

Burawoy, Michael. 1992. "The End of Sovietology and the Renaissance of Modernization Theory." *Contemporary Sociology* 21, no., 6 (November):774–85.

Chakrabarty, Dipesh. 1989. *Rethinking Working Class History: Bengal, 1890–1940.* Princeton, NJ: Princeton University Press.

Chatterjee, Partha. 1993. *The Nation and Its Fragments: Colonial and Postcolonial Histories*. Princeton, NJ: Princeton University Press.

Clifford, James. 1986. "Introduction: Partial Truths." Pp. 1–26 in *Writing Culture: The Poetics and Politics of Ethnography*, ed. James Clifford & George E. Marcus. Berkeley: University of California Press.

Cumings, Bruce. 1987. "The Origin and Development of the Northeast Asian Political Economy: Industrial Sectors, Product Cycles, and Political Consequences." Pp. 44–83 in *The Political Economy of New Asian Industrialism*, ed. Frederic C. Deyo. Ithaca, NY: Cornell University Press.

Dirks, Nicholas B. 1987. *The Hollow Crown: Ethnohistory of an Indian Kingdom*. Cambridge: Cambridge University Press.

Dirlik, Arif. 1992. "The Asia-Pacific Idea: Reality and Representation in the Invention of a Regional Structure." *Journal of World History* 3, no. 1 (Spring): 55–79.

———. (1994a). "The Postcolonial Aura: Third World Criticism in the Age of Global Capitalism," *Critical Inquiry* 20, no. 4 (Winter): 328–56.

———. 1994b. *After the Revolution: Waking to Global Capitalism*. Hanover, NH: University Press of New England for Wesleyan University.

Dixon, Chris. 1991. *South East Asia in the World-Economy: A Regional Geography*. Cambridge: Cambridge University Press.

Drakakis-Smith, David. 1992. *Pacific-Asia*. Routledge: London.

Dutton, Michael, & Elaine Jeffreys. 1993. "The Humanities, Humanism and Asian Studies." *Asian Studies Review* 16, no. 3 (April):2–9.

Emmerson, Donald K. 1984. "'Southeast Asia': What's in a Name?" *Journal of Southeast Asian Studies* 15, no. 1 (March): 1–21.

Errington, Shelley. 1989. *Meaning and Power in a Southeast Asian Realm*. Princeton, NJ: Princeton University Press.

Fenton, William N. 1947. *Area Studies in American Universities*. Washington, DC: American Council on Education, for the Commission on Implications of Armed Services Educational Programs.

Filene, Peter G. 1967. *Americans and the Soviet Experiment, 1917–1933: American Attitudes toward Russia from the February Revolution until Diplomatic Recognition*. Cambridge, MA: Harvard University Press.

Foucault, Michel. 1980. *Power/Knowledge: Selected Interviews and Other Writings*, ed. Colin Gordon. New York: Pantheon.

Gibb, Hamilton A. R. 1963. *Area Studies Reconsidered*. London: School of Oriental and African Studies.

Gibney, Frank. 1992. *The Pacific Century: America and Asia in a Changing World*. New York: Charles Scribner's Sons.

Gooding-Williams, Robert. 1993. *Reading Rodney King/Reading Urban Uprising*. New York: Routledge.

Gourevitch, Peter. 1989. "The Pacific Rim: Current Debates." *The Annals of the American Academy of Political and Social Science* 505 (September):8–23.

Grove, Linda, & J. W. Esherick. 1980. "From Feudalism to Capitalism: Japanese Scholarship on the Transformation of Chinese Rural Society." *Modern China* 6, no. 4 (October):397–438.

Habib, I. 1969. "Potentialities of Capitalistic Development in the Economy of Mughal India." *Journal of Economic History* 29, no. 1 (March):32–79.

Hall, Robert B. 1947. *Area Studies: With Special Reference to Their Implications for Research in the Social Sciences*. Washington, DC: Committee on World Area Research.

Harvey, David. 1989. *The Condition of Postmodernity: An Enquiry into the Origins of Cultural Change*. Oxford: Basil Blackwell.

Heginbotham, Stanley J. 1994. "Rethinking International Scholarship: The Challenge of Transition from the Cold War Era." *Items* 48, no. 2/3 (June–September):33–40.

Hough, Jerry F. 1977. *The Soviet Union and Social Science Theory*. Cambridge, MA: Harvard University Press.

Issacs, Harold. 1980. *Scratches on Our Minds: American Images of China and India*. White Plains, NY: M. E. Sharpe.

Jameson, Fredric. 1991. *Postmodernism, or the Cultural Logic of Late Capitalism*. Durham, NC: Duke University Press.

Johnson, Chalmers. 1982. *MITI and the Japanese Miracle: The Growth of Industrial Policy, 1925–1975*. Stanford, CA: Stanford University Press.

———. 1988. "Study of Japanese Political Economy: A Crisis in Theory." Pp. 95–113 in *Japanese Studies in the United States: 1. History and Present Condition*, ed. Japan Foundation. Ann Arbor, MI: Association for Asian Studies.

Koo, Hagen. 1990. "From Farm to Factory: Proletarianization in Korea." *American Sociological Review* 55, no. 5 (October):669–81.

Kopf, David. 1980. "Hermeneutics versus History." *Journal of Asian Studies* 39, no. 3 (May):495–506.

Koppel, Bruce M. 1995. *Refugees or Settlers? Area Studies, Development Studies, and the Future of Asian Studies*. Honolulu: East-West Center.

Kundera, Milan. 1981. *The Book of Laughter and Forgetting*, trans. Michael Henry Heim. Harmondsworth, UK: Penguin.

Lambert, Richard D. 1973. *Language and Area Studies Review*. Philadelphia: American Academy of Political and Social Science.

Lambert, Richard D., et al. 1984. *Beyond Growth: The Next Stage in Language and Area Studies*. Washington, DC: Association of American Universities.

Lyotard, Jean-Francois. 1989. *The Postmodern Condition: A Report on Knowledge,* trans. Geoff Bennington & Brian Masumi. Minneapolis: University of Minnesota Press.

Mafeje, Archie. 1971. "The Ideology of Tribalism." *Journal of Modern African Studies* 11, no. 2 (August): 353–61.

Marcus, George E., & Micheal J. Fischer. 1986. *Anthropology as Cultural Critique*. Chicago: University of Chicago Press.

Martin, William G. 1986. "Southern Africa and the World-Economy: Cyclical and Structural Constraints on Transformation." *Review* 10, no. 1 (Summer): 99–119.

———. 1991. "The Future of Southern Africa: What Prospects after Majority Rule?" *Review of African Political Economy* 50 (March): 115–34.

———. (1994). "The World-Systems Perspective in Perspective: Assessing the Attempt to Move beyond Nineteenth-Century, Eurocentric Conceptions." *Review* 17, no. 2 (Spring):145–85.

Marx, Karl. 1973. *Grundrisse: Foundations of the Critique of Political Economy*, trans. Martin Nicolaus. Harmondsworth, UK: Penguin.

McClintock, Anne. 1988. "Maidens, Maps, and Mines: The Reinvention of Patriarchy in Colonial South Africa." *South Atlantic Quarterly* 87, no. 1 (Winter):147–92.

Miyoshi, Masao, & Harry D. Harootunian, eds. 1989. *Postmodernism and Japan*. Durham, NC: Duke University Press.

Morishima, Michio. 1982. Why Has Japan "Succeeded"? Western Technology and the Japanese Ethos. Cambridge: Cambridge University Press.

Mudimbe, V. Y. 1988. The Invention of Africa: Gnosis, Philosophy, and the Order of Knowledge. Bloomington: Indiana University Press.

Mukhia, Harbans. 1981. "Was There Feudalism in Indian History?" Journal of Peasant Studies 8, no. 3 (April):273–310.

Munck, Geraldo L. 1993. "Between Theory and History and beyond Traditional Area Studies: A New Comparative Perspective on Latin America." Comparative Politics 25, no. 4 (July):475–98.

National Council of Area Studies Associations. 1991. Prospects for Faculty in Area Studies: A Report from the National Council of Area Studies Associations. Stanford, CA: American Association for the Advancement of Slavic Studies.

Oliver, Roland. 1991. The African Experience. London: Weidenfeld & Nicolson.

Palat, Ravi Arvind. 1993a. "The Making and Unmaking of Pacific-Asia." Pp. 3– 22 in Pacific-Asia and the Future of the World-Economy, ed. Ravi Arvind Palat. Westport, CT: Greenwood Press.

———. 1993b. "Transnationalization of Capital and the Paradox of Democracy: Free Markets, Decline of States, and Ethnic Conflicts." Paper presented at the conference on "The State in Transition: Reimagining the Local, National, International," La Trobe University, Melbourne, Australia, August 6–8.

———. 1996. "Pacific Century: Myth or Reality?" Theory and Society 25, no. 3 (June):303–47.

Picciotto, S. 1990. "The Internationalization of the State." Review of Radical Political Economics 22, no. 1 (Spring):28–44.

Pletsch, Carl E. 1981. "The Three Worlds, or the Division of Social Scientific Labor, circa 1950–1975." Comparative Studies in Society and History 23, no. 4 (October):565–90.

Ranger, Terence. 1983. "The Invention of Tradition in Colonial Africa." Pp. 211–62 in The Invention of Tradition, ed. Eric Hobsbawm & Terence Ranger. Cambridge: Cambridge University Press.

Research Working Group on World Labor. 1986. "Global Patterns of Labor Movements in Historical Perspective." Review 10, no. 1 (Summer):137–55.

Ross, Kristin. 1993. "The World Literature and Cultural Studies Program." Critical Inquiry 19, no.4 (Summer):666–76.

Ryckmans, Pierre. 1984. "Orientalism and Sinology." Asian Studies Association of Australia Review 7, no. 3 (April):18–20.

Said, Edward W. 1985. Orientalism. Harmondsworth, UK: Penguin.

———. (1989). "Representing the Colonized: Anthropology's Interlocutors." Critical Inquiry 15, no. 2 (Winter):205–25.

———. 1993. Culture and Imperialism. New York: Alfred A. Knopf.

Sassen, Saskia. 1990. The Mobility of Labor and Capital: A Study in International Investment and Labor Flow. Cambridge: Cambridge University Press.

———. 1991. The Global City: New York, London, Tokyo. Princeton, NJ: Princeton University Press.

Scott, Joan W. 1988. Gender and the Politics of History. New York: Columbia University Press.

Spate, Oskar Hermann Khristian. 1979. The Pacific since Magellan: 1. The Spanish Lake. Minneapolis: University of Minnesota Press.

Thompson, Edward Palmer. 1966. *The Making of the English Working Class.* New York: Vintage.

Tilly, Charles. 1990. *Coercion, Capital, and European States, AD 990–1990.* Oxford: Basil Blackwell.

Tomich, Dale W. 1990. *Slavery in the Circuit of Sugar: Martinique and the World-economy, 1830–1848.* Baltimore: Johns Hopkins University Press.

Vansina, Jan. 1961. *Oral Tradition: A Study in Historical Methodology.* Chicago: Aldine.

Wade, Robert. 1990. *Governing the Market: Economic Theory and the Role of Government in East Asian Industrialization.* Princeton, NJ: Princeton University Press.

Wallerstein, Immanuel. 1974. *The Modern World-System: 1. Capitalist Agriculture and the Origins of the European World-Economy in the Sixteenth Century.* New York: Academic Press.

———. 1991a. "The Cold War and Third World: The Good Old Days?" *Economic and Political Weekly* 26, no. 17 (April 27):1103–6.

———. 1991b. *Geopolitics and Geoculture: Essays on the Changing World-System.* Cambridge: Cambridge University Press.

———. 1991c. *Unthinking Social Science.* Cambridge: Polity Press.

———. 1992. "Geopolitical Strategies of the US in a Post-American World." *Humboldt Journal of Social Relations.* 18, no. 1, 217–23.

Ward, Kathryn, ed. 1990. *Women Workers and Global Restructuring.* Ithaca, NY: Cornell University Press.

Wolf, Eric. 1982. *Europe and the Peoples without History.* Berkeley: University of California Press.

PART TWO

International Studies and the Disciplines

RICHARD J. PERRY

Attack on the Straw Men

Postmodern Critiques of Anthropology and Vice Versa

A STRANGE AFFLICTION began to trouble anthropology in the early 1980s. The discipline had already passed through many decades of self-doubts, rowdy debates among its practitioners, and challenges from outside. For the most part these debates had been about improving, correcting, or redirecting the study of humankind, which most anthropologists would define as the purpose of the discipline. In the 1980s, though, a growing chorus of voices began to call into question the feasibility of the entire enterprise of cultural anthropology.

The challenge did not begin within anthropology but within the humanities, as a result of an intellectual development that many people have come to know as postmodernism. At a very basic level, postmodernists questioned the possibility of depicting human events with objective truth. Some went as far as to impute nefarious motives to those who claimed to do so or who seemed to claim such authority. These aspersions

Editor's Note: Richard J. Perry is Professor of Anthropology at St. Lawrence University. He makes a case for empirical research in the face of postmodernism by acknowledging the impossibility of absolute truth but insisting there is a standard of scholarship that allows communication to proceed nevertheless. In "Attack on the Straw Men: Postmodern Critiques of Anthropology and Vice Versa" Perry finds that standard in the term *accuracy*. Accuracy requires in-depth knowledge of specific cultures, and that in turn means knowledge of the appropriate language. Perry saves some of his most telling criticisms for "multiculturalists" in the humanities concerned about "the Other" but balking about learning about Others in depth. Their generalized concern, he charges, saves them from "the awkward position of having to read the works of their colleagues in history, anthropology, sociology, and political science." Postmodernists likewise escape the same homework by declaring all "stories" equal (cf. Gibbs's McVeigh paradox). One result, says Perry, is that "in many postmodernist courses the 'Other' is generically interchangeable as long as the 'Other' is different enough."

went to the heart of a discipline which rests almost entirely on ethnography: description of the lives and beliefs of people in various communities through firsthand observation. We began to hear of "ethnographic fictions" (Clifford 1988:92–113). The matter became especially contentious when a few anthropologists took up the cry, essentially disavowing (and perhaps exaggerating) their colleagues' claims to objective reportage and analysis (see, for example, Geertz 1973, 1988; Rosaldo 1986; Rabinow 1977, 1986).

Before examining the nature and validity of such charges, it will be useful to consider the intellectual basis of postmodern thinking. We can then trace some of the ways in which this view has generated serious postmodern critiques of anthropology, both from within the discipline and outside its borders, and assess their gravity. Finally, we can view the rise in popularity of postmodernism as a politico-academic development from the perspective of academic labor dynamics.

In an essay of this length, of course, it will not be possible to cite all of the many contributors to the debate or all of those at whom they have addressed their criticisms. Many of the general points, however, recur with great (perhaps even alarming) frequency. The aim here is merely to identify and address what, to this author, at least, seem to be some of the most important issues that have arisen during these conversations.

The "Truth" about "Reality"

Jean-Francois Lyotard has stated, "I define postmodernism as incredulity toward metanarratives" (1984:xxiv). Perhaps more clearly, an American scholar writes that "[p]ostmodernism is itself a notoriously difficult idea to pin down, but a simple definition would emphasize its skepticism toward any and all claims to truth" (Dettmar 1998:B4).

Who could take issue with that? Who among us would advocate gullibility? It does conjure the hoary question "what is truth," although we can set that aside for the moment. The issue of skepticism probably requires more immediate consideration. Skepticism could mean anything from cautious reservations to outright rejection of some assertion or representation. With regard to ethnography, some postmodern critics have been attracted to, flirted with, and even embraced the latter. Indeed, the issue has often gone beyond reservations regarding "claims to truth" and progressed to denial that *any* objective "truth" *exists* independent of competing versions of it.

This is hardly a new position. The *Oxford English Dictionary* defines a skeptic as "[o]ne who, like Pyrrho and his followers in Greek antiquity, doubts the possibility of real knowledge of any kind; one who holds that there are no adequate grounds for certainty as to the truth of any proposition whatever."

Perhaps we can see this from a more useful perspective if we set *truth* aside for a moment and focus on *reality*. Although the conventional meanings of these terms may overlap, they are not necessarily synonymous. One can speak of the "truth about reality," or for that matter, the "reality of truth." These phrases may be rather vapid, but they are not necessarily redundant. This is less clear with "real truth" or "true reality." When truth and reality take the form of nouns, their fields of meaning are more distinct.

Truth implies complex relationships, causative and other interacting, perhaps deeper, contextual factors that transcend the simpler meaning of *reality*. Truth is reality plus *why*. But if we have to start somewhere, reality is probably a good place.

And so we find ourselves facing a pair of ancient, interlocked questions. Is it valid to assume that a reality exists independent of human perceptions of it? If so, is it feasible to describe reality and "realistic" to hope to understand it, given the various factors that distort our perceptions and cognitive processes?

Unless we are willing to sink into utter solipsism, I suggest that we answer the first question provisionally in the affirmative. It may be that reality is an illusion; but if so, no one but myself will read what I (imagine that I am) writing, and any withering rebuttals will be nothing more than a bad dream.

Since that would leave us with nothing to discuss and no one with whom to discuss it, let us consider the alternative. Let us suppose that something we call reality does exist independently of our perceptions. Suppose that such phenomena as the force of gravity, the speed of light, molecular structures, the temperature at which water boils, and so on would be the same even if no human beings existed. The problem then would be how, if we wish to, we can perceive such aspects of reality *accurately*.

Accuracy is another useful concept. If truth in its absolute sense implies full knowledge of all there is to know about reality (or even some aspect of it), a moment's reflection will affirm that such understanding is not attainable even for such a simple event as a drop of water falling onto a smooth flat surface. *Truth*, in its absolute sense, is indeed unattainable. *Accuracy*, since it can accommodate gradation, is attainable to some degree. It can be relative. We can *approach* accuracy in perceiving such an event, noting the size of the drop, the speed at which it falls, the nature of the surface, and the splat it makes.

By watching multiple instances of comparable events, we can even gather enough information to *predict* what is likely to happen the next time, given a similar set of conditions. We can never get at the full truth of such an event, which is always immensely complex and never absolutely identical for other events. But we *can* achieve reasonable accuracy to the extent of giving assurance that the drop will fall rather than rise and fly away, that it will not remain intact when it hits, and so forth. We can never get it all, but we can be more accurate or less so.

Clearly, the attempt to describe human experience, especially the experience of others, is far more complex than describing a drip in the sink. Not only are the component aspects of the event far more numerous, but we also have the issue of interaction. The Heisenberg Uncertainty Principle notwithstanding, the act of observing the drop does not, in itself, affect the event in any discernible way. Most of us would agree that a drop of water does not have awareness or intention, nor does it knowingly interact with the observer. The observer, moreover, probably will not have the emotional reactions to the drop of water that he or she is likely to have in the presence of other humans. The participation of sentient beings in the observational process makes a difference.

The question is, how much difference does it make? Surely, it renders the task of description far more complicated, rife with distractions and potential errors. But it does not negate the postulate that the events and people are as real as the drop of water, however inaccurate the observer's perceptions and descriptions of them may be. Indeed, the problems of human interaction in shaping these perceptions underscore that reality. Interaction implies realities on both sides of the event—assuming, as we noted above, that the whole thing is not merely a solitary illusion.

Here we stand on the precipice of still another chasm of involuted reasoning, however. Possibly the reality in the mind of the "Other" is no more or less *accurate* than the ethnographer's. Yet this does not denote an *absence* of underlying reality. More important for present purposes, however, the ethnographer is not a physicist or someone of that sort for whom determining the nature of that underlying reality is the object. For the ethnographer, the conceptual reality of the Other *is* the object of interest *in itself*.

That leaves open the question of how *valid* ethnographic observations and their resultant descriptions can be. We have already disposed of the unattainable and therefore expendable criterion of absolute truth. Can we hope for a useful, albeit less than absolute, degree of accuracy? Since accuracy allows for a gradient of success, the question becomes "*how* accurate?" For now, however, we might reflect upon how we have arrived at the point at which it has been necessary to argue seriously for the existence of an independent reality. In any case, this question has been insistent enough to have provoked at least two recent books arguing the affirmative (Bohannan 1995, Searle 1995).

Postmodernism, Modernism, and Anthropology

Postmodernism, as the term suggests, opposes itself to modernism. It is worth considering what that means—particularly since, in conventional parlance, most of us would oppose "modern" to "old-fashioned." Whether we prefer one or the other may be a matter of our propensities for nostalgia. But certainly, postmodernists see *modernism* as old-fashioned. And as if that were not confusing enough, they sometimes link modernism with the Enlightenment, which was all the vogue over two centuries ago.

Postmodernism's roots are in literary criticism and art, in which *modernism* has a more distinct meaning. The historian Carl Schorske (1998) notes that among other things, modernism has denoted an emphatic departure from the past.

The very word "modernism" has come to distinguish our lives and times from what had gone before, from history as a whole, as such. Modern architecture, modern music, modern science—all have defined themselves not so much *out* of the past, indeed scarcely *against* the past, but detached from it in a new, autonomous cultural space. (304)

In the social sciences, allusion to the Enlightenment generally refers to the intellectual departure from theological explanation toward a celebration of rational, observational, scientific approaches to explanation. We can use the term *celebration* advisedly, since these developments involved a sense of optimism regarding human progress and the improvement of life through the triumph of reason.

A basic premise of this line of thinking is that the universe (or "reality") operates according to natural laws rather than the whims of some imponderable deity. An outgrowth of this was the development of positivism—the premise that these laws are discoverable and potentially comprehensible to the human mind.

This view retains a place in the contemporary intellectual milieu, although it has also provoked criticism, to the extent that "positivist" is a stinging epithet in many circles. Some of its manifestations, particularly the versions of functionalism which influenced much of sociology and anthropology over half a century ago, came to seem overly mechanistic and, in the opinion of many, simultaneously grandiose in their claims and simplistic in their findings. By the 1960s, functionalism suffered the devastating accusation of being "ultra-conservative" (a view that is hardly fair or accurate with regard to many of its politically left-leaning proponents).

Anthropology, however, already had a long history of alternative approaches to understanding the human experience. One of the most important found expression in the work of Franz Boas, beginning in the late nineteenth century.

Boas, who turned to the study of cultures after rigorous scientific training as a physical geographer, began with the hope that natural laws governing human life were indeed discoverable. But he reacted against what he considered to be premature excesses of the evolutionary theorists of his time, who posited elaborate and generally ethnocentric models of universal sociocultural development. As a classic inductivist, Boas insisted that sociocultural laws, if they do exist, can become apparent only through the exhaustive gathering of evidence. "This [deductive] method of starting with a hypothesis is infinitely inferior to one in which by truly inductive processes the actual history of definite phenomena is derived" (Boas 1896:89).

In this vein, Boas's search for evidence did not involve a quest for sweeping comparative similarities but, rather, focused on the fine-grained detail of specific cultural phenomena through firsthand fieldwork. As much as anything, this involved the quest for meaning, the attempt to grasp the perspectives of the people he was trying to understand. In espousing this approach, Boas was also acutely aware of the danger that the observer's own preconceptions were liable to distort interpretation. This was one basis for his advocacy of cultural relativism, the need to refrain from allowing one's value judgments to interfere with the understanding of other cultures.

It was Boas who was primarily responsible for adding the concept of culture as an extrasomatic phenomenon to the tool kit of the social sciences. Then, as now, this version of culture is far broader than the conventional references to the arts and literature ("high culture") and includes all learned, shared behavior, however trivial.

Boas's exacting standards and attention to detail ultimately dampened his search for broad laws governing human life, although many of his students were more willing to generalize about the human condition. With the development and diversification of anthropology as a discipline throughout the remainder of the twentieth century, a general dichotomy has remained, involving those who seek to identify and formulate broadly applicable principles and those who embrace a close-focused interpretation of the particular, unique case. (Contrast, for example, Harris 1968 and Geertz 1973.)

Most of Boas's early-twentieth-century insights apparently had little effect on other disciplines, however. One reason for this, no doubt, was that few scholars outside anthropology gave much notice to non-Western, nonindustrial populations as serious subjects of study during the first half of this century.

Scholars of the the Graeco-Roman and Egyptian spheres took note of "barbarians" as disruptive factors in the course of civilization but focused more on the disruptions than on the barbarians. American historians wrote at length of the "winning of the West," but with a few exceptions, they generally did so from the perspective of the winners. At most, a few examined the victimization of Native American peoples, but they rarely explored the cultures of these populations in much detail.

Sociologists, political scientists, and economists focused most of their attention on the complex nation-states of the West, whether at macro- or micro-levels. Historians concerned themselves with social, political, and economic trends and developments within the Euro-American sphere. Even when focusing on such issues as global imperialism, they generally did so from the perspectives of the home states. (See Edward Said's [1993] discussion of the role of colonialism in European thought. Green and Dickason (1989) address the Eurocentrism of the "Law of Nations" from a slightly different perspective.) The mid-twentieth-century rise of "social history" still, for the most part, focused on the common folk within European and American complex societies.

To the extent that the arts and humanities paid much attention to non-industrial peoples, they tended to use them as romantic, tragic, or savage foils without much attention to their social or historical realities. Philosophers grappled with "great ideas," which many of them took to be time-less and essentially culture-free. It would be fair to say that the serious study of small societies face-to-face—getting smoke in the eyes, eating strange foods, learning unwritten languages, and risking malaria—fell to anthropologists by default.

Critical analysis of Western society from within the ranks of its scholars, already well established at the beginning of the Enlightenment, became still more energetic late in the twentieth century in the presence of an established discipline of anthropology. In France, Jean-Paul Sartre and Simone de Beauvoir, friends of the anthropologist Claude Levi-Strauss, wrote scathing critiques of oppressive aspects of European society. The French philosopher and historian Michel Foucault examined the brutality of the European state in an essay titled "The Archaeology of Knowledge" (1969). It would be a gross misstatement, however, to argue that anthropology enjoyed center stage in these intellectual developments. On the contrary, even though more thinkers by the 1970s began to consider the comparative issues which had long furnished the workshop of anthropologists, they rarely paid much attention to anthropological work except as passing asides, using one or another ethnographic nugget to illustrate a point.

Eventually, this led to a rediscovery of ground that anthropologists had long since traversed. Upon finding anthropological footprints on the terrain, however, many intellectuals either ignored them or, like many earlier European "discoverers of new lands" that happened to be occupied, worked to discredit the earlier inhabitants.

Probably the most dramatic move in this direction arose from the work of the "deconstructionists," the best-known of whom is Jacques Derrida. A major inspiration for this approach arose from the work of the linguist Ferdinand de Saussure, who pointed out that "language is a system of interdependent terms in which the value of each term results solely from the simultaneous presence of the others. . . ." (1959:114).

Saussure asserted that ideas do not exist prior to, or independently of, language. The concepts through which humans categorize and engage reality are products and consequences of language. Saussure expressed this by noting that the linguistic unit, or "sign," consists of two components, which he called the "signifier," or "sound-image," and the "signified," or the concept to which the signifier refers. The relationship between signifier and signified is entirely arbitrary—that is, there is no intrinsic relationship between any signifier and signified. Any sound-image can be linked with any concept, although once established, signs are not subject to change through individual whim. Moreover, the meaning or "value" of any sign does not reside in the sign itself but derives from its contrastive or comparative relationships to other signs within the same system of signs.

Given the arbitrary nature of signs and their diverse possibilities of meaning and value within the field of other signs in the same language, signs are not easily translatable across language boundaries. Saussure (1959) offers the example of the French *mouton*, for which the conventional English translation is "sheep." But when the term refers to food, one dines on mutton, not on sheep. Hence the meaning of the terms, though similar, do not entirely coincide (115–16).

As to perceptions of reality, Saussure (1959) noted that "only the associations sanctioned by that language appear to us to conform to reality, and we disregard whatever others might be imagined" (65). To some, this has seemed to imply a cognitive universe in which signifier and signifed dance in a free-floating realm unanchored to concrete reality—a view that Saussure himself probably did not hold. As Paul Atkinson (1959) notes,

the post-Saussurean recognition that the linguistic sign is "arbitrary" does not condemn us to the view that we have lost everything in a sea of whimsical or random semioses . . . . The fact that linguistic signs derive their meaning from their relations with other signs—paradigmatic and syntagmatic—does not strip them of their referential function. (176)

Not all postmodernists seem to have shared this view, however. Some appear to have seized upon the relationships among signifiers while tending to ignore Saussure's discussion of the relationship between signifiers and signified.

The premiere revelation of the deconstructionists was that descriptive statements (or "texts"), being the products of humans who inevitably are immersed in specific cultural, social, and political milieux and enmeshed among their own signifiers, can never be taken at face value as objective or accurate accounts of reality. A reading of any text requires that it be "deconstructed." The layers of nuances arising from the author's biases, slants, and special interests (however unconscious these might be) require a peeling away to reveal the hidden agenda.

But there is a problem here. The deconstructor, being in the same situation as the author of the text (though perhaps in a different boat), cannot be a reliable authority either. The process of deconstructing any text creates another text which requires deconstruction. Logically, the concept seems to create a hall of mirrors in which "reality" is elusive and perhaps irretrievable.

This model also implicitly relegates those who adopt such an approach to the role of critiquing the work of positivists and other miscreants rather than producing their own fresh, insightful analysis of real-world phenomena.

Many scholars, nonetheless—particularly some in the field of literary criticism who apparently already were comfortable in such a role—found new energy in such a mission. Perhaps, as Arnold Krupat (1993) suggests, some of them had experienced "fatigue with New Critical textual explication" (56). Not only could they address a mass of existing texts ripe for critique, but they could also adopt a political posture rarely available to them before: the role of advocates of the weak and oppressed, exposers of hegemonic imposition. The premise of deconstructionism cultivated the defrocking of hidden agendas. As it turned out, texts dealing with politically and economically disadvantaged peoples provided a rich field for exposing the imposition of neocolonialistic, hegemonic structures on the "subaltern," the "Other."

Enter Multiculturalism

A catalyst for this development was the rise of "multiculturalism" as a cause celebre. The term itself has undergone several semantic metamorphoses which, beyond doubt, have exacerbated the controversy surrounding it. For this reason alone, it is worth our while to survey its history.

In its early form, multiculturalism seems to have grown out of the later stages of the civil rights movement in the United States. Among many other things, this movement stimulated a greater sensitivity to the under-representation of diverse populations in the standard college curriculum.

It also provoked a backlash. Perhaps one of the grumpiest appeared in the work of Allan Bloom, who became a poster child for those who argued that to stress non-Western history and literature somehow pre-cluded students' learning about Western civilization. The latter body of knowledge, in the process of discourse, became known as "the tradi-tional canon." Less kindly, perhaps, some multicultural and feminist pro-ponents of curriculum revision came to refer to it as the work of "dead white men."

As such characterizations suggest, the discussion soon left the grounds of reasonable discourse and launched into a series of bitter factional dis-putes, sometimes with individual tenure cases at stake. In the process, the issue often came to be framed in odd ways. The "West-firsters" pointed out that today's students often have a deficient grasp of Western history or "great literature." The implication, apparently, was that some zero-sum game operated between the "West" and the "rest" which determined that learning about one somehow precluded learning about the other. Proponents of a more diverse curriculum pointed out that many students have little basic knowledge even of global geography, let alone an appre-ciation of the vitality and complexity of other cultures.

More emotionally driven, however, was the issue of the *worth* of di-verse traditions. The increasing heterogeneity of American students, many of whose heritages had rarely if ever been represented in the tradi-tional curriculum, became a political element in the debates. The traditionalists' dismissive attitude toward non-Western cultures dripped from the remark of a renowned novelist who quipped "show me a Zulu Shakespeare." Such comments lent credibility to the multiculturalists' charges of arrogance, ignorance, and ethnocentrism.

In the meantime, the multicultural debate served some bureaucratic purposes among college administrations. Ever since civil rights and di-versity issues had come to the forefront in the 1960s and 1970s, many colleges had been hard-pressed to show progress in remedying past injus-tices and exclusionary practices. By publicly embracing "multicultural-ism," they could demonstrate that they were "dealing with" the issue. All too often, however, this meant investing in highly visible measures such as campus speakers, dance troupes, art exhibits, or international "foods of many lands" festivals rather than working toward structural changes in the curriculum or diversifying the faculty and student body. In effect, one could make the case that multiculturalism for public consumption dissipated much of the pressure for genuine improvements.

Somewhere in this process, an odd shift occurred among many academic professionals who had come to define themselves as multiculturalists. Having argued vehemently for the importance of recognizing other cultural systems and ways of life (the Other, as many came to refer to them), many of these scholars seemed to draw the line at investing serious time and effort in learning about these Others in depth.

Such an effort, after all, would require extensive reading about their histories and cultures, perhaps learning their languages, doing fieldwork among them, or preferably, all of those things. Not only would these amount to daunting tasks, but many other people had already been doing such things for a long time. It would have placed multiculturalists with backgrounds in the humanities in the awkward position of having to read the works of their colleagues in history, anthropology, sociology, and political science.

For postmodernists, however, it was possible to avoid this through deft reasoning. Since any text purporting to describe another's experiences was bound to be a distortion of "truth," why should anyone need to wade laboriously through ethnographies? They were only "stories," after all, and one story was no more or less valid than any other. For this reason, one could avoid painstaking studies of other peoples' customs, beliefs, subsistence patterns, child-rearing practices, social organization, or even their histories and instead look at such things as relationships between non-Western populations and their oppressors. Much postmodern scholarship came to emphasize power disparities or hegemonic relationships, conceived broadly and dynamically, as an alternative to what they described as "in-depth" studies of particular cases.

One essential strategy in staking out one's ground if it extends to neighboring fields of inquiry is to present one's approach as new and unique. This posture may not only stress the difference of one's own initiatives but attempt to discredit previous enterprises. In this case, postmodernists had to show that although some scholars had spent many years in studying non-Western cultures, the postmodernist attempts were superior. This was difficult, since theirs were not based on "in-depth" studies of these societies. The strategy, however, was to assert that "in-depth" studies have little value. Intercultural relationships were more salient.

To some this might have seemed similar to watching a tennis game by focusing only on the ball and ignoring the players. But it arose, let us recall, from the assertion that ethnography is misleading. Some also embellished their position by posing a simplistic either / or dichotomy. "Traditional" studies, they maintained, focused entirely on small, isolated cases without attention to broader context. The multiculturalists, on the other hand, were interested in the global interactions of intercultural dynamics.

Another line of reasoning developed from these premises as well. One of the primary values of attending to the Other, some asserted, was to learn more about ourselves. This reflexive value became an important pedagogical rationale for courses which they now presented as multicultural from a postmodernist perspective. Students could "experience" radically different slices of life or cultural samples briefly but vividly— not to begin to understand much about them for their own sakes but to feel how *different* they were. (A colleague refers to this as the "Oh, wow!" approach.)

Who Invited the Anthropologists?

The multicultural issue played a crucial role in these exchanges. The postmodernists already had an enemy in the defenders of tradition. Many postmodernists had no trouble placing anthropologists (as well as practitioners of other long-standing disciplines) among the villains.

Naively, perhaps, many anthropologists at first had placed themselves firmly and eagerly within the multiculturalist camp, believing they could make major contributions to the effort. Many were gratified to see that, at last, some of their colleagues had come to value cross-cultural issues and to realize the importance of studying other cultures. Surely, people who were newly interested in addressing the Other would want to talk to those colleagues on their campuses who had already spent years in other parts of the world living with other peoples and reading, writing, and teaching about these other ways of life.

If anthropologists expected warm invitations to join the effort, however, they soon began to realize that the phone would never ring. Before long, they discovered that things had been moving on without them. Their colleagues in English and other non–social science departments had been busy planning initiatives, proposing programs, and securing funding to address "cultural issues."

Many anthropologists still felt that this was what they had been doing all along, even though the vocabulary was somewhat different. Rather than *cross-cultural*, a term familiar to anthropologists, the words *multicultural* and even *intercultural* were now ubiquitous. The difference in terms represented a deeper difference in perspective, however.

These initiatives not only tended to bypass anthropology but in many respects were distinctly hostile to it.

This became apparent to many anthropologists by 1990. At the American Anthropological Association's annual breakfast meeting for department chairs, a number of attendees raised the issue with some alarm. Among their concerns, several saw an apparently naïve return to nineteenth-century concepts of culture and an inherent essentialism and superficiality in dealing with non-Western cultures. These concerns found expression in opinion essays in the *Chronicle of Higher Education* (Perry 1992, Weiner 1992) and in symposia at subsequent annual meetings.

Perhaps anthropologists had become complacent over the decades, secure in having achieved some authority in their own subject matter. There had been some warning shots from within (e.g., Rosaldo,1986; Marcus and Fisher, 1986; Rabinow, 1977). But generally, most anthropologists had treated these arguments as continuations of the long tradition of self-critique. As it turned out, however, a number of these internal criticisms became fuel for a more emphatic rejection of anthropology from outside, and the long tradition of internal critique in anthropology escalated to extreme divisiveness. This reached a level of crisis when, in the view of many, postmodernists "took over" the discipline's major journal, the *American Anthropologist*, and subscriptions dropped.

Do They Have a Point?

In assessing the critiques that postmodernists have leveled at anthropology, we can accept and therefore pass beyond the assertion that ethnographies do not represent the absolute truth about cultures. No reputable anthropologist, to my knowledge, has ever claimed that they do. The assertion that anthropologists have generally made such claims, therefore, requires correction.

It is not possible, of course, to offer absolute assurance that no one calling herself or himself an anthropologist has ever made such a claim, any more than we can be certain that no one professing to be a "scientist" has ever expounded delusional nonsense. For better or worse, anthropology, unlike law or medicine, has no formal means to address malpractice. Usually, though, we judge the worth of an enterprise by its foremost practitioners rather than its marginal claimants. With that in mind, let us examine some of the more common postmodern criticisms of cultural anthropology.

a. Anthropologists have presented their own versions of cultures as authoritative truths.

b. Anthropologists have failed to recognize or acknowledge the collaborative nature of fieldwork.

c. Fieldwork does not "privilege" the ethnographer's account.

d. Anthropologists have been complicit in the oppression of third world peoples by imposing an outsider's representation of their realities (see also a, b, and c above).

e. Anthropologists have focused on the small, isolated case rather than addressing global phenomena.

I will address these criticisms in order, beginning with point a. As we have noted above, when it comes to perception of events in the "real world," truth is best left to philosophers, and anthropologists might better pursue accuracy. A number of postmodern critics have asserted that the ethnographer's claim to "authority" (a) rests on constructing persuasive narratives, often distorting the truth in doing so. Referring to E. E. Evans-Pritchard's classic study of the Nuer of the southern Sudan, Renato Rosaldo (1989) criticizes the venerable anthropologist for, among other things, glossing over the complex variability of Nuer life in favor of generalization. "The author speaks interchangeably of the Nuer or of a Nuer man because, differences of age aside (questions of gender barely enter Evans-Pritchard's androcentric work), the culture is conceived as uniform and static" (43).

It is difficult to imagine how anyone who is at all familiar with Evans-Pritchard's career could mistake his general statements for an expression of an underlying assumption that Nuer society was static. One of the reasons he worked there, in fact, was that the Nuer were confronting more and more outside influences, some of them quite hostile (see, for example, discussions in Goody [1995] and Stocking [1995]). Far from being unaware of changes affecting the Nuer, Evans-Pritchard expressed concerns about the dangers they and other colonized peoples faced as a result of ignorance and lack of respect that characterized colonial policies (see, for example, Evans-Pritchard 1962:109–29).

The more pertinent issue here, though, is the merging of "the Nuer" with "a Nuer." To what extent is it legitimate to generalize from myriad discrete events and nuances? As James Clifford (1988) notes, "Experimental, interpretive, dialogical, and polyphonic focuses are at work, discordantly, in any ethnography, but coherent presentation presupposes a controlling mode of authority. I have argued that this imposition of coherence on an unruly textual process is now inescapably a matter of strategic choice" (54).

Indeed, the task of gathering complex information into a coherent and accurate report does inevitably involve summaries of disparate events, decisions regarding emphasis or omission, choices of ways to interpret ambiguous situations. Such is the stuff of humans working with other humans. As Mary Louise Pratt (1986) points out, the narrative form of ethnography "mediates a contradiction within the discipline between personal and scientific authority" (32). Ultimately, in other words, the ethnographer must arrive at a means to convey information effectively and credibly, resting on the "authority" (perhaps we might substitute "credibility") derived from having been there and done the work.

To convey information effectively, then, necessarily requires summarizing a sea of detail to depict a perceived pattern. Let us take an example from the Apache.

In the course of my fieldwork, an elderly Apache woman asked me, "Do owls speak to you in English?" Hearing that they do not, she said, "They speak in Apache real plain. One time an owl said to me, 'I'm your grandfather.' Another time I dreamed I saw an owl among the chickens. It said, 'You're going to cry.' A few weeks later, my little niece died."

On another occasion a young girl told me she had dreamed that an owl had told her that her father would soon die. When she pleaded with the owl, it said to her, "All right, if you all pray real hard, he'll be hurt, but he won't die." A month or so later, she said, her father was involved in a car accident, but he survived.

Small children sometimes scared one another by claiming to hear an owl. A man also told me that many Apache parents were disturbed by the logo of a national scholastic testing service, which was a stylized owl. In discussing such things, an elderly woman said, "We shouldn't be talking about owls. They hear everything we say."

As it turns out, earlier Apache ethnography dating from observations in the 1930s offers more indications that Apache associate owls with ghosts of deceased relatives and that they consider them harbingers of death (see, for example, Opler [1941:30, 229–31]). In John Bourke's (1886) account of a military campaign in the Sierra Madres in 1883, we learn that Apache scouts became upset when a packer kept an owl for a pet, and they demanded that he release it.

In light of such information, is it valid to assert that "the Apache" associate owls with death and view them with dread? Is it acceptable to do so despite an elderly Plains Apache man having said to me, as he recently did, that when he was young he was not afraid of owls and used to shoot them every chance he had?

To approach one form of accuracy, we might attempt to gauge which and how many Apache individuals share such a belief and to what degree. But this would miss another aspect of Apache "reality." This belief is shared and transmitted among individuals. As such, it displays many of the characteristics of a supraindividual phenomenon with an existence independent of particular persons who might or might not hold it. It is, in other words, a feature of Apache culture. This aspect is manifest even in the elderly Plains Apache man's divergent stance. Despite shooting owls and discussing it as he did many years later, his actions acknowledged the belief even in defying it.

Is it, then, a hegemonic imposition of an "observer's model" to speak of such a phenomenon as a cultural feature? Or is it merely an attempt to draw a reasonable conclusion from multiple events? Does the generalization rest primarily on the "authority" of the ethnographer, or does whatever *authority* the account may have arise from the gathering of evidence "on the ground," "at the scene," "in the field"?

Of the numerous anthropological straw men that postmodernists have stalked and picked off with deadly inaccuracy, few are more exasperating than the "discovery" of the anomalous role of the ethnographer. James Clifford (1986) urges that we all embrace and develop this as the "ethnography of conjuncture" (7), although elsewhere he hints at some nostalgia for the "lost authenticity" (however naïve) of earlier ethnographies (1988:4).

Like so many postmodern insights, this appears to be a case of discovering the new by renaming the old. A sociologist colleague has referred to this as "innovation through vocabulary." Perhaps this is an example of what some postmodernists mean by making the familiar strange.

In any case, only one who has never done fieldwork could imagine that those who have could be unaware of their anomalous position. Some old-timers have referred to it as marginality (see, for example, Freilich 1970). As every ethnographer knows, fieldwork involves continuous reminders that one can never be one of the community in the deepest sense, however successful one might be in getting along. Without having undergone childhood there and experienced the socialization process, learned the language as one's first speech with all the cognitive orientation that implies, absorbed the beliefs of the community as one's primary knowledge from birth, and become enmeshed in the web of kinship obligations and expectations, the stranger can rarely hope to be more than a familiar outsider—even if, perhaps, a congenial one.

Fantasies about being "adopted into the tribe" may appeal to the popular imagination, but they have little or no relationship to the realities of fieldwork. The ethnographer, inevitably carrying the baggage of his or her own upbringing and cultural immersion, can only hope to earn acceptance by the hosts and learn something about their reality, not to become part of it.

This does not preclude the possibility of *communicating* ideas and concepts across cultural fields, though it does mean that such communication may be a laborious, uncertain enterprise. Learning about another culture, even after a lifetime of effort, can resemble uncovering an infinity of Chinese nesting boxes. But rarely, if ever, can the ethnographer hope to achieve the assured cultural virtuosity of the average community member, who can say "Of course that's the way it is; what else could it be?" Instead, the fieldworker must hope for the occasional glimpse of insight, connection, or pattern, perhaps to be rewarded with the solitary flash of excitement: "So *that's* what it's about!"

What about point *b*? Have anthropologists failed to recognize the collaborative nature of field work? It was the anthropologist and linguist Edward Sapir (1929), student of Franz Boas, who pointed out seven decades ago that "[t]he worlds in which different societies live are distinct worlds, not merely the same world with different labels attached." In attempting to interpret and convey such worlds to a readership unfamiliar with them, most anthropologists have tried hard to be as accurate as possible. Fundamentally, this has involved living for extended periods with the people they have tried to understand, learning from them, and subjecting their own perceptions continuously to correction by their hosts. They have relied, in other words, on collaboration. (See *b* in list above.)

Anthropologists may not always have acknowledged collaboration as fully as they could have. In many cases this would have involved compiling almost a full roster of the members of a community. Given the political nature of the world, it might also, in some cases, have placed people in danger. Protecting the anonymity of people, or even communities, may take precedence over publicizing their identities.

Nonetheless, in many cases anthropologists have given full credit to their indigenous colleagues. Franz Boas acknowledged his debt to George Hunt in his many years of work with the Kwakwala speakers of British Columbia. Margaret Mead wrote extensively about Paliau in the Great Admiralty Islands of the Pacific. Napoleon Chagnon makes clear the help he received from a number of Yanomano, especially Rerebawa. Andrew Strathern wrote extensively about his colleague Ongka of the Kawelka of Papua New Guinea and advised in the production of an ethnographic film featuring Ongka. We could compile a lengthy and, eventually, rather tedious list of similar examples.

The more important issue, however, is that the charge of anthropologists' taking sole credit for their knowledge is a red herring. As Daniel Bradburd (1998) recently wrote about his work with Komachi pastoralists in Iran,

We would observe negotiations, disputes, and Komachi retellings of these events; we would attempt to analyze, contextualize, and understand what we had seen and heard; then we would seek out informants, either to try to gather additional information that would clarify the situation or to check our analyses. (165)

The centrality of collaboration in fieldwork has long been so self-evident that only recently have many anthropologists found it necessary to highlight it. Only in puerile adventure novels and old grade-B movies have fictional anthropologists made their way into "unknown territories" to "discover lost tribes," written author-as-lonely-hero descriptions of their "exotic customs," and presented them as authoritative truths.

What of point c above; does fieldwork "privilege" the enthnographer's account? Whether an ethnography is a privileged account depends on the field of comparison. One could argue quite reasonably and with the agreement of many anthropologists that the most privileged account of any cultural system would be one produced by a member of that society. Such an account, though, would not quite be the same thing as an account that an outsider might produce in collaboration with members of that community. Alexis de Tocqueville's description of U.S. society in the early nineteenth century offers an outsider's view of American values and customs that continues to fascinate us. Few members of any society can attain the perspective available to an observer who approaches from a different cultural experience. Nor have many chosen to interpret their own cultures to outsiders. The major exceptions in recent times have been the numerous indigenous people who have become anthropologists (see, for example, Beatrice Medicine for Lakota culture, Alfonso Ortiz for San Juan Pueblo culture, Francis Mading Deng for Dinka, Victor Uchendu for Igbo, Sir Peter Buck for Maori, Epeli Hau'ofa for Tonga, and numerous others).

The more important field of comparison, however, is description by other, nonanthropological outsiders. Does it much matter whether such accounts draw upon lengthy field research, observation, and consultation—or come from imaginative projections from a distance? The answer, no doubt, depends upon whether one can accept the premises that accuracy is important and reality is real.

Despite the interests of anthropologists in peoples beyond their own cultural systems, many indigenous peoples have not fared well during this century (see *d* in list above). To address postmodern criticisms, is this *despite* anthropology or *because* of it? Have the "strategic choices" of anthropologists writing their ethnographies done harm to the people with whom they have lived? Are anthropologists complicit in the oppression of "the Other"?

In the 1960s a significant number of anthropologists addressed this question. Many of them believed that anthropology's old posture of objectivity—based on the premise that the task was to understand and learn from indigenous peoples rather than to interfere with or try to change them in any way—had led to an unacceptable lack of involvement. They felt that anthropologists should become more active as advocates of the people whose cultures they studied.

This in turn has its problems. Many indigenous communities are far from united in their views on issues affecting them. Nonetheless, many anthropologists took the need for activism seriously. Anthropologists founded the organization Cultural Survival, which monitors issues and problems affecting indigenous peoples worldwide. Many anthropologists have placed themselves at the service of indigenous peoples, acting as consultants and expert witnesses and advisors in court cases or, as Terrance Turner and others did with the Kayapo, supporting land claim disputes and helping to gain access to the media.

The extent to which anthropology has helped or harmed indigenous peoples will no doubt remain subject to debate. To resolve that question once and for all, it would be necessary to know what the situation for indigenous peoples would have been if there had been no anthropologists but only engineers, political scientists, missionaries, development economists, and students of literature with whom to deal. One can only speculate what difference it would have made if no one had attempted to describe the ways of life of these small populations as viable, successful cultural systems developed by complex, three-dimensional human beings, rather than backward, underdeveloped impediments to progress or romantic children of nature.

Finally, let me consider point *e* above: The anthropologist James Boon (1982), in a postmodern critique of anthropology from within, notes that "[f]unctionalist monographs portrayed cultures as functionalists presumed them to be: islandlike, space-time isolates of interlocking, reinforcing systems of relationships" (14). The tendency of anthropology to focus intensely on small communities is long-standing (see *e* in list above). Does this mean that anthropologists have been unaware of the fact that cultures change? Does it substantiate the postmodern criticism that anthropologists ignore the big picture in favor of examining endless minutiae?

To help address these questions, let us grant that many anthropologists have indeed devoted themselves to what many would consider an inordinate focus on small research sites. Bronislaw Malinowski spent almost five years living among Trobriand Islanders off the coast of New Guinea. A. R. Radcliffe-Brown assiduously recorded and published the kinship system of Andaman Islanders. Franz Boas worked for over a decade, off and on, with a small Native American community of Kwakwala speakers on the coast of British Columbia, gathering information on aspects of their lives ranging from ceremonial exchanges to recipes. All of these have involved populations of no more than a few thousand people. None of them would come close to filling a modern football stadium.

On the face of it, this would hardly seem to be in the same league as studies of the rise of European and Asian socialism, the causes of the French Revolution, or the globalization of the economy after the Cold War. But to place these small-scale studies in perspective, let us consider what questions drove them. Just as it may be difficult to make sense of one end of a telephone conversation, it is difficult to appreciate these methods without taking into account the intellectual context of the times and the prevalent assumptions they were attempting to rebut.

Malinowski, Radcliffe-Brown, and Boas each worked with societies that most Europeans and Americans considered "savages," to the extent that the public were aware of them at all. The concept of savages arose from deeply rooted assumptions about the nature of humankind. Earlier writings, including treatises in early anthropology, characterized the customs and life-ways of people in such societies as backward, underdeveloped, and "primitive" in the sense that they represented antiquated and anachronistic stages of human development which were not only less fit but were doomed to extinction—the sooner, the better.

Perhaps among the major accomplishments of these early close, intimate ethnographic studies and others like them was to demonstrate the complexity and sustainability of such small societies and, above all, their situational rationality. The thrust of such studies, for anyone who cared to read them, was to demand for these societies a new level of respect.

Unfortunately, the more primitive views of Third World populations persist in modern Western popular thinking. Anthropological studies of small societies did, however, render these views far less defensible.

This did not, of course, mean that anthropologists were unaware of global phenomena impinging upon these societies. Such awareness, in fact, made the task of coming to understand them *as they were* all the more urgent. This task remains, even in the face of the good news that many of these local cultures have not entirely disappeared, as predicted, but have continued to adapt and survive.

Nonetheless, the need to address global processes which engulf such populations has also been of importance in anthropology. Perhaps among the most significant works of this nature have been Eric Wolf's *Europe and the People without History* (1982) and Peter Worsley's *The Three Worlds* (1984). Concerns with state dynamics, particularly as they impinge on indigenous populations, is a well-established anthropological concern (see, for example, Bodley 1999, Perry 1996).

What about the Postmodernists?

But enough about anthropology for the moment. Perhaps we should afford some attention to postmodern approaches to cross-cultural issues. Since critique is the order of the day, let us continue with a critique of postmodern studies of "the Other." Among them, we could list the following:

a. Many postmodernist studies display a proclivity toward essentialism.
b. The central point of many postmodern studies seems to be reflexive, rather than being aimed at achieving any serious understanding of the culture studied.
c. In the same vein, postmodern approaches carry the assumption that one can discuss global relationships without attention to sociocultural specifics.
d. Many postmodern studies privilege moralistic critique over substantive attention to the "Others'" cultures.
e. Notwithstanding postmodernists' posture of unmasking oppression and injustice, the approach confuses cultural relativism with moral relativism.
f. In questioning the validity of privileged knowledge, the postmodern approach assaults indigenous peoples' own histories and cultures.

Again, I will take up these points in order, beginning with *a.* Essentialism is an old problem in European intellectual traditions. Basically, it derives from an assumption that a fundamental, inherent essence distinguishes one category from another. Applied to concepts of humanity, of course, it emphasizes (some might say "celebrates") profound differences.

Anthropology has long dealt with differences. The thrust of twentieth-century anthropology, however, has been to explore causes for human differences in situational, historical, environmental, and cultural factors acting on a common human substance. Perhaps one of the major achievements of recent anthropology has been to assert and demonstrate a common humanity, to promulgate the idea that understanding diverse ways of dealing with shared human issues offers a useful way of understanding ourselves and others. Postmodern approaches, in contrast, celebrate the exotic without analysis, glorying in the differences without going deeper into the common substance.

b. At the level of the college classroom, this thrill of experiencing difference reflects the main purpose of much postmodern pedagogy. The main thrust is not to *understand* the Gahuku Gama, the Jale, or some other small populations of which few people have ever heard, but to experience how *different* they are from us. This helps us see ourselves as one group among many, but it tells us very little about the many. The use of the term "Other" is revealing in this respect. The Other is "other" only in reference to "us."

Many an anthropology professor has also told students that the discipline allows us to understand more about ourselves. But the rationale in this case has been somewhat more complex. From an anthropological perspective, we try to understand as much as we can about the Shuar, the Dani, the Samburu and so on because they are humans, as *we* are humans. Their different experiences and approaches to life can help us better grasp what it means, *collectively,* to *be human.* The postmodern approach, however, is often to sample some essentially different human phenomena without delving too deeply into the details of the peoples' lives, merely to savor how different they are. This appears to be one reason why, in many postmodernist courses, the Other is generically interchangeable as long as the Other is different enough.

c. The idea that interrelationships, particularly those involving power disparities, are more significant than the specific nature of the parties involved tends to reduce the study of complex human phenomena to formulaic mantras. Certainly, power disparities are crucial in understanding the historical experience of most third world peoples. But for anthropology (not to mention history and other disciplines), the latter component—the lives and experiences of the peoples involved—remains a significant part of the equation.

Beyond the psychological interplay between oppressor and oppressed, the pillage of resources also has been a salient factor in such situations. Few postmodernists have focused on such materialistic issues, perhaps because they carry the taint of political economy with its positivist associations. Once postmodernists have exposed the ill-kept secret that powerful interests have systematically exploited innocent peoples, should we not try to learn something about the people beyond their status as victims?

d. This leads, of course, to moralistic critique as pièce de résistance. Certainly, we may decry colonialistic and neocolonialistic outrages, as many have for a long time—including such politically innocuous academics as anthropologists. Moral outrage does pose a problem with the postmodern agenda, however, since to be consistent one must recognize that such sensibilities can only arise from a culture-specific, unanchored set of perceptions on the part of the observer—a matter of imposing one's own framework on another's reality. To argue otherwise would be to rub elbows with absolute values, which the emphatically relativist postmodernists have disdainfully abandoned.

e. In the minds of some postmodernists, apparently, relativism itself approaches the status of an absolute. Moral relativism, however—the inability to pass judgment on anything, no matter how atrocious and cruel it may appear to the unenlightened—is a difficult position to maintain consistently. In practical terms, it would render one all but useless as a contributing human being. But perhaps consistency itself is merely a delusional artifact of positivistic thinking.

In any case, extreme moral relativism has little to do with cultural relativism. As noted earlier, cultural relativism merely involves the attempt to keep one's own preconceptions from inhibiting the quest to understand human phenomena. It does not prevent one from deploring or confronting injustice. It attempts to look beyond revulsion and try to understand the causes of the observed phenomenon.

f. The unbuttoned relativism and rejection of "privileged texts," finally, does great injustice to the many Others who have drawn the attention of postmodern multiculturalists.　The Others do have real histories and cultural systems. To treat these as negotiable texts is to vandalize a fundamental aspect of their identities. Far from being consistent with the moralistic exposure of injustice, the misrepresentation of peoples' cultural and historical realities has long been a major tool of their oppression.

It would be difficult to put it more effectively than the Third World scholar Ziauddin Sardar (1998):

Postmodernism does not mark a break, a discontinuity from oppressive modernity; rather, it represents an underlying continuity of thought and actions about Other cultures, which formed the bedrock of colonialism, was the foundation of modernity and is now housed in postmodernism. Colonialism signified the physical occupation of the territory of Others, the non-Western cultures. Modernity signaled their mental occupation. Postmodernism now moves in to take possession of their total reality. (20)

Troubled Reflections

One should not impugn the motives and integrity of colleagues merely because they see things differently, even if these perceptions have dire implications. Notwithstanding some compelling critiques of postmodern writings such as Sokal and Bricmont's (1998) exposure of habitual obfuscation in phony pseudoscientific verbiage, in many respects postmodernists have sought to bring a freer critical perspective to some tired paradigms. As in any field, however, it is useful to distinguish the leading intellectual contributions from the secondary strategies of those who see opportunity in taking advantage of innovative developments. On many college campuses, this is not merely an issue of people pursuing new ideas and challenging old assumptions. It is also a matter of many faculty teaching subjects in which they have little background in order to exploit the postmodern / multicultural academic growth industry.

This is puzzling, since it is not the norm in academia. One seldom hears of faculty trained in English literature deciding to teach chemistry or anthropologists choosing to offer courses in literature. Up to this point, the accepted standards in most reputable colleges would have left such eventualities out of the question. Most colleges and universities evaluating candidates for faculty positions scrutinize the applicants' credentials for evidence of competence in the fields they will teach.

Somehow, though, teaching about other cultures has come to be exempt from such criteria. The Third World seems to have become fair game—not merely in world politics, as in the past, but now in academia as well.

One possible reason seems to be that some academics and administrators see these subjects as "easier," somehow, than others in the curriculum—a field of inquiry for which one need not have extensive preparation to teach. (There is little point in even discussing publication here, since most published works of the new converts seem to be about "how to teach multiculturalism," not about cultures.)

Among the processes at work here is yet another insidious phenomenon—the devaluation of academic labor and a concomitant erosion of its integrity. The devaluation of labor in general has been a global process for many years. In academics it has manifested itself in a growing tendency toward the interchangeability of faculty. Ultimately, college faculty have no particular value except for their possession of specialized knowledge. In general, they are not necessarily bigger, stronger, better looking, snappier dressers, more charismatic, or even smarter than the average person. Their only credentials are based on what they have taken the time and effort to learn about some subject. The short-term benefits that faculty can gain from exploiting the postmodernist fashion of discrediting the "traditional" study of other cultures plays into the hands of those who tend to see college faculty as generic, individually expendable eccentrics.

This is not the most important problem, however. Perhaps a more serious issue, in the long run, is that the political maneuvering of these academic games works to the detriment of the serious study of complex human issues and the attempt to understand them.

Postmodernists have tried to claim the high ground by characterizing the painstaking study of other cultures as "traditional" and "conservative," with all of the baggage that implies. We might ask, at the end of all this, why it is "progressive" to deal with most of the world's peoples in a superficial way? Why is it "reactionary" to insist that other societies and cultures are important enough and complex enough to warrant serious study?

Ultimately, such aspersions distract attention from the substantive issue, which is how we can better understand the human experience in all its diversity and complexity. That purpose is ill-served by declaring accuracy delusional and observational data irrelevant.

Note

The author would like to express his deep appreciation to Dr. Alice Pomponio, Professor of Anthropology and spouse, for her patient reading and helpful comments

References Cited

Atkinson, Paul. 1990. *The Ethnographic Imagination: Textual Constructions of Reality*. London and New York: Routledge.

Bloom, Alan. 1987. *The Closing of the American Mind*. New York: Simon & Schuster.

Boas, Franz. 1896. "The Limitations of the Comparative Method in Anthropology." *Science* 4; no. 103. Reprint: Pp. 85–93 in *High Points in Anthropology*, ed. Paul Bohannon and Mark Glazer. New York: Alfred A. Knopf, 1973. Bodley, John. 1999. *Victims of Progress*. Mountain View, CA: Mayfield.

Bohannon, Paul. 1995. *How Culture Works*. New York: Free Press.

Boon, James A. 1982. *Other Tribes, Other Scribes: Symbolic Anthropology and the Comparative Study of Cultures, Histories, Religions, and Texts*. Cambridge: Cambridge University Press.

Bourke, John. 1886. *An Apache Campaign in the Sierra Madres. An Account of an Expedition in Pursuit of the Hostile Chiricahua Apaches in the Spring of 1883*. New York: Charles Scribner's Sons.

Bradburd, Daniel. 1998. *Being There: The Necessity of Fieldwork*. Washington: Smithsonian.

Clifford, James. 1988. *The Predicament of Culture: Twentieth Century Ethnography, Literature, and Art*. Cambridge: Harvard University Press.

Clifford, James, and George Markus. 1986. *Writing Culture: The Poetics and Politics of Ethnography*. Berkeley: University of California Press.

Dettmar, Kevin J. H. 1998. "An Introduction to Postmodernism: Just Let Them Hear Some of That Rock n' Roll Music." *Chronicles of Higher Education* (September 25): B4–B5.

Evans-Pritchard, E. E. 1962. *Social Anthropology and Other Essays*. New York: Free Press.

Foucault, Michel. 1972. *The Archaeology of Knowledge*. London: Harper Colophon.

Freilich, Morris, ed. 1970 *Marginal Natives: Anthropologists at Work*. New York: Harper and Row.

Geertz, Clifford. 1973. "Thick Description: Toward an Interpretive Theory of Culture." Pp. 3–32 in *The Interpretation of Cultures*. New York: Basic Books.

——. 1988. *Works and Lives: The Anthropologist as Author*. Cambridge: Polity.

Goody, Jack. 1996. *The Expansive Moment: The Rise of Social Anthropology in Britain and Africa 1918–1970*. Cambridge: Cambridge University Press.

Green, L. C., and Olive Dickason. 1989. *The Law of Nations and the New World*. Edmonton: University of Alberta Press.

Harris, Marvin. 1968. *The Rise of Anthropological Theory*. New York: Thomas Y. Crowell.

Krupat, Arnold. 1992. *Ethnocriticism: Ethnography, History, and Literature*. Berkely: University of California Press.

Lyotard, Jean-Francois. 1983. *The Post-Modern Condition: A Report on Knowledge*. Minneapolis: University of Wisconsin Press.

Marcus, George and Michael Fisher. 1986. *Anthropology as Cultural Critique*. Chicago: University of Chicago Press.

Opler, Morris E. 1941. *An Apache Life-Way. The Economic, Social, and Religious Institutions of the Chiricahua Indians*. Chicago: University of Chicago Press.

Perry, Richard J. 1992. "Why Do Multiculturalists Ignore Anthropologists?" *Chronicle of Higher Education* (March 4): A52.

———. 1996. *From Time Immemorial: Indigenous Peoples and State Systems*. Austin: University of Texas Press.

Pratt, M. L. 1986. "Fieldwork in Common Places." Pp. 27–50 in *Writing Culture*, ed. James Clifford and George Marcus. Cambridge: Harvard University Press.

Rabinow, Paul. 1977. *Reflections on Field Work in Morocco*. Berkeley: University of California Press.

———. 1986. "Representations Are Social Facts: Modernity and Post-Modernity in Anthropology." Pp. 234–61 in *Writing Culture,* ed. James Clifford and George Marcus. Cambridge: Harvard University Press.

Rosaldo, Renato. 1986. "From the Door of His Tent." Pp. 77–97 in *Writing Culture,* ed. James Clifford and George Marcus. Cambridge: Harvard University Press.

Said, Edward. 1993. *Culture and Imperialism*. New York: Knopf.

Sapir, Edward. 1929. "The Status of Linguistics as a Science." *Language 5*, no. 4: 207–14.

Sardar, Ziauddin. 1997. *Postmodernism and the Other: The New Imperialism of Western Culture*. London: Pluto Press.

Saussure, Fernand de. 1955. *Course in General Linguistics*. New York: McGraw-Hill.

Schorske, Carl E. 1998. *Thinking with History: Explorations in the Passage to Modernity*. Princeton: Princeton University Press.

Searle, John R. 1995. *The Construction of Social Reality*. New York: Free Press.

Sokal, Alan, and Jean Bricmont. 1999. *Fashionable Nonsense: Postmodern Intellectual Abuse of Science*. New York: Picador USA.

Stocking, George W. Jr. 1995. *After Tylor: British Social Anthropology 1888–1951*. Madison: University of Wisconsin Press.

Weiner, Annette. 1992. "Anthropology's Lessons for Cultural Diversity." *Chronicle of Higher Education* (July 22): B1–B2.

Wolf, Eric R. 1982. *Europe and the People without History*. Berkeley: University of California Press.

Worsley, Peter. 1984. *The Three Worlds*. Chicago: University of Chicago Press.

Additional Readings

Abu-Lughod, Lila. 1991. "Writing against Culture." Pp. 137–60 in *Recapturing Anthropology. Working in the Present,* ed. Richard G. Fox. Santa Fe, NM: School of American Research.

Adair, Gilbert. 1992. *The Postmodern Always Rings Twice.* London: Fourth Estate.

Anderson, Walter Truett. 1990. *Reality Isn't What It Used to Be.* San Francisco: Harper.

Appell, George N. 1993. "Scholars, True Believers, and the Identity Crisis in American Anthropology." *Reviews in Anthropology* 21:193–202.

Asad, Talal, ed. 1973. *Anthropology and the Colonial Encounter.* London: Ithaca Press.

Barber, Benjamin. 1994. *Jihad vs. McWorld.* New York: Time Books.

Baudrillard, Jean. 1993. *The Transparency of Evil.* London: Verso.

Bauman, Zygmunt. 1993. *Postmodern Ethics.* Oxford: Blackwell.

———. 1995 *Life in Fragments: Essays on Postmodern Morality.* Oxford: Blackwell.

Bernstein, Richard J. 1995. *The New Constellation: The Ethical-Political Horizons of Modernity / Postmodernity.* Cambridge, MA: MIT Press.

Best, Steven, and Doublas Kellner. 1991. *Postmodern Theory: Critical Interrogations.* London: Macmillan.

Borofsky, Robert. 1996. *Assessing Cultural Anthropology.* New York: McGraw-Hill.

Brightman, Robert A. 1997. "Forget Culture: Replacement, Transcendence, Relatxification," *Cultural Anthropology* 10:509–46.

Bush, Ronald. 1998. "The Presence of the Past: Thinking / Literary Politics." Pp. 32–41 in *Prehistories of the Future: The Primitivist Project and the Culture of Modernism,* ed. Elazar Barkan and Ronald Bush. Stanford, CA: Stanford University Press.

Callinicos, Alex. 1989. *Against Postmodernism.* Cambridge: Polity Press.

Escobar, Arturo. 1993. "The Limits of Reflexivity: Politics in Anthropology's Post–*Writing Culture* Era." Review article based on *Recapturing Anthropology,* ed. Richard G. Fox. *Journal of Anthropological Research* 49:377–91.

Feyerabend, Paul. 1974. *Against Method.* London: New Left Books.

———. 1987. *Farewell to Reason.* London: Verso.

Forster, Peter. 1973. "Empiricism and Imperialism: A Review of the New Left's Critique of Social Anthropology." Pp. 23–38 in *Anthropology and the Colonial Encounter,* ed. Talal Asad. London: Ithaca Press.

Fox, Richard G. 1991. *Recapturing Anthropology: Working in the Present.* Santa Fe, NM: School of American Research.

Gibbons, John R. ed. 1989. *Contemporary Political Culture: Politics in a Postmodern Age.* London: Sage.

Griffin, Ray. 1988. *The Reenchantment of Science: Postmodern Proposals.* Albany, NY: SUNY Press.

Harvey, David.1989. *The Condition of Postmodernity.* Oxford: Blackwell.

Jameson, Fredric.1990. *Postmodernism, or the Cultural Logic of Late Capitalism.* Durham, NC: Duke University Press.

Jencks, Charles. 1986. *What Is Postmodernism?* London: Academy Editions.

Kroken, Arthur, and David Cook. 1986. *The Postmodern Scene.* London: Macmillan.

Knauft, Bruce. 1994. "Pushing Anthropology Past the Posts: Critical Notes on Cultural Anthropology and Cultural Studies as Influenced by Postmodernism and Existentialism." *Critique of Anthropology* 14:117–52.

Kuper, Adam. 1993. "Post-Modernism, Cambridge and the Great Kalahari Debate." *Social Anthropology* 1:57–71.

Lewis, Herbert S. 1999. "The Misrepresentation of Anthropology and Its Consequences." *American Anthropologist* 100:716–31.

Marcus, George E. and Michael D. Fischer. 1986. *Anthropology as Cultural Critique: An Experimental Moment in the Human Sciences*. Chicago: University of Chicago Press.

McGrane, Bernard. 1989. *Beyond Anthropology: Society and the Other*. New York: Columbia University Press.

Rabinow, Paul. 1987. "Beyond Ethnography: Anthropology as Nominalism." *Cultural Anthropology* 3:355–64.

Reyna, S. P. 1994. "Literary Anthropology and the Case against Science." *Man* 29:55–581.

Ricoeur, Paul. 1984. *The Reality of the Historical Past*. Milwaukee, WI: Marquette University Press.

Rosaldo, Renato. 1995. "Whose Cultural Studies?" *American Anthropologist* 96:525–29.

Rosenau, Pauline M. 1992. *Post-Modernism and the Social Sciences: Insights, Inroads, and Intrusions*. Princeton, NJ: Princeton University Press.

Said, Edward. 1989. "Representing the Colonized: Anthropology's Interlocutors," *Critical Inquiry* 15:205–25.

Sangren, P. Steven. 1988. "Rhetoric and the Authority of Ethnography: 'Postmodernism' and the Social Reproduction of Texts." *Current Anthropology* 29:405–35.

Spencer, J. 1989. "Anthropology as a Kind of Writing," *Man* 24:145–64.

Spiro, Melford. 1996. "Postmodern Anthropology, Subjectivity, and Science: A Modernist Critique." *Comparative Studies in Society and History* 38:759–80.

Strathern, Marylin. 1989. "Out of Context: The Persuasive Fictions of Anthropology." *Current Anthropology* 28:251–81.

Tibbetts, Paul. 1990. "Representation and the Realist-Constructivist Controversy." *Human Studies* 11:117–32.

Woolgar, Steve, ed. 1991. *Knowledge and Reflexivity: New Frontiers in the Sociology of Knowledge*. London: Sage.

Yearly, Steven. 1981. "Textual Persuasion: The Role of Social Accounting in the Construction of Scientific Arguments." *Philosophy of the Social Sciences* 11:409–35.

JOHN AGNEW

Disputing the Nature of the International

Geographies of Sameness and Difference

IN INTERNATIONAL STUDIES, *geography* usually has one or both of two meanings. The first one refers to a fixed and objective physical geography constraining and directing the activities of states and other actors (such as businesses, migrants, and international organizations). By way of example, such fixed geographical features as the disposition of states in relation to the distribution of continents and oceans (land powers versus sea powers) or resource bases in relation to military strength are seen as determining or conditioning the possibilities and limits of specific states as players in international relations. Even more mundanely, *geography* is also used in a second meaning in reference to the terms and labels used to designate states, regions, and places on the world map. The world's geography thus becomes reduced to a list of names applied to places, near and far, familiar and exotic, in which "events," "situations,"

Editor's Note: John Agnew is a member of the Department of Geography and Center for European and Russian Studies at UCLA and is concerned with bridging a bifurcation within the discipline of geography and, in the process, enhancing its contributions to geopolitical studies. In "Disputing the Nature of the International," Agnew argues that the fundamental split in geography is between the "realists" and the constructionists"; the former group analyzes the actions of states in terms of physical factors deemed to be "out there" regardless of human will (proximity to the sea, contiguity with other states, etc.), while the latter, deeply suspicious of the hegemony of nation-states, sees virtually all geopolitical categories as "constructed" by human will. The split is so sharply defined, Agnew maintains, that both sides lose: "If one neglects the crucial role of human consciousness in making and describing the world, the other misses the verifiable existence of a material world with which human consciousness and practices must work." His solution is a historical approach to geopolitics that makes use of both realist and constructionist insights and recognizes that the "international" is not necessarily the dominant geographical scale of world politics.

or "crises" occur that demand a recognition, reaction, or response from a home state or international agency.

Within the field of academic geography today these meanings, long taken for granted, have begun to excite considerable interest as topics of study in their own right. In some contemporary human geography courses, therefore, students will find much of their time devoted to studying how thinking by politicians and intellectuals about the world's physical geography and division into state territories and labeling of world regions and places affects the character and course of international and domestic affairs. In particular, the presumed universal effects of relative location (ocean-fronting or continental interior) on state potential and the seeming political neutrality of geographical labels (such as the West or Pacific Rim) are called into question. These are seen as dangerous oversimplifications of a more complex world in which cultural and political *difference* is systematically obscured in favor of a predictable *sameness* in behavior and outcomes. In many other courses, however, more of a "problem-solving" approach than conceptual analysis tends to prevail. The division of the world into territorial states is seen as a given, powerful states are seen as having predictable territorial sources of their power and behavior, and a struggle for primacy between powerful states animates international politics. In other words, the world as it is conventionally described is more or less as it is. It has also been this way since time immemorial. International political practice is based on the clash of state-territorial forces mandated by locational and/or environmental imperatives.

Among geographers, therefore, the *international* in international studies has come to refer to either (1) ways in which the world's physical geography and the labeling practices of powerful states and other institutions are used to create, direct, and justify actions outside the boundaries of one's home state in violation of the world's actual complexity, or (2) the predictable impacts of the world's physical geography (the relative location of states on the world map, the geographical juxtaposition of states one to another, the state-by-state distribution of major resources, etc.) on the likelihood of conflict between states. What distinguishes them are competing understandings of the *nature* of the international. In the first case the international is understood as the application of a category really involving inter*state* relations, by means of which "essential" features (really a selected set of elements) of the natural order of things (adjacency of states, resources, strategic significance, etc.) are invoked as directing relations between states. This is nature as the invention of human volition. In the second case the essential character of the world is seen as residing in its physical geography, with the international referring to the level or geographical scale beyond that of individual states at which the resource and locational characteristics of states determine relations between them. This is nature without benefit of human volition.

These positions are akin to those in political science and other fields staked out, respectively, by so-called poststructuralists and neorealists.[1] The first suggests a sensitivity to the connection between power and knowledge; how what we presume to know reflects a political bias that cannot recognize the experiences and understandings of subordinated people and places but which records the "common sense" of the power-ful—above all state elites and the "intellectuals of statecraft"—who give advice to political leaders in powerful states about the conduct of foreign policy. The second represents a rationalist understanding of behavior: that irrespective of location or culture a set of material conditions (in-cluding geographical influences) will elicit similar response from persons or states. To the liberal understanding of individual persons as rational actors (usually implying a considered pursuit of ordered preferences for goods and beliefs) is added the sense of states as unitary entities engaging in a like-minded pursuit of utility or status, inevitably at the expense of each other.

The purpose of this essay is to provide a discussion of the philosophi-cal perspectives these positions reflect, critique the total opposition between "constructionism" and "realism" that is the basis of the argu-ment between them, give a brief overview of the logic of "critical" and "classical" understandings of geopolitics (or geographies of international relations) that have emerged within academic geography, and offer an al-ternative to them that both "historicizes" (puts in historical perspective) and "spatializes" (identifies the changing geographical practices that in-form) international politics. A historical understanding of how global space is produced and used by states and other actors, therefore, provides a real alternative to either the purely discursive or the fixed materialist understandings of the world's geography that currently prevail within geographical approaches to international studies.

Constructionism versus Realism

The terms *state* and *world region* (such as Latin America or the Middle East) conjure up an image of relatively homogeneous blocks of terrestrial space that have persisting distinctiveness due to physical and/or cultural and political characteristics. The claim is that they exist "out there" in the world, even if there is a prior requirement to think that the world is actu-ally divided up in this way. This combination of a claim to real existence and the necessity for prior thought on the part of an observer/designator has caused major difficulty for geographers and others using geographical designations and descriptions. It has also led to the unfortunate opposition in contemporary human geography between those who claim the mantle "real" for their regions and those who regard all regions and geographical descriptors as inventions of observers whose definitions say more about who they are and where they are from than the phenomena they purport to classify. This is how geographers have tended to construe realism, on the one hand, and constructionism, on the other.[2]

I see the opposition as unfortunate because it makes little or no sense to regard regions (or any mode of classification, for that matter) as if they are either simply "out there" or all in the mind of observers imposing their designations on everyone else. These perspectives rest on drawing a total opposition between realism and constructionism as positions on what exists and how it comes about. On the one side, the world's geography is causally efficacious, and the terms used to describe it have a universal applicability. On the other side, regions and other geographical designations are the result of linguistic categories produced by social conventions *without* universal applicability.

There is undoubtedly a visceral tension between the idea that something is real and the idea that it is constructed. The history of Western philosophy could be seen to a large degree in terms of the competing claims of the two—between realism and idealism. The real is like the body in the mind-body problematic in philosophy; it is tangible, touchable, and empirically knowable with a minimum of assumptions. The constructed is like the mind at work making sense of itself and the body. Consciousness is prior to the working of the body because the body can only be understood by the mind.

The main problem here is that an object or a thing (such as a body or a mind) and *an idea about* that object or thing are not the same. Neither can be reduced to the other. Yet that is precisely what the opposing positions do. If one neglects the crucial role of human consciousness in making and describing the world, the other misses the verifiable existence of a material world with which human consciousness and practices must work. If theoretical, cultural, and political differences of opinion provide evidence of the former, then the workings of gravity, the finiteness of terrestrial space, the biology of sexual desire, and the decline of biodiversity attest to the latter. The critical issue is *human reflexivity*, which means that although humans react to objects, they also have ideas about those objects to which they also react. Human reflexivity applies as well to regions, which reflect both differences in the world and ideas about those differences. *They cannot be reduced entirely to one or the other.* Observers and people in the world use regional designations to make sense of the world because some degree of simplification is inevitable given the mass of information about particulars potentially available. These designations draw on real differences between parts of the world, but they cannot claim total fit to the world because they are based on ideas about geographical differences that are not simply about those differences *per se* but also about ideas about how the world as a whole works.

Much contemporary philosophical discussion in human geography is organized around the realism-constructionism opposition. Two recent widely reviewed works serve to illustrate this take on the philosophy of the field: books by Robert Sack (1997) and by Martin Lewis and Kären Wigen (1997).[3] Sack offers an abstract framework for understanding places that takes nature, self, social relations, and moral awareness as constitutive elements of places in which "forces" (the real) and "perspectives" (the constructed) jointly produce the experience and awareness of place. Lewis and Wigen provide a sophisticated critique of the continental, three worlds, East-West, and other schemes for dividing up the world into regions. They criticize conventional wisdom by drawing attention to its inherent cultural and political biases. They propose a "better" basis to world regionalization than those manifested by existing schemas.

Despite their acknowledgment of the effects of ideas about place and regions on awareness and experience, both works insist on associating constructionism with relativism (the idea that knowledge is dependent on experience, social standpoint, or a pet theory) and deconstructionism (the idea that language determines what we can know). They self-consciously champion the realist position that "the world" can be known and causally explained. Yet each also depends crucially on a constructionist approach to the impact that ideas about places and regions have on people's experience and awareness, and on the meaning of places and regions. They cannot avoid doing so if they are to take human reflexivity into account. But at the level of explicit philosophy they refuse to acknowledge their own practical incorporation of constructionism.

In research and teaching practice, therefore, the distinction between realism and constructionism often breaks down. But authors continue to write as if they are opposites, without possibility of conciliation. An intellectually deadening philosophical template has descended on the field in which authors sensitive to the mutual impact of both feel the need to publicly refuse one or the other. Away from philosophically sensitive books such as those of Sack or Lewis and Wigen the opposition grows more intense. Understandings of the international in the work of political geographers exemplify the drawing of a particularly acute distinction between the real and the constructed.

Geographies of International Relations

As long as professional geographers have studied the international, it has always been subsumed by the global. For much of the twentieth century this has involved relating relations between states to the global positioning of states and their relative access to the resources upon which competition between states is based. So-called classical geopolitics has been based squarely within this tradition of understanding. Its adherents see classification as a sea- or land-power with respect to the global distribution of oceans and continents as driving international relations. A more recent school of spatial geopolitics has continued this approach but with an explicit emphasis on the role of relative location of states in generating conflict between them. I use an example of the influential work of John O'Loughlin to illustrate this perspective.[4]

Beginning in the 1980s, but with intellectual antecedents going back to anarchist geographers such as Kropotkin and under the influence of the linguistic turn in the social sciences in the 1970s, a self-consciously "critical" geopolitics began to emerge whose proponents were skeptical of the conventional wisdom about the geography of international relations. Two intellectual elements distinguish this approach from the classical one. The first is an explicit suspicion of state power, particularly that of the most powerful states, such as the United States. The second is a joint focus on the language and practices of state elites and their supporting intellectuals as not only suggestive but determinative of activities carried on in the name of the state. In geographical terms, this orientation celebrates a world of diversity suppressed and disciplined by established geopolitical discourse and practices and identifies the role of conventional geographical reasoning as crucial in maintaining current structures of power. I use the seminal work of Gearóid Ó Tuathail to illustrate this perspective.[5]

Obviously, the pieces of writing I refer to by O'Loughlin or Ó Tuathail do not constitute a random sample of available writing within the various genres of contemporary political geography. For example, they are both Irishmen who teach at American universities. They are selected purposefully to illustrate the intellectual practice of the realism-constructionism opposition. Much writing does not in practice neatly fit the template even as writers, more often than not, tend to publicly situate themselves in one "box" or another rather than on a continuum from one extreme to the other.

Spatial Geopolitics

A good example of a realist take on international relations (as defined above) would be O'Loughlin (1986).[6] This paper maps the incidence and severity of wars involving states for the period 1816–1982, in terms of number of years at war, and proceeds to measure the effects of relative location on the production of this map. The geographic causes of war, such as number of borders and location in different geopolitical zones, are weighed against nonspatial attributes, such as military expenditures, type of government, and global ideological alignment (which side in the Cold War?). O'Loughlin adds to existing analysis in three ways. He specifies that not only immediate neighbors but also more distant ones should be included in measurement, insists that regional location in relation to global geopolitics should be estimated, and argues that spatial and nonspatial variables must be included within the same analysis to show their relative importance.

O'Loughlin takes great care in defining and finding appropriate data for his key indicators, such as state contiguity and military expenditures. Accurate measurement has a high priority, as does quantitative estimation of the relative weight of variables in accounting for the incidence of war in different historic periods identified to fit different features of international relations, such as colonialism and the Cold War, that might otherwise "complicate" the structural analysis of the incidence of war. Measures of spatial autocorrelation (testing whether the spatial arrangement of values is random or clustered) reveal that there is no simple contiguity-war relationship. Rather, it seems that geographic contiguity is mediated by a range of nonspatial variables such as military strength, alliance membership, political ideology, and war history.

A more inclusive spatial-structural model of war is then used to test for the relative importance of geographic and state-structural variables in determining the incidence and severity of wars. This model is compared to one lacking in spatial variables. Multiple regression analysis is applied to the sets of spatial and nonspatial predictor variables with number of months at war, battle deaths, and years at war as war indicators (dependent variables). States with high scores on the three dependent variables tend to cluster, and thus their contiguity can be seen as a predictor of their prevalence as combatants. Location within a global "shatterbelt" region—sub-Saharan Africa, the Middle East, and Southeast Asia—is also of statistical significance; though this is weakened when the contiguity measure is present. The main conclusion O'Loughlin (1986) draws is that "spatial factors [contiguity relations] are as important as military expenditures and are more important than the commonly used political and economic predictors in explaining war behavior."[7]

Throughout, the following assumptions are operative. First, a world divided into states is taken as given. Second, war between states can be explained in terms of the workings of factors that do not involve human volition—for example, war, like the weather, can be predicted if only the right variables are identified in the right combination. Third, history, in the sense of changing constellations of states, other actors, and ideologies, is a source of complication in understanding rather than the actual source of the causes of war. Fourth, all states are fundamentally conflictual in orientation, irrespective of their other differences. Fifth, and finally, domestic and alliance sources of external behavior are systematically excluded because of difficulties of measurement and the tendency to see states as unitary actors.

Critical Geopolitics

Ó Tuathail is a complex writer whose views have changed somewhat as he has confronted a number of critiques of the poststructuralist rendering of geopolitics with which he has been primarily concerned. The full range of his perspective is on view in his book *Critical Geopolitics* (1996) and in his contributions to a special issue of the journal *Political Geography*.[8] His work at its most explicitly constructionist is illustrated by a 1994 paper entitled "(Dis)placing Geopolitics: Writing on the Maps of Global Politics."[9]

In this paper, Ó Tuathail criticizes geopolitical thinkers and politicians for categorizing and labeling the world and its parts and at the same time interrogates the term *critical geopolitics* to suggest its limitations as a perspective. The terms *critical* and *geopolitics* sit uneasily together, the former indicating a suspicion of power and state-centric thinking, the latter assuredly associated intimately with *raison d'état*. From the start, therefore, the terms of geopolitics (including the word itself) are seen as situated in a set of discourses about statehood, state sovereignty, and the divisions of the world upon which international relations depends for its theory and practice. Language is defined as the expression of collective meanings invested in terms that, rather than being accepted as constructed, are typically understood as representing "deep" or "essential" features of an external reality. Drawing on such thinkers as Jacques Derrida and Michel Foucault, Ó Tuathail sees the mapping of the world by academic theorists and political practitioners as involving a "geographing" in which meaning is never completely mapped even though that is the claim they make. The goal of the paper is to provide an analysis of the ways in which conventional geopolitics can be called into question or "displaced" from its intellectual-political pedestal.

The paper has three main sections. In the first section Ó Tuathail criticizes the traditional maps of geopolitics in two ways. One is that they treat terms as self-evident when they are anything but. For example, the term *international* "presupposes a geographical distinction between an inside domestic sphere and an outside international sphere"[10] that though historically variable is never absolute. The other involves the exclusion of the term *geopolitics* as a legitimate word within the discipline of geography (because of its links to imperialism and Nazi ideology), even as geopolitics continued to be integral to the field while its excluders preached their own innocence of politics or geopolitical views.

A second section regards geopolitics as a type of "governmentality," a term coined by Foucault to refer to a means of organizing population, security, and territory. From this point of view, geopolitics is understood as "[t]he endeavor . . . to make the features, realities, and enduring laws that supposedly account for global politics visible to statesmen and the general public."[11] The tasks of a critical geopolitics are

(1) to problematize the delimitation of the relationship between geography and politics to essential identities and domains; (2) to document the strategies by which maps of global politics are produced by governmental sites; and (3) to disrupt the infrastructural functioning of such maps by "displacing their boundaries, blotting out their cardinal reference points, thus making it more difficult to read off the coordinates."[12]

A third and much longer section explores the techniques of seeing "that make maps of global politics possible."[13] Rather than "mirrors of nature," maps select and order information according to authoritative sources emanating from sites of global power. Attention focuses on the institutions that produce geopolitical knowledge and the corresponding types of knowledge produced. First is the disciplinary (i.e., geography) site of knowledge. Particular ways of seeing the world have been sponsored by academic geography. These privilege travel accounts and cartographic portrayals, a "spatial accounting" that surveys and documents place-characteristics of the world-at-large, and continuous monitoring with respect to global norms articulated by powerful states and international organizations. The second site is that occupied by foreign-policy makers. Places are constructed to fit into global schemas of security interests and commitments as politicians and their advisors engage in the day-to-day problem solving that later appears on the evening news or in tomorrow's newspaper. The third and final site of geopolitical knowledge is that of popular culture. Within capital cities, for example, monuments represent sites of ritual celebration that memorialize colonial and other geopolitical commitments. Films and magazines also convey images of threat and commitment by means of which popular ideas of geopolitics circulate and gain currency. Ó Tuathail favorably cites Paul Virilio's notion that cinema is a technology of perception that has grown up alongside warfare.[14] Maps, aerial photographs, and photogrammetry have all become interconnected as a result of the explosion of aerial and satellite surveillance. In turn, these techniques have had applications in cinematic film and video game production.

The thrust of the article is to "displace" the logic of conventional geopolitics by pointing to the means of its production. Geopolitics does not just "happen." It is practiced by agents who occupy discrete sites where geopolitical knowledge is produced and from where it is enforced. Moreover, critical geopolitics is not simply an alternative theory to that of classical geopolitics. It "cannot be written from a beyond of geopolitics, from a place outside or beyond the infrastructure of mapping, geo-graphing, seeing." Yet, it aspires to refuse the geopolitical tradition's "teleological drive towards homogeneity, decidability, certainty. The identity of place and the place of identity are problematized."[15]

The article has a number of features that are themselves problematic. The first is its reliance on the word/text as a singular guide to action. This is not to say that language is never revealing of intentions and activities. Rather, it is to suggest that written language or textuality is an imperfect guide to the practices of geopolitics. For example, is what is said necessarily the same as what is actually driving a specific policy? Words mask as much as they enlighten. This suggests the limits of models for understanding geopolitics drawn from the literary field. Discursive reasons only give clues to the operation of practical reason.[16]

Second, though the logic of the argument suggests that geopolitics need not be named to have a presence within international relations, there is an implied nominalism that would suggest it must.[17] Writing global space, therefore, is unique to the century since the invention of the word. In my view, this position is plainly absurd, defying the attempt to invoke practice as the ultimate arena of geopolitics. If images and representations of global space predated the 1899 invention of the word *geopolitics*, then why not explore and examine them?

Third, the representations of geopolitical discourses do not exist in a material vacuum. They both reflect and inform judgments and interpretations about the ways of the world. People are practical as well as imagineering animals. The world is a joint creation of practical pressures and ideological impositions. It cannot be reduced satisfactorily to one or the other. Thus, the urge or passion of some to consume, accumulate capital, control other people and places, or achieve intellectual approbation have sociological and psychological origins that are bracketed in constructionist accounts of geopolitical knowledge. Knowledge may often serve power, but its workings do not tell anything about who has power and why.

Fourth, and finally, implicit in critical geopolitics as formulated in the specific article in question is an ontological undercurrent that surfaces episodically in allusions to military surveillance and technology. This suggests a rendering of state security that privileges the military aspects of state activities over, say, economic or financial ones. But the public hostility to the concept of a set of material constraints channeling or limiting state activities leaves any particular inference as problematic. Absent a thorough airing of possible commitments to an external reality beyond the pages of texts and maps, any inference must remain tentative and contestable.

Historical Geopolitics

A number of crucial certainties about fixed and unquestioned boundaries between states, the division of the world into mutually hostile armed camps on the basis of political ideology, the centrality of states to world politics, and the primacy of fixed national identities in political psychology have all either disappeared or are in question. The end of the Cold War, the growing importance of trading blocs such as the European Union, and the proliferation of ethnic and regionalist movements within established states have undermined both the seemingly stable international order and the intellectual perspectives that described and served it. It is not surprising, therefore, to find increased scrutiny of conventional wisdom about the nature of the international.

Power and Geopolitics

The history of the word *geopolitics* began about one hundred years ago, in 1899, when it was coined by the Swedish political scientist Rudolf Kjellén. The word formally linked the process of thinking globally on behalf of particular states (your own) to the potential of those states to act globally, as indicated by global location, resources, and the like. In practice, however, such linkage had begun much earlier, when European political elites had begun to consider their strategies in terms of global conditions revealed to them by the European encounter with the rest of the world. The onset of the capitalist world economy and the growth of European territorial states gave rise to new understandings of the division and labeling of global space.

The layering of the globe from the world scale downward—only possible once the entire world was available for consideration—created a hierarchy of geographical scales through which the emerging political-economic reality was seen and understood. The four scales were the global (the scale of the world as a whole), the international (the scale of the relations between states), the domestic/national (the scale of individual states), and the regional (the scale of parts of the state). Political problems and policies were defined in terms of the geographical scales (either domestic/national or international/foreign) at which they were seen as operative. World politics worked from the global scale down. It was at this scale that the term *geopolitics* came to be applied. But the term rested on assumptions about the relative importance of different scales that were already in place. In particular, the national and the international were already privileged within the context of the global framework.

What underpinned this bias was a dominant perception of the nature of power. Power had two attributes that never changed: (1) it was an ability to make others do your will and reflected state advantages of location, resources, and populations, and (2) it was a feature of territorial states that attempt to monopolize it in military competition with other states. Today, however, military force is less significant than in the past as economic power becomes an end in itself more than a means to enhance military capability. Similarly, technology, education, and economic growth have become more important than conventional geopolitical attributes of power in determining relative state success in the international system. In addition, more intangible aspects of power, such as the capacity to impose ideas or shape preferences, have become more obviously important. International and supranational organizations, including multinational business, have also acquired power assets that challenge state-power monopolies.

The changing nature of power, therefore, requires a critical reevaluation of the meaning of geopolitics from that invested in it at the turn of the last century. First of all, the primacy of the territorial state is not a trans-historical given but is specific to different historical periods and different world regions. States differ historically and from world region to world region in their external powers and in their ability to control their own territories. Second, history is not the repetition or unfolding of a constant set of geopolitical imperatives. Rather, there are historic shifts in the character of economic development, from territorial (autarkic) to interactional (open) strategies, for example, and in the efficacy of state-sponsored warfare. Today, relative openness favors economic growth among industrialized countries, and disciplined armies are at a disadvantage in conflicts with amateur but fanatical opponents. Third, territorial resource endowments seem to have little or nothing to do with contemporary economic and political success on the part of states, regions, or localities. Positioning within an evolving world of flows, transfers, and interactions is more important than ready access to the resources needed to fuel large-scale military production. Fourth, and finally, geopolitical discourses or understandings shift or adapt together with the material practices they both inspire and reflect. Though existing representations of the world and how it is ordered are recycled, they do not remain unchanged. Current talk of globalization and an emerging world of flows, for example, point to both a new way of thinking about states and the declining significance of the international as a dominant scale in contemporary world politics.[18]

Geopolitical Periods

A periodization of geopolitics rests on a number of premises. One is that, over the years since the emergence of a world of territorial states in the early nineteenth century, the rules, practices, and ideas governing their relationships and those with other actors have changed historically. A second is that these rules, practices, and ideas are sociologically grounded in the interaction between states and other actors. They are not the result of such transcendental drives as rational choice or *raison d'état*. The identities and interests of actors arise out of historically specific contexts of action. Third, and finally, practices and ideas are inherently geographical. Different periods produce different balances between territorial and interactional modes of economic operation, different hegemonic states (or none whatsoever), different rankings of world regions with respect to economic and security interests, and different weightings of military as against economic power.

Using these criteria, four periods of geopolitical order and associated geopolitical discourse can be identified over the years 1815–1998.[19] The first period (1815) is one of a European balance of power in which Britain came to command and define the nature of the growing world economy outside Europe. Britain held the balance of power in Europe, enjoyed a significant edge in sea power that allowed a coercive role in imposing its policies around the world, and sponsored a set of economic ideas—comparative advantage, free trade, and the gold standard—that, while appearing universal in applicability, benefited influential groups in Britain.

By the beginning of the period 1875–1945 this combination of European concert and British domination outside Europe gave way to a destabilization of the European balance of power as other states (particularly a newly unified Germany) challenged British policies. National economies became increasingly autarkic and protectionist, and the world economy slowly lost its emphasis on free trade and the gold standard and divided into economic blocs. The two world wars were an integral part of this period of interimperial rivalry.

In the third period (1945–1990), a Cold War contest of political-economic ideologies arose out of the ashes left by the previous round of geopolitical competition. The two principal victors, the United States and the Soviet Union, divided the world into two spheres of influence, with political economies that they advertised as total opposites (a First World of democratic capitalism and a Second World of state-planned socialism), and competed for influence in a third (the Third World of states emerging from colonialism). American hegemony in its part of the world involved a structure of power not dissimilar to that of Britain in the nineteenth century. But it also had a much greater commitment than had Britain to opening up the world to direct investment and trade, organizing it multilaterally through international organizations (such as the IMF, World Bank, and GATT) and operating a security apparatus that was both more extensive and intrusive than that operated by Britain in its day.

The net impact of American hegemony has been to set the rules for a system of transnational liberalism that, with the collapse of the Soviet Union and its sphere between 1989 and 1992, has now become worldwide in operation. This still emerging geopolitical order is one in which flows of goods, services, and investment draw together cities and their hinterlands as primary units more than autonomous national economies interacting with one another at an international scale. The "free" world economy invoked by American leaders during the Cold War has now emerged as a hegemonic global project sponsored by multinational business, agents of global financial integration, and their supporters in powerful states.

Paralleling this sequence of geopolitical periods have been a series of geopolitical discourses or sets of representations of world politics that have both inspired and justified political practice by elites.[20] The first, prevalent in much of the nineteenth century, was a civilizational geopolitics, in which Europe's unique and superior civilization was compared to the sloth, paganism, and backwardness of elsewhere and offered both guide and justification for state activities, particularly outside Europe. The second arose to prominence alongside the development of racial and environmental determinism from the late nineteenth century on. This was a naturalized geopolitics, in which the "natural" character of states as predators and competitors, with relative rankings determined by "racial dynamism" and global location, came to prevail in academic and practical discussion of international relations. The third, operational during the Cold War, displaced much of what had gone before with an ideological geopolitics based on dividing up the world between zones organized differently in terms of politics and economics. The present period is one in which the victorious American model has deterritorialized into a logic of globalization and incipient global regulation.

Though distinctive in composition, each dominant geopolitical discourse has had elements in common with the others. These elements of continuity constitute what I have called the "modern geopolitical imagination." One is the vision of the globe as a frame of reference or action space. Without this visualization of the world as a whole and the divisions that are imposed upon it, there would be neither the ability to identify a hierarchy of scales at which different policies are directed nor the capacity to identify and name the world in relation to securing a domestic identity and a set of national interests. A second is the identification of different regions at different "stages" of political-economic development relative to the past experience of the dominant states or world region. Typically, modern geographical taxonomy involves the naming of different areas as advanced or primitive, modern or backward. Europe and its immediate progeny (such as the United States) are seen as defining modernity, and other parts of the world are ranked according to how they appear relative to Europe's past. This provides a norm for judging the nature of a potential adversary and the potential for exporting one's model of development. The third element has been the key assumption that the division of global space into the territories of actual and potential states of has been necessary and inevitable. Territorial states are the individual actors of the geopolitical imagination. Even though this vastly oversimplifies the large variety of actual polities to be found around the world (from empires to city-states and confederations), the ideal type of territorial state serves to anchor geopolitical discourse in a specific spatial form. Finally, the dynamic force holding together the other elements is devotion to the idea of states engaged in a pursuit of primacy. The modern world is seen as one of unremitting competition to dominate either militarily or economically, depending on the period. What the most recent transformation in geopolitics suggests, however, is that this perception is breaking down as states no longer are effective masters of their own fate.

Geopolitical discourses, therefore, are not manifestations of thought prior to practice, as much poststructuralist writing might make them appear. Nor are they determined by practice or functional to it, in the typical sense of ideology, as realists might claim. Rather, as modes of representation, they are both implicit in practice and subject to revision as practice changes. It is inadequate to claim, therefore, that world politics can be understood as either "out there," independent of human thought and practice, or textually driven by perpetually recycled tropes and metaphors. It is the outcome of sociological praxis based on rules, practices, and ideas (including geopolitical discourses) that are not set for all time but change as a result of the contingencies of world history.

Conclusion

Rigid adherence to the realism-constructionism opposition serves to obscure what each has to offer to the other as a geographical contribution to understanding of the nature of the international. Such an adherence forces an unnecessary choice between a fixed, physical geography and an invented, textual one. In its place I have suggested a historical approach to geopolitics that endeavors to explicitly recognize the joint effects of geographical representations and the spatial distribution of material conditions on political practice. From this point of view, the international is neither, as in realist accounts, set for all time as the dominant geographical scale of world politics nor, as in constructionist ones, purely an invention of textual authority. Rather, its theoretical and practical importance shifts historically as the practices of states and other actors change. The typical mundane renderings of the contribution of geographical understanding to international studies, therefore, are extremely misleading to the field as a whole. They reproduce competing realist and constructionist accounts. The very intellectual basis to *international* studies itself requires attention to the historical-geographical conditions and understandings that make it possible and perhaps, as under current conditions of globalization, call its sufficiency into question altogether.

Notes

1. These terms cover a range of positions, but the former focuses on the construction of action through discourse or sets of representations that inform action and the latter on the behavior of individual states as unitary actors within a system of states.

2. The term *social construction* is sometimes used to represent the social determination of a given outcome, such as economic activities producing a certain regional distribution of incomes. Irrespective of terminology, philosophically this is a realist, not a constructionist, position. In human geography many (former)

Marxists have become advocates of social construction, adopting a term implying a degree of human agency but remaining attached to social determinism.

3. R. D. Sack, *Homo Geographicus: A Framework for Action, Awareness, and Moral Concern* (Baltimore: Johns Hopkins University Press, 1997); M. W. Lewis and K. E. Wigen, *The Myth of Continents: A Critique of Metageography* (Berkeley: University of California Press, 1997).

4. J. O'Loughlin, "Spatial Models of International Conflicts: Extending Current Theories of War Behavior," *Annals of the Association of American Geographers,* 76, no. 1 (1986):63–80.

5. G. Ó Tuathail, "(Dis)placing Geopolitics: Writing on the Maps of Global Politics," *Society and Space* no. 12 (1994): 525–46.

6. This is an example of a fairly large literature involving geographers and political scientists that focuses on such international phenomena as interstate wars and such domestic-level phenomena as the character of political regimes (democratic, etc.) in terms of the adjacency of states and the diffusion of antagonism and influence between them. See, for example, M. D. Ward, ed. *The New Geopolitics* (London: Gordon and Breach, 1990), and J. O'Loughlin, M. D. Ward, C. L. Lofdahl, J. S. Cohen, D. S. Brown, D. Reilly, K. S. Gleditsch, and M. Shin, "The Diffusion of Democracy, 1946–1994," *Annals of the Association of American Geographers* 88, no. 4 (1998):545–74.

7. O'Loughlin, "Spatial Models of International Conflicts," 78.

8. G. Ó Tuathail, *Critical Geopolitics: The Politics of Writing Global Space* (Minneapolis: University of Minnesota Press, 1996), and S. Dalby and G. Ó Tuathail, *Critical Geopolitics,* Special Issue of *Political Geography* 15, no. 6/7 (1996).

9. G. Ó Tuathail, "(Dis)placing Geopolitics," 525–46. In this paper Ó Tuathail situates his work in close relationship to the so-called dissident international relations theory of R. K. Ashley, "The Geopolitics of Geopolitical Space: Towards a Critical Social Theory of International Politics," *Alternatives* 12 (1987): 403–34; R. Walker, *Inside/Outside: International Relations as Political Theory* (Cambridge: Cambridge University Press, 1993); and C. Weber "Something's Missing: Male Hysteria and the U. S. Invasion of Panama," *Genders* 19 (1994): 171–97. In his 1996 book and in his contributions to the 1996 symposium (Dalby and Ó Tuathail, *Critical Geopolitics*), however, he criticizes this literature for what he sees as its focus on academic theorists at the expense of actual political practice and the workings of the world economy.

10. Ó Tuathail, "(Dis)placing Geopolitics," 532.

11. Ibid., 538.

12. Kamupf 1991, xix (quoted in Ó Tuathail, "(Dis)placing Geopolitics," 535).

13. Ó Tuathail, "(Dis)placing Geopolitics," 535.

14. Ibid., 541.

15. Ibid., 542.

16. Ó Tuathail himself makes much the same point in his 1996 book, *Critical Geopolitics,* 73.

17. Indeed, Ó Tuathail seems to suggest as much in *Critical Geopolitics,* p. 16.

18. These points are dealt with at greater length in S. Agnew and S. Corbridge, *Mastering Space: Hegemony, Territory and International Political Economy* (London: Routledge, 1995), chapters 5–7.

19. Ibid., chapters 2, 3, and 7.

20. There is variation around the global norms established under a specific global hegemony. National "geopolitical visions" make distinctive contributions to overall practice. On this see G. Dijink, *National Identity and Geopolitical Visions* (London: Routledge, 1996).

References

Agnew, J., and S. Corbridge. 1995. *Mastering Space: Hegemony, Territory and International Political Economy.* London: Routledge.

Ashley, R. K. 1987. The Geopolitics of Geopolitical Space: Towards a Critical Social Theory of International Politics." *Alternatives* 12: 403–34.

Dalby, S., and G. Ó Tuathail. 1996. *Critical Geopolitics.* Special issue of *Political Geography* 15, no. 6/7.

Dijkink, G. 1996. *National Identity and Geopolitical Visions.* London: Routledge.

Lewis, M. W., and Wigen, K. E. 1997. *The Myth of Continents: A Critique of Metageography.* Berkeley, CA: University of California Press.

O'Loughlin, J. 1986. "Spatial Models of International Conflicts: Extending Current Theories of War Behavior." *Annals of the Association of American Geographers* 76, no. 1, 63–80.

O'Loughlin, J., M. D. Ward, C. L. Lofdahl, J. S. Cohen, D. S. Brown, D. Reilly, K. S. Gleditsch, and M. Shin. 1998. "The Diffusion of Democracy, 1946–1994." *Annals of the Association of American Geographers,* 88, no. 4, 545–574.

Ó Tuathail, G. 1994. "(Dis)placing Geopolitics: Writing on the Maps of Global Politics." *Society and Space* 12, no. 5, 525–46.

Ó Tuathail, G. 1996. *Critical Geopolitics: The Politics of Writing Global Space.* Minneapolis: University of Minnesota Press.

Sack, R. D. 1997. *Homo Geographicus: A Framework for Action, Awareness, and Moral Concern.* Baltimore: Johns Hopkins University Press.

Walker, R. 1993. *Inside/Outside: International Relations as Political Theory.* Cambridge: Cambridge University Press.

Ward, M. D., ed. 1990. *The New Geopolitics.* London: Gordon and Breach.

Weber, C. 1994. "Something's Missing: Male Hysteria and the U.S. Invasion of Panama. *Genders* 19: 171–97.

PAUL STREETEN

What's Wrong with Contemporary Economics?

∽⁀∽

> Economics used to be written in English by Scotsmen;
> today it is written in mathematics by Hungarians.
> —Overheard in the common room.

> If you can analyse—and not make models your master;
>   If you can think—and not make algebra your aim;
> If you do not consider plain words a disaster
>   And treat words, figures, symbols all the same;
> If you can talk to crowds and keep your virtue
>   Or walk with econometricians—nor lose the common touch;
> If neither facts nor theories can hurt you
>   If all costs count with you, but none too much
> If you can fill the unforgiving minute
>   With sixty seconds' worth of distance run
> Yours is the Earth and everything that's in it,
>   And—what is more—you'll have a lot of fun!
>   —(With apologies to Rudyard Kipling)

Educating Economists

THE QUESTION IN THE TITLE of this essay is open to two opposite interpretations, one implying approval, the other criticism. It can be interpreted in an aggressively defiant, pugnacious mode: what's *wrong*

Editor's note: Development economist Paul Streeten is even harder on his own discipline than is Agnew on geography. In "What's wrong with Contemporary Economics?" Streeten takes the field to task for its tendency to privilege theory as an entity itself, unsullied by reference to the "real" world. Streeten quotes with approval Kenneth Boulding's indictment of modern economics as "the celestial mechanics of a non-existent world." He maintains that economists need to be rescued from an involuted fate by learning more about philosophy, anthropology, and history and by conducting joint empirical research with practitioners of those disciplines. He is especially scathing when describing denial of tenure to an economist who resisted pigeonholing by combining empirical and theoretical work.

with contemporary economics? The implication would be that everything is for the best in this best of all possible worlds, or at least for the second best in this best of all feasible worlds. Or it can be interpreted in a matter-of-fact, quietly inquisitive mode: what *is* wrong with contemporary economics? I shall opt for the second interpretation.

Most of us would agree that he is a poor economist who is only an economist. Yet, the pressures for appointments, promotion, tenure, and publication have become such that economists have to cultivate ever narrower fields, if not little patches. As a result, they tend to become narrow-minded specialists, without training in the understanding of institutions, of the history of economic thought, of economic literature, of the handling and evaluation of quantitative and nonquantitative data, and of how to weigh evidence, and they are without wider visions. And frequently they are not able to communicate even their narrow vision successfully. In his obituary of Frank Ramsey, J. M. Keynes wrote: "If he had followed the easier path of mere inclination, I am not sure that he would not have exchanged the tormenting exercises of the foundations of thought and of psychology, where the mind tries to catch its own tail, for the delightful paths of our own most agreeable branch of the moral sciences, in which theory and fact, intuitive imagination and practical judgment, are blended in a manner conformable to the human intellect." Economics has strayed a long way from those delightful paths since Keynes wrote this.[1]

In his essay on Alfred Marshall, Keynes wrote:

The study of economics does not seem to require any specialized gifts of an unusually high order. Is it not, intellectually regarded, a very easy subject compared with the higher branches of philosophy and pure science? Yet good, or even competent, economists are the rarest of birds. An easy subject, at which very few excel! The paradox finds its explanation, perhaps, in that the master-economist must possess a rare *combination* of gifts. He must reach a high standard in several different directions and must combine talents not often found together. He must be mathematician, historian, statesman, philosopher—in some degree. He must understand symbols and speak in words. He must contemplate the particular in terms of the general, and touch abstract and concrete in the same flight of thought. He must study the present in the light of the past for the purposes of the future. No part of man's nature or his institutions must lie entirely outside his regard. He must be purposeful and disinterested in a simultaneous mood; as aloof and incorruptible as an artist, yet sometimes as near the earth as a politician.[2]

Undergraduate and graduate education has moved a long way from these types of skills. Judged by its own criteria, it can be said to be a great success. Most members of the profession think they are making important contributions. Economists can get good jobs and are sought after; the discipline attracts good minds, it is rigorous and unified, and, in spite of occasional sniping from the outside, it is widely admired. Yet, there is considerable unease, both inside and outside the profession, expressed by its most senior members in presidential addresses and on similar ceremonial occasions. Among them are Kenneth Boulding, Ragnar Frisch, Wassily Leontief, David Worswick, Henry Phelps Brown, Lawrence Klein, and G. S. L. Shackle.[3] The critique is summed up in Kenneth Boulding's statement that modern economics is "the celestial mechanics of a nonexistent world."[4]

The Commission on Graduate Education in Economics, consisting of very distinguished American mainstream economists, reported in 1991 that tools and theory were emphasized in graduate education at the expense of "creativity" and problem solving and that the principal weakness of graduate education was an underemphasis of the linkages between tools, both theoretical and econometric, and real-world problems. Graduate students who come to economics from other fields can obtain Ph.D.'s with little or no knowledge of economic problems and institutions. There were also criticisms of the lack of writing and communication skills of many graduate students. "The weakness [of graduate education in economics] is *not* an excessive use of mathematics. If there is a central theme to our concerns, it is that we believe there is considerable scope for improvement in ensuring that students' knowledge of economic problems and institutions enables them to use their tools and techniques on important problems" (pp. 1039–40).[5]

My criticisms, like those of the commission, do not apply so much to excessive teaching of mathematics (although it can crowd out other activities and interests and be quite useless in the later career of the student, especially if he or she seeks a nonacademic job), but, as David Colander has pointed out, to what is left out and to what is illegitimately appropriated. Arrogance (often combined with a feeling of inferiority vis-à-vis mathematicians and physicists) with respect to a lack of awareness of these limitations may be a tolerable flaw, but intolerance of any other approaches commonly found, whether alternative or complementary to the orthodox approach, is not. Scholars should be, above all, open-minded and tolerant and, if possible, humble.

What is left out of the curriculum can be divided into areas from inside and outside economics. Inside economics, the study of institutions, economic literature, the history of economic thought, the interpretation of quantitative and qualitative data, how to weigh evidence, and economic history are neglected. Outside economics, philosophy, politics, history, and anthropology are candidates for inclusion.

Those of us who accept Keynes's descriptions (or are they prescriptions?) of economics and economists may reflect on what type of education is most conducive to producing a good economist. I suggest that we should sacrifice some of the more technical aspects of economics, on which graduate education so much insists (which can be learned later), in favor of the compulsory inclusion of (a) philosophy (b) political science, and (c) economic history. Although each of these disciplines has its own justification, I shall argue for them on the narrower ground that they are essential for making a better economist. If we also get, in the process, more civilized human beings, this is a bonus. Let me say a few words about each.

Philosophy consists of logic and epistemology and of moral and political philosophy. A good grounding in logic and the theory of knowledge will make the economist a better economic theorist. The distinction between an identity and an equality (because of the identity of indiscernibles, equality is possible only between nonidenticals), elementary to a philosopher, would have saved many pages of print in the early controversy over savings and investment. It is amazing how much wasted effort could have been avoided, had the disputants been aware of the significance of the third little stroke, added to the equality symbol. The philosophical analysis of causality is another area from which economists (and economic statisticians) would benefit. There was an article, I think in *Econometrica* or in the *Southern Economic Journal,* not to be taken entirely seriously, proving that business cycles cause sun spots.

A training in logic would teach students to distinguish between, on the one hand, tautologies and deductions from axioms, which may be valid or invalid, and, on the other, empirical facts and their relation, which may be true or untrue. Mistaking validity for truth, and the easy transition from tautology to falsehood (e.g., the Laffer curve, some treatments of utility and profit maximization), are frequently the bane in economics. The same mistake also lies at the heart of the alleged precision and rigor (a friend of mine used to call it rigor mortis) of mathematical economics. Conclusions may be valid but are frequently untrue.

A good education in moral and political philosophy would avoid, or at least reduce, the all too numerous hidden biases in economic reasoning, the smuggled-in value premises, and the frequent naturalistic fallacies (the jump from an "is" to an "ought"). Again, it would save reams of wasted disputations. So I conclude, for knowing philosophy, the economist becomes a better economic theorist.

In 1982 an exchange took place between the Nobel laureate and Yale professor James Tobin and the Harvard philosopher, sometimes called the rich man's Rawls, Robert Nozick on "social justice in the Reagan era." Tobin said: "There's nothing more dangerous than a philosopher who's learned a little bit of economics." To this Nozick immediately responded:

"Unless it's an economist who hasn't learned any philosophy." On this occasion, I confess, I agree with Nozick.

Political science, or, less ambitiously, politics, as it is known in England, makes the economist a better applied economist. The knowledge of political institutions and processes and of political history makes the economist aware of the constraints and opportunities for getting policies implemented. What I have in mind is not the usurpation and narrowing of political science by economic method (or methodology as it is, regrettably, nowadays always called), as illustrated by the writings of Gary Becker[6] and the Public Choice School, which uses a brain transplant from the narrowest economic doctrines to politics,[7] but its broadening, as was done, for example, by Albert Hirschman, when he enriched economics with political categories by exploring "voice" as an alternative to "exit."

Thomas Schelling talks of "the absent colleague" when it comes to applying economic advice. We economists have to take over the investigation into the political variables in economic policy. And we should supplement the positive political economy by a normative branch, concerned with analyzing what pressure groups, what reformist alliances, what types of progressive coalitions, can be mobilized for desirable policies and reforms.

Economists are trained in the study of the operation of economic forces within political, social, and moral constraints. This approach has to be supplemented (and in some cases replaced) by the study of the operation and manipulation of political, social, and psychological forces within economic limits. More fundamentally, the distinction between economic and noneconomic variables may not be tenable if the aim is to understand social problems. I shall say more of this below.

The inclusion of some social and economic (as well as political) history hardly needs a defense, although it is sadly neglected. The discussion of outward-looking versus inward-looking strategies and of import substitution versus export promotion would have gained in depth had the participants taken into account the historical phasing of these processes. Every point on our demand and supply diagrams should have an added time dimension, for memories of the past inevitably affect movements from this point to any other. The widely accepted dictum "bygones are bygones" misses entirely the mark, for bygones affect our expectations and therefore our current behavior. So I conclude that the economist qua economist is a better theorist for knowing philosophy and a better applied and empirical economist for knowing political science and history.

Education is, of course, more than acquiring skills or *aptitudes*; it involves also the acquisition of *attitudes*. We prefer our students to be not methodology-driven but reality- and problem-driven, to know the scope as well as the limits of the techniques we teach them, to have some skepticism and humility, as well as pride in their subject. The brightest will probably acquire these traits in any case. But how do we make the modal men and women use the box of tools with which we equip them properly and prevent them from falling victims to the law of the hammer, according to which a little boy, given a hammer, finds everything worth pounding, not only nails but also Ming vases?[8] I suggest that the added education in philosophy and politics may also contribute to the right attitudes.

Does this broadening not mean that we have to sacrifice specialized education in a subject that is all the time becoming more technical, specialized, professional, and fragmented? Unless we lengthen the time of study, clearly some sacrifice is involved. It is to be hoped that mathematics will be taught more effectively in high schools so that universities can be spared this remedial training. Other, more specialized branches, now included in the graduate curriculum, can be acquired later or may not be necessary for economists entering public administration, the civil society, the media, and business.

When I was a student, I went through the Oxford school of PPE, which stands for philosophy, politics, and economics (with an additional paper on social and economic history in the final examination). Since those days the pressures toward specialization have removed the compulsory philosophy and politics papers and the economic history paper from PPE. I compared my teachers and the successful older generation of economists who had sprung from this education with those who had gone through the then more specialized economics tripos at Cambridge. (Since those days there has been convergence, Oxford giving more specialized options, Cambridge fewer.) And I found that the Oxford products did not lag behind the Cambridge products in professionalism. Comparing only Nobel Prize winners, the score is 2 to 1 in favor of Oxford: Hicks and Meade were Oxford-trained, Richard Stone was Cambridge-trained. Roy Harrod, a should-have-been Nobel laureate (someone should publish a "Who Should Be Who" and perhaps a "Who Would Be Who"), was Oxford-trained. Keynes himself, a genius, though Cambridge-trained, transcended its educational limitations.

The problem with American *undergraduate* education is that most American schools (with a few notable exceptions) teach so badly that the young people have to go through remedial training in their early university years. They are often almost illiterate when they enter university. At the same time, these youngsters are often eager to learn, have open minds, and are asking big questions. But while their minds are open and while they are eager to ask these large questions, they do not have the basic training to explore them.

By the time they reach *graduate* studies, the groundwork has been done, but the need to chase after credits and learn the required techniques tends to drive out time and interest in exploring wider areas, asking interesting questions. As a result, only very few exceptional young people are led to approach the subject with a sense of reality and vision. The majority is stuck in the mold of narrow experts.

There are some signs of a rising demand for a more realistic economics that is more relevant to policy issues. Sniping from the sidelines is done by feminist economists, who emphasize argument by rhetoric, analogy, metaphor, pattern recognition, imagination, and dialectical reasoning against the "rigor" of mathematics and the "hard science" of masculine economics. The "new" institutional economists, the school of experimental economics, some radical economists, and others have also criticized the narrowness of mainstream economics. In particular the environmental economists have questioned the narrowness and the blindness of conventional approaches. But by and large, they have left the main structure unaffected.

Recently a "Petition to Reform Graduate Education" was signed by 463 American undergraduate economics professors who are involved in hiring new economists. They say that good teachers of undergraduates do not receive currently necessary training in certain fields. Specifically, they would like anyone they hire to have

1. a background in the economic debates and literature of the past twenty years and how those debates have shaped what we as a profession believe;
2. a solid training in the models which they will be teaching to undergraduates;
3. a knowledge of economic institutions and the role institutions play in the economy;
4. an ability to communicate orally and in prose the central ideas conveyed in introductory and intermediate micro- and macro-economics;
5. knowledge of the alternative approaches in economics and an ability to compare and contrast different approaches;
6. a knowledge of econometrics but also of the limits of econometric testing.

These characteristics are very rare in the current requirements for academic appointments.

Interdisciplinary and Multidisciplinary Studies

There are three reasons for interdisciplinary, multidisciplinary, transdisciplinary, or supradisciplinary work in economics. Each has different methodological implications. First, specialists in different disciplines may work together on a specific practical problem. Improving nutrition, introducing new varieties of crops, controlling population growth, reducing pollution, planning a new town may call for drawing on several disciplines and applying their contributions to the problem. In this cooperative effort the disciplines are not transcended but brought together for a practical purpose. This practical need to draw on all relevant disciplines does not affect the methods or the content used in the contributing disciplines. On the contrary, it is just because they are specialists in their fields that the different members of a team have a contribution to make to an integrated solution. We may think of them as members of a royal commission or a presidential task force, investigating problems of controlling environmental pollution, deciding on a family planning program, planning a new town, or investigating how to combat hunger.

This kind of interdisciplinary work, though highly desirable for certain purposes, runs the risk of strengthening disciplinary borders instead of abolishing them. One member of the team provides the economic perspective, another the demographic one, a third the political one; the result is that each is confirmed in his own territory, without an advance in theoretical knowledge.

Second, it may be the case that certain assumptions, concepts, methods, or techniques, hitherto applied only to one area of study, yield illuminating results when applied to another, previously analyzed in quite different ways. There has been a considerable invasion of economic concepts and techniques into the territory of political scientists, anthropologists, sociologists, and psychologists. Principal-agent theory, the "new institutional economics," and work on the family and on racial and gender discrimination have dealt with areas traditionally discussed by sociologists. The assumption of maximizing behavior under constraints has been fruitful, up to a point, in illuminating the behavior of consumers, firms, and farms. Its success in these fields has encouraged its application to political activities such as voting, party formation, and government decision making. Calculations of economic returns and cost-benefit analysis have been extended from profit-seeking investments to education, health, birth control, the allocation of time between work and leisure and among different leisure activities, decisions about marriage and divorce, the size of the family, and even to extramarital affairs. Occasionally, though much less frequently, concepts used in political theory have been applied to economic problems. Albert Hirschman's (1970) use of "voice" as an alternative to "exit" is an example already mentioned.[9]

There is a third and deeper reason for interdisciplinary work. It may be that for a particular time or region the justification for having a separate discipline does not hold. This justification for a discipline consists in the contingent fact that between the variables encompassed by this discipline and those treated by another, there are few interactions, and the effects of any existing interactions are weak and dampened. Only then are we justified in analyzing causal sequences in one field, without always and fully taking into account those in others.

We may agree that society is a system and that all social phenomena are related, but with growing differentiation of functions and standards, some relationships become stronger than others. This justifies us (some would argue) in, say, separating business responses from family responses or economics from anthropology. The need for interdisciplinary studies arises not because people in developing countries, particularly in subsistence households, perform many functions normally separated in rich countries but because there is interdependence between variables normally analyzed separately. "Lack of specialization among the people being studied in no way justifies lack of specialization among the students. A student of Michelangelo could well confine attention to his sculpture, while caring little for the architecture and painting in which Michelangelo also excelled."[10] The fact that functions in developing societies are less differentiated does, of course, have a bearing on the interdependence.

There are numerous illustrations of such interdependence in economics. One is the relationship between income per head and population growth. High or accelerating rates of population growth are often presumed to reduce income per head, and higher income per head may be presumed in certain conditions to reduce population growth. Or consider the relationship, examined by Gunnar Myrdal, between the level of living of a deprived minority group—for example, a low caste or a racial minority—and an index of prejudice against it. Prejudice is a function of the level of living—the less educated, the less healthy, the stronger the grounds of prejudice; and the level of living is a function of prejudice— the stronger the prejudice, the stronger the discrimination in jobs, education, and so forth. Or consider the relation between productivity per worker and the ratio of investment to income. The higher the productivity, the higher will tend to be the savings and hence the investment ratio; and the higher the investment ratio, the more capital per worker and hence the higher productivity. One could also trace interdependence between the quality of interdisciplinary studies and the quality of the scholars they attract.

If interdependence between variables normally studied separately is strong, or, though weak, if reaction coefficients are large; or, though small in the neighborhood, if they change size for moves above a critical level, there is a case for breaking down the boundaries between disciplines. This is sometimes called transforming parameters into dependent variables. Family ties and economic calculus, land tenure and responses to incentives, religious beliefs and commercial motivation, prejudice and income level may interact in this way. When interdependence of this kind occurs and when the interdependent variables belong to different disciplines, there is a case for interdisciplinary work.

The third kind of interdisciplinary work, at a deep level, is the most difficult and is best done either under one skull or by a group of closely associated colleagues who stimulate and complement one another and have simultaneously a similar basic outlook. Some of the best economic research is a social activity that progresses most rapidly where a small group of like-minded scholars are not at all troubled by being out of step with the profession as a whole.

It is possible to draw two quite distinct conclusions from such interaction. First, it may be said that what is called for are not interdisciplinary studies but *a new discipline* that constructs concepts, builds models (or paradigms, as the current phrase has it), and designs theories appropriate to the conditions of the developing societies. In this case, we may have to discard concepts such as employment, unemployment, underemployment, income, savings, and investment and construct altogether new, more appropriate concepts. Second, and less radically, the existing concepts, models, and theories may continue to be used, but their content may have to be changed or their definitions modified.

How would these three approaches to interdisciplinary studies work out between, say, economists and anthropologists? In the first case—the team approach—anthropologists would be used for their traditional training. If a land reform or a family planning program or a tourist project or even a research project is proposed, they will be able to point to "constraints" in the beliefs and mores of the people or to beliefs and institutions that can be mobilized and on which the proposed reforms or projects can be built. Nothing new or radical is required here.

The second case is more interesting. I suspect that economic methods could illuminate some anthropological work and probably the converse too. The most interesting possibilities, however, are opened up by the third case, whether in its reformist or radical version. An agricultural production function in many developing countries should count among its inputs not only the conventional economic factors of production, land, labor, fertilizers, equipment, water, and power but also levels of education of the farmers, their nutritional status, their health, their distance from town, and systems of land tenure and of family kinship. All these variables are likely, in some societies, to be systematically related to agricultural production.

A status-conscious anthropologist will complain that he is being used only to provide fodder for the cannons of the economist. A self-respecting anthropologist may refuse to have all the important questions asked by the economist and to be reduced to a handmaiden, supplying low-class empirical data for the high-class analytical structure of another discipline.

Questions of status and precedence are, of course, not the concern of serious scholars. But it may turn out that the whole notion of a production function is wrong or misleading. Perhaps there is no systematic relationship between inputs, whether of fertilized, irrigated land or of physical capital or of educated farmers and human capital, on the one hand, and crops on the other. It may be that output depends on variables that have been observed and analyzed by anthropologists: the relationship between majority and minority groups; religious beliefs, the Protestant ethic; or kinship systems.

Or again, at a different level of discourse, it may be that increases in output beyond a decent minimum are not valued as a crucial component of development. The society may have opted for an alternative style of development, in which the ever-growing production of material goods is rejected. Or, through a shift in valuations, negatively valued unemployment may be converted into positively valued leisure. Or the way in which individual or cooperative agricultural work and its accompanying rites and ceremonies are performed are valued for themselves, not only as means to producing crops. Production and consumption then cease to be distinct spheres. Or the result of any given input could crucially depend on a series of preceding historical events, giving rise to different expectations and making it quite impossible to draw up a two-dimensional functional relationship. Each point on the supply curve would be located in a different place according to its history.

If any of this is the case, the crucial questions will have to be asked by the anthropologist or sociologist or historian. He or she has to construct the concepts, and it is then the economist's turn to fill the boxes built by the anthropologist, sociologist, or historian. Which of these possibilities should be realized will depend partly on empirical conditions and ultimately on valuations and the choice of lifestyles.

American education and, I suspect, European education also, is extremely hostile to multi- and interdisciplinary studies, whatever the professions of scholars may be. Charles Roos[11] reported a case that suggested the difficulties of combining mathematics, statistics, and economics. A young economist sought to extend static economic theory into a testable dynamic structure. His paper used technical mathematics and statistics. A leading American economics journal refused to publish the paper unless he removed the mathematics and statistics. A mathematics journal would publish it only without the statistics and economic theory. A statistics journal demanded that he eliminate the mathematics and the economics. The article is more than fifty years old, but nothing has changed since then, as the following recent experience shows.

I have known of a fine scholar who combined macro-political analysis with village studies and the impact of these on intrafamily relations. It was a combination of anthropology, political science, and economics. She was refused tenure at an American university on the ground that the subject did not fit into any single discipline.

Realism would call for all relevant disciplines to be brought to bear on the solution of a problem. Gunnar Myrdal used to say there are not economic and other, noneconomic problems; there are only problems. "In fact the problems are not economic, social, ecological, psychological, etc., but just problems, intermingled and complicated."[12] Some scholars, mostly of the older generation, have investigated the real world: Herbert Simon, Wassily Leontief, and Albert Hirschman are examples. But few among the younger generation of tenured American economists have followed in their steps.

E. F. M. Durbin, a brilliant British economist who drowned when young, wrote an article in 1938 in which he pleaded for (1) a union between abstract and empirical research, between theory and observation, and (2) cooperation of economists with specialists from other fields.[13] He found that in prewar Britain there was no shortage of empirical work. But theoretical and empirical work were done separately and distinctly, without illuminating each other. He quoted the philosopher Immanuel Kant: "Thoughts without content are void; intuitions without conceptions, blind."

In arguing for interdisciplinary work, Durbin says that, of course, subdivisions of an area of work are necessary. But, unlike the natural sciences, the subdivisions in the social sciences are largely *abstractions* from reality rather than *sections* of reality. Botany is the study of plants; zoology, of animals; crystallography, of crystals. But economics is the study of the *economic aspect* of social behavior, law, of the *legal aspects;* political science, of the *political aspects,* and so on. The subdivisions turn on the definitions of terms, not on subdivisions inhering in the objects of study. The conclusion does not point to large cooperative teams doing research on a subject. Durbin calls them "white elephants in labour to produce platitudinous mice." We all know that the best interdisciplinary research is carried out under one skull.

The rejection of the need for interdisciplinary studies is another aspect of the turning inward of modern economics, and this is a specifically

American feature. The universe is not divided along the same lines as the university. But it is university departments that dictate what should be incorporated in research, appointments of faculty and their promotion, not the problems of the real world. And the work will be judged, not by criteria of relevance but by the standards of excellence evolved from within the discipline.[14]

The Use of Mathematics

Frank Hahn, on his retirement, recommended to young economists "to avoid discussions of 'mathematics in economics' like the plague." I shall risk the danger of infection and say something about it.

Paul Samuelson, in *Foundations of Economic Analysis,* quotes J. Willard Gibbs: "Mathematics is a language." There can be no objections to the use of this language or jargon where it is appropriate. But users of it should know its limitations as well as its scope. Some economists and writers of articles should perhaps be reminded that English, also, is a language. The objections to the use of mathematics in economics do not relate to what it includes but to what it excludes from consideration. The complaint is both about what has to be left out of other disciplines and about the spread of mathematics beyond its legitimate boundaries. What is needed is addition and containment. Kenneth Boulding has said that "I know of no mathematical expression for the literary expression 'I love you.'"[15] In a more recent paper, Boulding wrote: "[Mathematics] is a language—or perhaps we should say a jargon—with an extraordinary paucity of verbs—it is hard to think of more than four: equals, is greater than, is less than, and is a fraction of."[16]

It is also true that, from its beginnings, economics has been couched in formal arguments. The models were often implicit rather than explicit. Even the politician, the official and the practical man, when putting forward some explanation or recommendation, has some kind of model at the back of his mind. Joan Robinson once said, "I don't know mathematics, therefore I have to think." But it can be rightly argued that it is a virtue to make relationships explicit rather than leave them implicit.

It is often claimed that the virtue of mathematics is that assumptions, deductions, and conclusions are spelled out precisely, whereas verbal economics permits fuzziness. Abstraction is, of course, necessary in all thinking. But not all abstractions are equally useful, and some are definitely misleading. Nor is mathematical reasoning exempt from fuzziness. Fuzziness enters into mathematical economics when a, b, c are identified with individuals, firms, or farms. The identification of the precise symbol with the often ambiguous and fuzzy reality invites lack of precision and blurs the concepts. Mathematical economists are also unrigorous in spelling out what would have to be the case for their exercises to be applicable. There is often a lack of realism in their assumptions. This may be a virtue, for all theory has to abstract, has to leave out many features of a complex reality; but if the abstractions are of the kind that pours out the baby instead of the bath water, it is damaging to an understanding of reality. Accusation that economics is the science that argues from unwarranted assumptions to foregone conclusions then become justified.

The correct inference from clearly stated premises leads to valid conclusions. The correct analysis of states and events in the world is called truth. There are two dangers in an overuse of mathematics in economics. First, as we have seen, validity can be mistaken for truth. Deductions from artificial models can be mistaken descriptions and analyses of the real world. Second, the time and effort devoted to deducing theorems can be at the expense of investigations of real events. The result is the exclusion of certain questions and techniques of understanding the world. There is evidence that economics has suffered from both dangers.

In a frequently quoted passage, Alfred Marshall wrote: "In my view every economic fact whether or not it is of such a nature as to be expressed in numbers, stands in relation as cause and effect to many other facts, and since it *never* happens that all of them can be expressed in numbers, the application of exact mathematical methods to those which can is nearly always waste of time, while in the large majority of cases it is positively misleading; and the world would have been further on its way forward if the work had never been done at all."[17]

In another letter to Bowley he wrote: "I had a growing feeling in the later years of my work at the subject that a good mathematical theorem dealing with economic hypotheses was very unlikely to be good economics: and I went more and more on the rules—(1) Use mathematics as a shorthand language, rather than as an engine of inquiry. (2) Keep to them until you are done. (3) Translate into English. (4) Then illustrate by examples what are important in real life. (5) Burn the mathematics. (6) If you can't succeed in (4), burn (3). This last I did often."[18]

Keynes, himself no mean mathematician, wrote: "[s]ymbolic pseudo-mathematical methods of formalizing a system of economic analysis . . . allow the author to lose sight of the complexities and interdependencies of the real world in a maze of pretentious and unhelpful symbols."[19]

Many other distinguished mathematical economists, from Simon Kuznets to Kenneth Arrow, Gerard Debreu, Lawrence Klein, Kenneth Boulding, Ragnar Frisch, E. H. Phelps Brown, David Worswick, and Wassily Leontief have been similarly critical of the abuse and excessive use of mathematics in economics. Some of these repent in presidential addresses but then go away and sin again. The criticism is directed at the triumph of technique over substance, of form over content, of elegance over realism. It is true that mathematics has a simplicity, beauty, and elegance that are seductive. But as contrasted with evolving its own standards of excellence, one may ask: what does it contribute to either understanding or prediction or prescription? Mathematics should be the servant of economics, not its master.

Wassily Leontief, in his presidential address to the 1970 meeting of the American Economic Association, condemned "preoccupation with imaginary, hypothetical, rather than with observable reality."[20] In a letter to *Science* magazine he wrote, "Page after page of professional economic journals are filled with mathematical formulas leading the reader from sets of more or less plausible but entirely arbitrary assumptions to precisely stated but irrelevant theoretical conclusions." As a good empiricist, Leontief then investigated recent articles in the *American Economic Review*. He found 54 percent of articles were "mathematical models without any data." Another 22 percent drew statistical inferences from data generated for some other purpose. Another 12 percent used analysis with no data. Half of 1 percent used direct empirical analysis of data generated by the author.

One may be forgiven if one feels some forms of mathematical economics should be an activity permitted only between consenting adults in private, or that it resembles masturbation in that it yields enjoyment to the practitioner without having to make any contact with outside reality.

Yet, it is true that training in mathematics should probably be a condition for a training in economics. The reason for this is that otherwise the economist would not be able to see through the flawed reasoning. When the nonmathematical economist picks up an issue of a current economics journal, he may feel like Diderot at the court of Catherine the Great when Leonhard Euler said to him: "Sir $(a+b)/n = x$, hence God exists; reply!" And, like Diderot, he may slink away in shame. Or (as Samuelson has pointed out) he may disbelieve the next mathematician who later comes along and gives him a true proof of the existence of the Deity.

What are the reasons for this dominance of mathematics, for the priority of form over content, of technique over relevance and realism? Some blame Milton Friedman's "as if" doctrine (that assumptions need not, indeed should not, be realistic) and the romantic desire to pass as a scientist.[21] To adapt a term from psychoanalysis, economists suffer from physics envy. At the end of the nineteenth century, with the marginal revolution, mathematics was introduced into economics by Walras, Cournot, Jevons, Pigou, Fisher, Edgeworth, and others to make it more like physics and raise the status of economists. Since then and particularly since the 1950s, it has come to dominate the subject.

Some of the reasons are internal, others external. The doctrine of Milton Friedman that lack of realism of assumptions is a virtue has already been mentioned. Lack of realism may have two quite distinct meanings. All thinking and theorizing has to select, to abstract, from reality. It is like making a map, which can never incorporate all features of reality.[22] This is its virtue, for without leaving out irrelevant features, we could not find our way, and the map would be useless. This type of "distortion" of reality, which selects relevant features and leaves out irrelevant ones, is indeed a virtue.

This is not what Friedman's doctrine says. According to Friedman, only the predictive power of the theory is relevant; if it yields correct prediction, the assumption may be as far removed from reality as we wish— indeed, fly in its face. But first, theories may have other functions than prediction; they may explain, illuminate, or prescribe. Second, it is hard to see why incorrect assumptions should yield systematically correct predictions. Be this as it may, the Friedman doctrine was one ground on which mathematical economists could proceed without testing the correspondence of their symbols to real entities.

Among other internal reasons is the already mentioned beauty and elegance of mathematics, the prestige attached to it, and the standards of excellence evolved from within mathematics. But I suggest that among the external reasons there may be one to which little attention has been paid. The political pressures of McCarthyism in the 1950s played, I think, an important part. Economics deals with people's pockets and their ideals: a highly explosive mixture. To be accused of criticizing the capitalist system and pandering to socialism was very dangerous in the 1950s. Yet, any honest economist looking at the real world would have had to come up with some criticisms. So mathematics provided a safe escape mechanism that drove economists away from political and economic reality.[23]

The proof of the pudding is in the eating. Has mathematics advanced the subject? yielded new insights? provided deeper analysis? contributed to more accurate predictions or better prescriptions and policies? I suggest that, on the whole, and with the exception of some important and applicable insights from game theory, the results have been quite puny compared with the sophistication of the apparatus. Those not able to handle the mechanics of modern mathematical economics may feel like the handloom weavers when the power loom was introduced. But they can find comfort in the fact that the power-loom weavers have been weaving the emperor's clothes.

I conclude that mathematics has its place in economics but that it should be kept in its place. We should use mathematical analysis like grafting body parts onto a living body in spare-parts surgery. Quantitative and qualitative arguments can then be combined, formal and nonformal methods can be used, historical and anthropological insights can be added, and a fuller understanding can thus be reached.

The Current State of Economics

What is the difference between a specialist and a generalist? According to a well-known quip, the specialist knows more and more about less and less, until he knows everything about nothing; the generalist know less and less about more and more, until he knows nothing about everything. The real question behind this quip is, should a well-trained economist concentrate on a few areas or spread his research widely?

The obvious answer is that this should be left to the preferences of the individual in question. The spark of good, original work is so rare that it should be fanned wherever it strikes, whether in a concentrated or diluted form. But there are professional pressures for appointments and promotions that guide a scholar in his or her preferences. To the question "What is your field?" the economist eager to advance his career must have an answer. And it is often better for his or her advancement if the field is a little patch.

Modern economics has become too narrow, as well as too far removed from reality. The German word for the product of many economics graduate schools is *Fachidiot;* the French, *idiot savant*. Robert Kuttner wrote: "Departments of economics are graduating a generation of *idiots savants*, brilliant at esoteric mathematics yet innocent of actual economic life."[24]

Jacob Viner once said that "men are not narrow in their intellectual interests by nature; it takes special and rigorous training to accomplish that end."[25] And when graduate students in the elite universities' economics departments were asked what they disliked most about their graduate schools, the majority of comments mentioned the heavy load of mathematics and theory and a lack of relevance of the material they were learning.[26]

I agree with Amartya Sen that juggling lots of balls clumsily is superior to displaying virtuosity with only one ball. If this means that some precision may have to be sacrificed, the broad-gauged economist may prefer to be vaguely right to being precisely wrong. If I could choose between being accused of reductionism and fuzziness, I think I would prefer to be accused of fuzziness. Robert Solow said that reductionism is not the occupational disease of economists, it is their occupation. I find this regrettable.

Economics is not a science in which controlled experiments can be conducted. No economic theory has ever been falsified by an experiment.

There is the widespread impression among economists that there is a high degree of consensus on modern economics in the profession. An interesting article by Bruno Frey and others tested the degree of consensus and dissensus of economists in different countries.[27] American, Swiss, and German economists tend to support competition and free markets and hence neoclassical economics, while French and Austrian economists are more inclined to support government interventions. (The Austrian view on these questions is, of course, quite different from the "Austrian school" in economic theory.) The results suggest a good deal of inbreeding among American economists. They mistake their views for generally accepted ones. This is largely the result of the provincialism of American economists, in turn partly the result of the large size of the country. They have little notion of what is being thought and written outside their borders.

Robert Frank and others investigated whether studying economics (in America) inhibits cooperation and makes students less cooperative and more self-interested.[28] After surveying several other studies and conducting their own, they found that economics students are more self-interested than others and that it is not self-interested people who are attracted to the study of economics but it is the study of economics that makes people more self-interested.[29] They conclude that emphasis in teaching on the self-interest model inhibits cooperation. As the authors point out, self-interested responses can be counter-productive. The ultimate victims of noncooperative behavior may be the very people who practice it. The authors conclude that "economists may wish to stress a broader view of human motivation in their teaching."[30]

A survey by Arjo Klamer and David Colander asked American students at a few top universities what they regarded as the conditions for success in the economics profession.[31] "Knowledge of the economy," "knowledge of economic literature," and "being interested in, and good at, empirical work" ranked low and in this order, from the bottom up ("knowledge of the economy" being the lowest), compared with "being good at problem solving," "excellence in mathematics," "being very knowledgeable about one particular field," ranked from the top down.

The problem with this narrow, unrealistic, self-satisfied, often intolerant approach to economics is not only that those educated in America and the consumers of their product suffer professional debilitation, but the influence is worldwide. Students from overseas, including many developing countries, if they return to their homes, are imbued with the spirit. But this is not all. Even those who never leave their home countries are powerfully influenced by the thrust of what is being published in the top journals in America. This form of diversion of brain power adds to the losses suffered from the external brain drain (the loss of educated, professional manpower to the rich countries) and may be called the internal brain drain. Its pernicious influences are a multiple of those of the external drain.

There are, however, signs that things may be changing for the better and that the crest of the wave of unreal and escapist economics may be passed. The journal *Economic Perspectives* communicates to a wide audience and raises important real-world questions. The award of the John Bates Clark Medal to the labor economist David Card from Princeton is another sign. David Card with Alan Krueger—ex-Labor Secretary Robert Reich's chief economist—has done important empirical, unconventional work on subjects such as minimum wages and the impact of education on earnings. Yet another sign is the appearance of articles in the *American Economic Review* on subjects such as economic growth and income distribution, which also use empirical data. The National Bureau of Economic Research set a whole day apart in 1998, the National Security Day, to discuss pensions, drawing on experts from different fields.

Science and Crypto-science

If the social sciences, including economics, are regarded as a "soft" technology compared with the "hard" technology of the natural sciences, development studies have been regarded as the soft underbelly of "economic science." I have heard it being equated to economics minus logic. In the attempt to emulate the colleagues practicing "hard" economics, we have seen that mathematical methods are brought to bear on issues for which they are not appropriate.

In his Romanes Lectures, Sir Isaiah Berlin illustrates, by citing Turgenev's *Fathers and Children,* how what was once revolutionary doctrine has become establishment doctrine.

The victorious advance of quantitative methods, belief in the organisation of human lives by technological organisation, reliance on nothing but calculation of utilitarian consequences in evaluating policies that affect vast numbers of human beings, this is Bazarov, not the Kirzanovs. The triumphs of the moral arithmetic of cost effectiveness which liberates decent men from qualms, because they no longer think of the entities to which they apply their scientific computations as human beings . . . this today is rather more typical of the establishment than of the opposition.

Growing concern with social objectives—employment, poverty, women, equality, the environment—has led in the past to calls for the "dethronement of GNP," which (erroneously) has been regarded as an *economic* objective. But the fault in the preoccupation with GNP was excessive attention to a simple quantitative index, irrespective of the valuations implicit in its sets of weights, that is, of its composition, distribution, and the manner in which it was produced. The danger is that the same fault is repeated when simple indexes are constructed for social and human objectives. The proportion of the GNP earned by the bottom 40 percent, or the Gini coefficient, or the Human Development Index of the United Nations Development Programme's Human Development Reports are just as inadequate and, if used only by themselves, just as misleading measures of what we are getting at when we try to eradicate poverty or reduce inequality or remove unemployment, as GNP is an inadequate measure of productive capacity or economic welfare.

Inequality of income distribution touches only a small portion of the vast, multidimensional problem of inequality. There is also inequality of ownership of assets; of access to assets and to earning opportunities; of satisfaction from work; of recognition, status, and prestige; of ability to enjoy consumption; of access to power; of participation in decision making; of freedom of choice, and many other dimensions. The call for greater equality, for a genuine community of equals, cannot be answered simply by measures that reduce the Gini coefficient or any other simple measure of inequality, which are inadequate even in expressing what concerns us in grossly unequal income distribution. It is possible to envisage a technocratic society in which decisions are highly centralized and in which a few enjoy the satisfactions from power and creativity while the many carry out boring or disagreeable tasks or are unemployed, in a hierarchic structure and in which the Gini coefficient is zero or in which at least there is no poverty. Kurt Vonnegut describes vividly such a society in his novel *Player Piano*. The materially satisfied but otherwise deprived underclass eventually rebel.

The danger of research in economics that attempts to emulate the "hard" sciences is that it selects the measurable and neglects the rest: only what can be counted counts or even exists. (A secondary danger where statistics are very unreliable is to say "any figure is better than none.") Some of the most important obstacles to the eradication of poverty and the reduction of gross inequality lie in areas in which measurement is still very difficult or perhaps impossible. Among these are the following:

1. Unwillingness of governments to grasp the political nettles: land reform, tax reform, labor mobilization, widening access to education and health services.
2. Linked with these, elitism, nepotism, corruption.
3. Behind these again, various forms of power concentrations in the form of oligopoly and monopoly power: the power of large landowners, of big industrialists, of multinational corporations.
4. In a different field but sometimes equally disruptive, the power of organized labor unions and the obstacles to an incomes and employment policy that would create full employment without inflation.
5. Restricted access to educational opportunities, the imbalance in education and the resulting job certification that both reflects and reinforces the unequal structure of power and wealth.
6. Weak entrepreneurship and defective management and administration of public enterprises, private firms, the civil service, and some NGOs.
7. Lack of coordination between central government and regional, local, and project administrations. Too many countries are better on planning than on administration and implementation.
8. The weakness of the structure, area of competence, recruitment, training, and administration of the UN agencies charged with development, combined with an often narrowly technocratic approach, encouraged by the location, origin, and organization of these agencies and their politically "noncontroversial" approach.
9. Finally, there are the terrible facts of mass slaughter of ethnic or religious minorities (often entrepreneurial and therefore hated) and political opponents, torture, imprisonment without trial, expulsion, and the vast sums spent on armies and the police and other horrors.

The list is not exhaustive but merely illustrative. But it shows that the temptation to select the quantified and quantifiable at the expense of other, possibly more important areas reinforces political reasons for avoiding these problems and strengthens the vested interests that benefit from the status quo.

In a famous passage in *Value and Capital,* John Hicks wrote that the assumption of perfect competition must be retained, or else the whole of economic theory would be a wreck. In his later days he regretted this and turned to a plea for a more realistic economics; but the priority of preserving an abstract, theoretical structure that yields to techniques over understanding the real world has permeated economics. Equilibrium analysis takes a central place, although its lack of realism is generally recognized. Amartya Sen has pointed out that the *use* of equilibrium-based reasoning is subject to criticism. In particular, questions should be asked about its (1) existence (2) uniqueness (3) stability, and (4) efficiency.[32]

Equilibrium may not exist. Even if it does exist, it may not be unique. Even if it exists and is unique, it may not be stable. And it may exist, be unique, and be stable but be inefficient in the sense of not achieving Pareto optimality. As Sen goes on to say, frequently the mere presence of competition is taken to entail the existence, uniqueness, stability, and efficiency of a general equilibrium. The difficulties of equilibrium economics are not primarily with the idea itself. They lie in the way the idea is applied. Among the critics of the competitive equilibrium approach to economics have been John Kenneth Galbraith[33] and Janos Kornai[34] but their writings have not been accepted by the profession.

Similarly, the rejection of the assumption of increasing returns, ubiquitous in reality, by equilibrium analysts has made economics lose touch with reality. The importance of increasing returns has been recognized by great minds like Adam Smith, Allyn Young, Piero Sraffa, and Nicholas Kaldor but has not found the place it deserves in the analysis of mainstream economists, because the formal analytical apparatus is absent.

In development economics the important question is, what are the springs of development? Many would stress the importance of entrepreneurial and managerial motivation and attitudes, of education of the right kind, and of appropriate institutions. But we do not know what characteristics make for the social selection of an innovating, entrepreneurial group, while many papers are written on years, months, days, and hours of schooling or the number or proportion of engineers and scientists. Neither innate characteristics nor education nor religion can explain why some societies at certain periods are better and quicker at innovating than others at other times. Innate characteristics are distributed according to normal distribution curves. The level of scientific education is quite high in many societies, such as India, in which innovation is poor, and vice versa; and all kinds of religion besides Protestantism have proved to be consistent with innovative behavior: Roman Catholicism in Austria and Malta, Hinduism in East Africa, Confucianism and Buddhism in East Asia. What we need is an explanation of why, in some societies, with the right education, innate characteristics, and religion, the ablest and fittest, the "Best and the Brightest," the creative innovators, are not attracted to production and business but, instead, to politics, universities, or the civil service.

At the end, we must confess that we cannot answer the most important question in development economics, that we do not know what causes successful development. But we must try to resist the temptation to which so many have yielded, to behave like the drunk who has lost his key and looks for it not where he dropped it but under the street lamp— because this is where the light is.

Notes

1. J. M. Keynes, *Essays in Biography*. (New York: W. W. Norton, 1951), 239.
2. Keynes, *Essays in Biography,* 140–41.
3. K. E. Boulding, "The Economics of Knowledge and the Knowledge of Economics," in *Economics of Information and Knowledge,* ed. D. M. Lamberton (Harmondsworth, England: Penguin Books 1971); R. Frisch, "Econometrics in the World of Today," in *Induction, Growth and Trade: Essays in Honour of Sir Roy Harrod,* ed. W. A. Eltis, M. F. Scott, and J. N. Wolfe (London: Clarendon Publishing, 1970); W. Leontief, "Theoretical Assumptions and Nonobserved Facts," *American Economic Review* 61(1) (1971):1–7; G. D. N. Worswick, "Is Progress in Economic Science Possible?" *Economic Journal* 82 no.325 (1972): 73–86; E. H. Phelps Brown, "The Underdevelopment of Economics," *Economic Journal* 82 (1972):1–10; G. S. L. Shackle, *Epistemics and Economics: A Critique of Economic Doctrines* (Cambridge: Cambridge University Press, 1972).
4. See David Colander, "Reform of Graduate Economics Education," ed. David Colander and Reuven Brenner, in *Educating Economists* (Ann Arbor: University of Michigan Press, 1992), pp. 213–31. Also his *Why Aren't Economists as Important as Garbagemen?* (Armon, New York, 1991). This essay is greatly indebted to David Colander's incisive critique of economics.
5. Anne Krueger et al. "Report of the Commission on Graduate Education in Economics," *Journal of Economic Literature,* 29, no.3 (September 1991): 1035–53.
6. G. S. Becker, *The Economic Approach to Human Behavior* (Chicago: University of Chicago Press, 1976); *A Treatise on the Family* (Cambridge, MA: Harvard University Press, 1987).
7. Charles K. Rowley, Robert D. Tollison, Gordon Tullock, eds., *The Political Economy of Rent-Seeking* (Boston: Kluwer Academic Publishers, 1987).
8. This applies to all the criticisms of the education of economists made in this essay. The truly top people will always overcome these handicaps and teach themselves; it is the average student with whom we should be concerned.
9. A. O. Hirschman, *Exit, Voice and Loyalty* (Cambridge, MA: Harvard University Press, 1970).
10. Michael Lipton, "Interdisciplinary Studies in Less Developed Countries," *Journal of Development Studies* 9 (October 1970): 5–18.
11. Charles Roos, "A Future for the Econometric Society in International Statistics," *Econometrica* 16.2 (April 1948): 127–34.
12. Gunnar Myrdal, "The Unity of the Social Sciences," *Human Organization* 34, no. 4 (1975): 327.
13. E. F. M. Durbin, "Methods of Research: A Plea for Cooperation in the Social Sciences," *Economic Journal* (June 1938): 183–95.
14. My friend Hugh Stretton wrote to me after reading an earlier draft of this essay:

As I finished reading the paper, one more argument occurred to me . . . To come to economics from another discipline, with another structure of social theory in one's head, induces an instrumental, perhaps more sceptical view of theory itself. All but the brightest Economics I undergraduates tend to learn that national income, opportunity cost, marginal value (and all the rest) are facts out there in the economy, to be observed and respected. That is harder to swallow if you come to class with Parsonian sociological theory or Austinian theory of law or pluralist political science in your head. If the theory you bring is mostly bad, that prompts scepticism about economic theory; if it is good . . . *that* prompts scepticism too. The effect is not necessarily pragmatic anti-theoretical; on the contrary it may rub in the lesson that one *must* select, simplify, distill (etc.) to grasp such complicated life. But it can teach people to think of theory as a tool kit, useful in relation to their purposes of study and action; with the need to change some of the tools as either the life out there changes, or the student's social purposes do. They should be less prone to hit Ming vases with the hammer—or try to understand relations between employer and employee by means of theory designed to explain the supply, demand and price of carrots.

15. Kenneth Boulding, "Samuelson's Foundations: The Role of Mathematics in Economics," *Journal of Political Economy* (June 1948): 187–209; quoted in Munir Quddus and Salim Rashid, "The Overuse of Mathematics in Economics: Nobel Resistance," *Eastern Economic Journal* 20, no. 3 (Summer 1994): 257.

16. Kenneth Boulding, "Economics as an Institution," in the *The Fifth Annual Kenneth Parsons Lecture Series* (Boulder, CO: IBS, 1989); also cited in Quddus and Rashid, "Overuse of Mathematics."

17. Alfred Marshall, letter to A. L. Bowley, 3 March 1901 in A. C. Pigou, ed., *Memorials of Alfred Marshall* (New York: Augustus M. Kelley, 1966), 422.

18. Pigou, *Memorials*, 427.

19. John Maynard Keynes, *The General Theory of Employment, Interest and Money* (New York: Harcourt, Brace, 1936): 297–98.

20. Quoted by Robert Kuttner in "The Poverty of Economics," *Atlantic Monthly*, February 1985, 74–84.

21. Frank Hahn, "An Intellectual Retrospect," *Banca Nazionale del Lavoro Quarterly Review* (September 1994): 246.

22. Salim Rashid commented: "I do not like the analogy with a map. Chicago remains in Ilinois regardless of scale. I am not sure this applies to economics." He is quite right that in economics, as we have seen, there is a lot of throwing out of babies instead of the bath water.

23. Interestingly, Gordon Tullock also considers mathematical economics as escapism, but in his case it is an escape from the antimarket sentiments that he regards as characteristic of most American universities, especially outside the economics departments.

24. Robert Kuttner, "The Poverty of Economics," *Atlantic Monthly*, February 1985, 74–84.

25. Quoted in Arjo Klamer and David Colander, *Making of an Economist* (Boulder, CO: Westview Press, 1990), 16.

26. Klamer and Colander, *Making of an Economist*, 14.

27. Bruno S. Frey, Werner W. Pommerehne, Friedrich Schneider, and Guy Gilbert, "Consensus and Dissension among Economists: An Empirical Inquiry," *American Economic Review* 74, no. 5 (December 1984): 986–94.

28. Robert H. Frank, Thomas Gilovich, and Dennis T. Regan, "Does Studying Economics Inhibit Cooperation?" *Journal of Economic Perspectives* 7, no. 2 (Spring 1993):159–71.

29. Amartya Sen raises the interesting question of whether the presumption of exclusive self-interestedness is more common in America than in Europe, without characterizing *actual* behavior. Alexis de Tocqueville thought so:

The Americans . . . are fond of explaining almost all the actions of their lives by the principle of self-interest rightly understood; they show with complacency how an enlightened regard for themselves constantly prompts them to assist one another and inclines them willingly to sacrifice a portion of their time and property to the welfare of the state. In this respect, they frequently fail to do themselves justice; for in the United States as well as elsewhere people are sometimes seen to give way to those disinterested and spontaneous impulses that are natural to man; but the Americans seldom admit that they yield to emotions of this kind; they are more anxious to do honour to their philosophy than to themselves.

Amartya Sen, "Rationality and Social Choice," *American Economic Review* 85, no. 1 (March 1995): 15.

30. Ibid., p. 171.

31. Klamer and Colander, *Making of an Economist.*

32. Amartya Sen, "Economic Methodology: Heterogeneity and Relevance," *Methodus,* 3 no. 1 (June 1991): 70.

33. J. K. Galbraith, *American Capitalism: The Concept of Countervailing Power* (Cambridge, MA: Riverside Press, 1952), *The Affluent Society* (Boston: Houghton Mifflin, 1958), and *The New Industrial State* (Boston: Houghton Mifflin, 1967).

34. J. Kornai, *Anti-Equilibrium* (Amsterdam: North Holland, 1971).

References

Becker, G. S. *The Economic Approach to Human Behavior.* Chicago: University of Chicago Press, 1976.

———. *A Treatise on the Family.* Cambridge, MA: Harvard University Press, 1987.

Boulding, Kenneth. "The Economics of Knowledge and the Knowledge of Economics." *Economics of Information and Knowledge.* Ed. D. M. Lamberton. Harmondsworth, England: Penguin Books, 1971.

———."Samuelson's Foundations: The Role of Mathematics in Economics," *Journal of Political Economy* (June 1948): 187–209.

———."Economics as an Institution." In *The Fifth Annual Kenneth Parsons Lecture Series.* Boulder, Co: IBS, 1989.

Brown, Henry Phelps. "The Underdevelopment of Economics." *Economic Journal* 82 (1972): 1–10.

Colander, David. *Why Aren't Economists as Important as Garbagemen?* Armonk, New York: M. E. Sharps, 1991.

Colander, David, and Reuven Brenner, eds. *Educating Economists.* Ann Arbor: University of Michigan Press, 1992.

Durbin, E. F. M. "Methods of Research: A Plea for Cooperation in the Social Sciences." *Economic Journal* (June 1938): 183–95.

Frank, Robert H., Thomas Gilovich, and Dennis T. Regan. "Does Studying Economics Inhibit Cooperation?" *Journal of Economic Perspectives* 7.2 (Spring 1993): 159–171.

Frey, Bruno S., Werner W. Pommerhne, Friedrich Schneider, and Guy Gilbert. "Consensus and Discussion among Economists: An Empirical Inquiry." *American Economic Review* 74.5 (December 1984): 986–94.

Frisch, Ragnar. "Econometrics in the World of Today." Pp. 152–66 in *Induction, Growth, and Trade, Essays in Honour of Sir Roy Harrod,* ed. W. A. Eltis, M. F. G. Scott, and J. N. Wolfe. London: Clarendon Press, 1970.

Galbraith, John Kenneth. *The Affluent Society.* Boston: Houghton Mifflin, 1958.

———. *American Capitalism: The Concept of Countervailing Power.* Cambridge, MA: Riverside Press, 1952.

———. *The New Industrial State.* Boston: Houghton Mifflin, 1967.

Hahn, Frank. "An Intellectual Retrospect." *Banca Nazionale del Lavoro Quarterly Review* (September 1994): 246.

Hirschman, Albert O. *Exit, Voice and Loyalty.* Cambridge, MA: Harvard University Press, 1970.

Keynes, John Maynard. *Essays in Biography.* New York: W. W. Norton, 1951.

———.*General Theory of Employment, Interest, and Money,* 297–98.

Klamer, Arjo, and David Colander, *The Making of an Economist.* Boulder, CO: Westview Press, 1990.

Kornai, J. *Anti-Equilibrium.* Amsterdam: North Holland, 1971.

Krueger, Anne, et al. "Report of the Commission on Graduate Education in Economics." *Journal of Economic Literature* 29.3 (September 1991): 1035–53.

Kuttner, Robert. "The Poverty of Economics." *Atlantic Monthly,* February 1985, 74–84.

Leontief, Wassily. "Theoretical Assumptions and Nonobserved Facts" (Presidential Address to the American Economic Association, 29 December 1970) *American Economic Review* 61.1 (1971): 1–7.

Lipton, Michael. "Interdisciplinary Studies in Less Developed Countries." *Journal of Development Studies* 9.1 (October 1970), 5–18.

Marshall, Alfred. "Letter to A. L. Bowley" (3 March 1901) P. 422 in A. C. Pigou, ed, *Memorials of Alfred Marshall.* New York: 1966.

Myrdal, Gunnar. "The Unity of the Social Sciences." *Human Organization* 34.4 (1975): 327.

Quddus, Munir, and Salim Rashid. "The Overuse of Mathematics in Economics: Nobel Resistance." *Eastern Economic Journal* 20.3 (Summer 1994): 257.

Roos, Charles. "A Future for the Econometric Society in International Statistics," *Econometrica* 16.2 (April 1948): 127–34.

Rowley, Charles K., Robert D. Tollison, and Gordon Tullock, eds. *The Political Economy of Rent-Seeking.* Boston: Kluwer Academic Publishers, 1987.

Sen, Amartya. "Economic Methodology: Heterogeneity and Relevance." *Methodus* 3.1 (June 1991): 70.

———."Rationality and Social Choice." *American Economic Review* 85.1 (March 1995): 15.

Shackle, G. S. L. *Epistemics and Economics: A Critique of Economic Doctrines.* Cambridge: Cambridge University Press, 1972.

Worswick, G. D. N. "Is Progress in Economic Science Possible?," *Economic Journal* 82.325 (1972): 73–86.

JAMES N. ROSENAU

Confessions of a Pre-Postmodernist; or Can an Old-Timer Change Course?

∽o∾

When the mind is forced to repudiate the immediate past, the intellectual community splits in two. On one side stands the majority, the great mass, who cling to established ideas; on the other side, the scant few who venture forth alone, the minority of alert souls who glimpse, somewhere in the distance, a zone never seen, a skin never touched. These amazing sights inspire them to gesture in ways that most people can make little sense of, for the sluggish majority has not yet climbed to the heights from which terra incognita can be discerned. Thus, the forward-moving few are doomed to be misunderstood. They must face the dangers of the unconquered lands that lie ahead and at the same time endure harassment from those who lag behind. While creating the new, they must defend themselves against the old.
—Jose Ortega y Gasset[1]

LIKE REALISTS, behavioralists, neorealists, and liberals before them, postmodernists and poststructuralists in the field of international relations (IR) give voice to the perspective summarized in this epigraph. As one of them put it, "Recognition of the extraordinary lengths to which one must go to challenge a given structure of intelligibility, to intervene in resident meanings by bringing what is silent and unglimpsed into

Editor's note: James Rosenau, a well-known international relations scholar at The George Washington University, is the author of "Confessions of a Pre-Postmodernist." Rosenau writes an engaging account of his own days as a "young turk" in a field then dominated by "realists" such as Hans Morgenthau, and of his current position as an empiricist besieged and bemused by postmodernists and poststructuralists. He describes a pattern of insularity and involution that once afflicted his own group and now characterizes the new wave of postmodernists. He acknowledges that there is merit in some postmodernist positions, but he rejects the proposition that empirical inquiry is inherently biased to the point that it is useless. Rosenau, like Richard Perry, agrees with postmodernists that perfect and unbiased communication may be impossible but advances his own neologism, "checkableupableness," as "the antidote to the inevitable tainting of truth with nonobjective values."

focus, is an essential step towards opening up possibilities for a politics and ethics of discourse."[2] Both the challenge and the impulses underlying it, that sense of being under siege for glimpsing what others fail to see, give rise to the questions that drive the ensuing analysis: What does the proliferation of postmodern, poststructuralist, postpositivist, and post-or-neo-anything-that-is-long-standing approaches to the field signify? Intellectual ferment? A growing wisdom? A sense that deep understanding is not possible? A need for polarities? A generational transformation? A political move? A fragmenting world? Questions such as these are worth probing, but here I can only hint at the answers by addressing a persistent bewilderment over why the lines between the newer and older schools of IR thought are drawn so tightly and, alternatively, why so few efforts are made to achieve synthesis among them.[3]

Nor is the bewilderment new or naive.[4] It has plagued the author across five decades of IR teaching and research. The content of the competitive schools has changed substantially, but the lack of efforts at synthesis is hardly less conspicuous. Unaffected by mushrooming complexity, unawed by transformative dynamics, unwilling to concede we may be in error, and ever ready to denigrate other approaches, most of us either remain ensconced in our own paradigmatic world or we slug away at other worlds. For an old-timer who was a vigorous participant in earlier slugfests, the time has come to resort to bridge building, to seek to span the gulfs that divide us.

It might be asked why efforts should be made to bridge—and perhaps even synthesize—theoretical and methodological differences between the older and newer schools? It is merely a wishy-washy, idealistic aspiration to minimize needless tensions and conflicts? Or are there sound substantive reasons to undertake bridging and synthesizing efforts? Conceding that ontological and epistemological differences can be inherently contradictory—not to mention that an idealistic preference for cooperation and an emotional distaste for energy wasted on sustained tensions may underlie my response to these questions—I nevertheless believe that a good, substantive case can be made for bridge building. The case is founded on the premise that knowledge building is a consensual process, that understanding derives from shared, intersubjective agreements as to how the world works, and that therefore the seemingly conflictual approaches can benefit from converging with each other, or at least from remaining open to, rather than condemning, alternative theories, methodologies, and findings. None of us has a corner on ultimate truth. All of us undertake inquiries with a point of view, with values and agendas that we may not fully appreciate are operative. So we ought to be appreciative of alternative perspectives that highlight how our analyses may suffer from exaggerated and unrecognized premises and procedures. Put more specifically, surely those who articulate the newer perspectives can draw on the insights and findings of their predecessors even as they tailor them to their own inquiries and methodologies. Likewise, surely those who employ the older perspectives can profit from pondering the interpretations and critiques of the newer approaches even as they maintain their theoretical and methodological premises.

Some Credentials

Aside from the alleged perspective that goes with being an old-timer, I view myself as loaded down with credentials that attach some legitimacy to this effort at synthesis. The main credential—but not the only one—derives from having been an early warrior in the battle to establish behavioral/quantitative perspectives as legitimate approaches to the study of IR. It does not require much effort to recall either the unqualified convictions and enthusiasm with which we waged that struggle in the 1950s or the thoroughgoing obstinacy and ridicule with which our arguments were dismissed by the early realists. We were, or at least we felt we were, a small band of renegades who dared to question the prevailing wisdom that states predominated in an anarchical world and that they did so by seeking to maximize their power. The early realists (and the designers of their book jackets) stressed that states were either like chess pieces or billiard balls in the sense that they all moved in the same way when subject to the same situations or provocations. The writings of Arnold Wolfers and Hans Morgenthau were among those who served as the targets of our angst.[5] The latter drove us to distraction with his contention that "as disinterested observers we understand his thoughts and actions perhaps better than he, the actor on the political scene, does himself."[6] No, we vigorously insisted, this was much too simple. The only way you can grasp why states do what they do is to look inside the billiard ball and ascertain how their policy makers view the world, an exercise that leads quickly to the conclusion that not all states react the same way when subjected to the same external stimuli. What is needed, we argued, is empirical inquiry—not just a case study (since one never knows whether the single case represents the exception or the rule) but numerous cases so that one can tease out central tendencies and how these can vary under varying conditions. This reasoning led directly to valuing quantification and scientific methods as prime means of inquiry.

And as we became more articulate in advancing our case and carrying out studies that supported it, so did we evoke more articulate and intense criticism and ridicule,[7] an escalatory process that seemed to acquire greater momentum with each publication and each counterreaction. Indeed, we had to devote considerable energy to defending our flanks and answering the more extreme of the criticisms,[8] a process that doubtless led us to be insular and aggressive, to convene conferences and read journals in which we quoted each other and avoided open interaction with other than like-minded colleagues. And the more we fed off each other, the tighter did we draw the lines that divided us from our critics and the more did we become convinced that we had discovered the royal road to "truth" that had eluded others. That royal road was paved with expectations in which the application of scientific methods would enable us to uncover quantified patterns that would demonstrate how the underpinnings of world politics functioned or, in my case, how and why different countries pursued different foreign policies on the basis of their size, their degree of economic development, and their form of political accountability.[9] To be sure, we acknowledged, there were exceptions and anomalies—or, in statistical terms, outliers—but we did not attach much importance to them as long as the central tendencies embedded in large bodies of data were unmistakable in their direction.

Needless to say, imbued with a spirit of righteousness and adventure, these were heady times. There was satisfaction, even exhilaration, to be had in feeling we were fighting the good fight—the fight for "truth," for understanding founded on the secure footings of a rigorous methodology, for systematic inquiry rather than intuitive and unsubstantiated observations.[10] Moreover, there was a sense of triumph in pointing out how the traditional approaches yielded findings that were questionable because they could be interpreted in so many ways.

Partly because we were successful and began to be defined as the mainstream, partly because our claims for the virtues of a scientific approach proved to be premature as our inquiries raised as many questions as they answered, and partly because new schools of IR research evolved that seem to hold greater promise than did ours, by the mid-1970s our élan began to wane; and instead of affirming their scientific commitments, some of those in our ranks began to deny they ever were "behavioralists"—as if the word represented an outmoded and far-fetched approach to the study of world politics. In some quarters, especially those that began to turn to postmodern perspectives, the notion of "behavioralism" or "positivism" came to be used pejoratively. I do not recall any of those in our ranks referring to themselves as positivists—in fact, I had never heard the term until I was accused of being one—but for the critics there seemed to be a special pride in insisting they were postpositivists or poststructuralists, as if such a label indicated they had cleansed the impurities from their inquiries and had moved on to become serious scholars free of the silliness of science. Indeed, I have the impression that many of those who saw themselves as postpositivists latched on to postmodernism or poststructuralism because they seemed to offer a philosophical perspective, an intellectual structure and rationale, that infused substance into their rejection of behavioral and scientific approaches. In short, postpositivists and poststructuralists became as rigid and ideological with respect to behavioralists as we had been in our rejection of Morgenthau and other versions of realism. And in neither paradigmatic transition were voices heard that sought to bridge the differences and achieve syntheses. Reinforced by the publication of Kuhn's persuasive argument that paradigms are all-encompassing and mutually exclusive,[11] we saw no need to reach out across the paradigmatic divides for greater understanding.

A Caveat

Looking back on my participation in the early debates and the writings I contributed to them, I find comfort in a perspective I articulated that more than offsets the subsequent postpositivist, poststructural, and postmodern criticisms. The latter fault those committed to scientific inquiry for claiming objectivity when in fact they have hidden political agendas and are endlessly making what the postmodernists call political moves. Indeed, as I understand their paradigm, it is a central tenet of postmodernism that all observations, even those consisting of statistically affirmed quantified patterns, are rooted in values and thus can never claim objectivity. The trouble with behavioralism, positivism, and science, the argument would appear to be, is that the findings uncovered can never tell the whole story, that inevitably they rest on values and premises that are pervaded with silences not revealed by their patterns and that therefore it is profoundly deceptive to contend that "truths" have been uncovered even by the most careful and systematic of inquiries. From postmodern and poststructural perspectives, scientists deceive themselves as well as their audiences when they cast their results in the language of established facts.

There is truth in this line of reasoning—except that in my case it does not hold. In the very earliest of my works,[12] and consistently thereafter, I reiterated the caveat that it was not possible to engage in objective analysis; that we practiced a value-explicit, not a value-free science; that the scientist had the obligation to explicate the value, conceptual, and methodological bases of his or her analysis. Time and again, I stressed that the core of science involved explicitness so that the reader could check up on whether the purported findings held up in the context of other values, concepts, or methodologies (I even coined a term for this process that several generations of students still recall, namely, the term "checkable-upableness"). If others concluded that a set of findings did check out, then they could join a consensus in support of the understandings thereby generated; if their checkableupableness resulted in a rejection of the findings, then no consensus would form around the findings, and they would probably disappear into an ever widening dustbin of failed inquires. Thus, I argued, did knowledge evolve: it consists of an ever evolving series of competitive consensuses which are not objective but intersubjective in nature. I have never come upon objective results and I never will; the postmodernists and poststructuralists are right: such results do not and cannot exist. And they are also right in arguing that the prevailing consensuses may overlook matters of concern, silences to which attention needs to be paid. But they are wrong, I would argue, in claiming that those committed to scientific inquiry presume they can uncover objective truths. Our early enthusiasm for behavioralism may have conveyed such a presumption, but it was not long before our subsequent "truth" claims were couched in probabilistic terms that acknowledged the intersubjective nature of any conclusions derived from systematic analyses. To repeat, be they in the hard or soft sciences, the best that scientists can do is uncover findings that are the focus of widespread consensuses.

Toward Synthesis

This caveat, I would argue now with the hindsight of an old-timer, has the makings of a workable synthesis that can bridge some of the paradigmatic divides. If it is the case that most or all versions of postmodernism and poststructuralism presume that interpretations are inevitably subjective and reflective of the values and/or goals of those who offer them, then that is not far removed from the position of those who view science and scientific methods as rooted in intersubjectivity. Scientists care more than postmodernists or poststructuralists about establishing widespread agreements among observers about the nature of what they study, but they acknowledge that their findings do not exist prior to their interpretation of them and that the widespread agreements can dissipate as new findings refute them and observers flock to the new findings and form a consensual interpretation of them. "Wait a minute," a postmodernist or poststructuralist might respond, "we don't care about consensuses. Every interpretation is unique to the interpreter, and it doesn't matter if different interpreters come to similar conclusions." Even if this response is accurate—and I doubt that it is, as one can readily cite convergences among postmodernists and poststructuralists—it skirts the essential point that both scientists and their opponents share a view that interpretation derives from subjective sources which channel observations. That scientists aspire to broadening support for their interpretations, while postmodernists and poststructuralists say they have no such aspirations, does not alter the conclusion that all three schools of thought allow for the intrusion of personal biases, values, and convictions. Nor is the conclusion undermined by the commitment of scientists to an elaborate methodology for checking out their findings while such a methodology tends to be an anathema to postmodernists and poststructuralists, who believe that "checkableupableness" can never fully explicate the interpretations hidden in the methods of science.

On the Nature of Pre-Postmodernism

It is precisely the commitment to moving from subjective to intersubjective understanding through a methodology that allows consensuses to form that prevents my crossing the line into the world of postpositivists, poststructuralists, and postmodernists. I have changed course in the sense that I share their view that science's preoccupation with parsimony narrows the field within which they can engage in observations, and indeed, elsewhere I have argued the time has come to relax the strictures of parsimony.[13] And I also agree that the silenced voices need to be heard, that some scientists are unmindful of the need for explicitness and thus deceive themselves into viewing their findings as objective reality, and that some of them also have implicit political agendas that guide their inquiries. Still, to concede these points is not to negate my view of science as an explicit, consensus-building enterprise. It is merely to acknowledge that some scientists fit the postmodernist and poststructuralist stereotype of modernist procedures. Even though the shoe fits some practitioners, however, it remains the case that at their core the scientific methodologies of the modernist, the critical discourse methodologies of the postpositivist, and the deconstructionist methodologies of the postmodernist are essentially identical insofar as their readiness to proceed explicitly is concerned as they probe whatever problems of world politics they deem significant.

To be a prepostmodernist or a prepoststructuralist, then, is to straddle the two schools of thought and to discern a mechanism for synthesizing them. It is to acknowledge that many of the charges against modernism, behavioralism, and positivism are not without merit, but it is also to retain a commitment to empirical inquiry that is founded on explicitness. This is the unifying mechanism. While the several approaches may differ on the virtues of empiricism, intersubjectivity, and the relevance of power, they share a deep-seated belief in checkableupableness. Admittedly, this does not mean they will accept each other's knowledge that checks out and thus may never subscribe to the same consensuses; but each arrives at his or her interpretations through a shared commitment to explication, and therein lies the basis for pre-postmodernism and/or pre-poststructuralism. They are empirical enterprises committed to a relaxed view of scientific methods and a readiness to concede that values shape the questions asked by investigators and the answers they offer subsequent to their analyses.

Notes

1. Quoted in Oded Balaban, *Politics and Ideology: A Philosophical Approach* (Aldershot, UK: Ashgate Publishing Co., 1995), xiv.

2. Michael J. Shapiro, quoted in Roland Bleiker, *Retracing and Redrawing the Boundaries of Events: Postmodern Interferences with International Theory* (Copenhagen: Danish Institute of International Affairs, No. 17, Working Papers, 1997), 2.

3. An earlier version of this chapter was presented at the annual meeting of the International Studies Association (Minneapolis, March 21, 1998). I am grateful to David Johnson and Hongying Wang for their critical reactions to an earlier draft of this paper.

4. See, for example, O. C. McSwite, *Legitimacy in Public Administration: A Discourse Analysis* (Thousand Oaks, CA: Sage Publications, 1997), chap. 1.

5. Cf. Hans J. Morgenthau, *Politics among Nations: The Struggle for Power and Peace*, 5th ed. (New York: Alfred A. Knopf, 1973), and Arnold Wolfers, *Discord and Collaboration* (Baltimore: Johns Hopkins University Press, 1962).

6. Morgenthau, *Politics among Nations*, 5.

7. See, for example, Hedley Bull, "The Case for a Classical Approach," in Klaus Knorr and James N. Rosenau, eds., *Contending Approaches to International Politics* (Princeton, NJ: Princeton University Press, 1969), 20–38.

8. An insightful example is provided in Robert C. North, "Research Pluralism and the International Elephant," in Knorr and Rosenau, eds., *Contending Approaches to International Politics*, 218–42.

9. James N. Rosenau, "Pre-Theories and Theories of Foreign Policy," in R. B. Farrell, ed., *Approaches to Comparative and International Politics* (Evanston, IL: Northwestern University Press, 1966), 27–92.

10. For an autobiographical account of "the good fight," see James N. Rosenau, "The Scholar as an Adaptive System," in Joseph Kruzel and James N. Rosenau, eds., *Journeys through World Politics: Autobiographical Reflections of Thirty-four Academic Travelers* (Lexington, MA: Lexington Books, 1989), 53–67.

11. Thomas S. Kuhn, *The Structure of Scientific Revolutions*, 2nd ed., enlarged (Chicago: University of Chicago Press, 1970).

12. See, for example, Rosenau, "Pre-Theories and Theories of Foreign Policy," and James N. Rosenau, "Moral Fervor, Systematic Analysis, and Scientific Consciousness in Foreign Policy Research," in A. Ranney, ed., *Political Science and Public Policy* (Chicago: Markham, 1968), 197–236.

13. James N. Rosenau, *Turbulence in World Politics: A Theory of Change and Continuity* (Princeton, NJ: Princeton University Press, 1990), 23–25.

References

Balaban, Oded. *Politics and Ideology: A Philosophical Approach.* Aldershot, UK: Ashgate Publishing Co., 1995.

Bleiker, Roland. *Retracing and Redrawing the Boundaries of Events: Postmodern Interferences with International Theory.* Copenhagen: Danish Institute of International Affairs (Working Papers, No. 17), 1997.

Bull, Hedley. "The Case for a Classical Approach." Pp. 20–38 in *Contending Approaches to International Politics,* ed. Klaus Knorr and James N. Rosenau. Princeton, NJ: Princeton University Press, 1969.

Kuhn, Thomas S. *The Structure of Scientific Revolutions,* 2nd ed., enlarged. Chicago: University of Chicago Press, 1970.

McSwite, O. C. *Legitimacy in Public Administration: A Discourse Analysis.* Thousand Oaks, CA: Sage Publications, 1997.

Morgenthau, Hans J. *Politics among Nations: The Struggle for Power and Peace,* 5th ed. New York: Alfred A. Knopf, 1973.

North, Robert C. "Research Pluralism and the International Elephant." Pp. 218–42 in *Contending Approaches to International Politics,* ed. Klaus Knorr and James N. Rosenau. Princeton, NJ: Princeton University Press, 1969.

Rosenau, James N. "Moral Fervor, Systematic Analysis, and Scientific Consciousness in Foreign Policy." Pp. 197–236 in *Political Science in Public Policy,* ed. A. Ranney. Chicago: Markham, 1968.

———. "Pre-Theories and Theories of Foreign Policy." Pp. 27–92 in *Approaches to Comparative and International Politics,* ed. R. B. Farrell. Evanston, IL: Northwestern University Press, 1966.

———. "The Scholar as an Adaptive System." In *Journeys through World Politics: Autobiographical Reflections of Thirty-Four Academic Travelers,* ed. Joseph Kruzel and James N. Rosenau. Lexington, MA: Lexington Books, 1989.

———. *Turbulence in World Politics: A Theory of Change and Continuity.* Princeton, NJ: Princeton University Press, 1990.

Wolfers, Arnold. *Discord and Collaboration.* Baltimore: Johns Hopkins University Press, 1962.

IAN J. BARROW

Agency in the New World History

༄০৵

THE PAST FIFTY YEARS have seen dramatic changes within the discipline of history. Prior to the Second World War, historians primarily concerned themselves with diplomacy, war, and politics; whether they were imperialist, nationalist, or even Marxist, the overriding objective was to explain or account for high political actions. Since the war, as new generations of historians searched for nonelite perspectives, the variety of history writing increased, which added depth to understanding and range to vision. No longer compelled to focus on policy and great men, many historians increasingly identified themselves by those whom they studied—labor historians or peasant studies scholars, for instance. Others followed schools—the Annales or Marxist or Subaltern schools, for example—while still others characterized themselves as thematic historians, including environmental or representational historians. At first sight it would seem that the discipline is now so segmented that there are no overarching paradigms.

Editor's note: In "Agency in the New World History," Ian Barrow of Middlebury College looks for a link between the particular and the general—"area studies specialists" and "world history" practitioners—within the discipline of history. He implies that the dispute between these two groups within the discipline of history is a microcosm of the conflict between area studies practitioners in many disciplines and those who call themselves globalists.

The two groups of historians, says Barrow, have found coexistence possible because they both reify disembodied entities such as governments, nation-states, civilizations, and world systems, treating them as if they had independent will. The accommodation between world historians and area studies historians, however, is illusory, because the reification that unites them is itself flawed. Barrow takes the reader on a tour of the ideas of leading scholars of world history, civilizations, and world systems, including Oswald Spengler, Fernand Braudel, William McNeill, Samuel Huntington, Immanuel Wallerstein, and Janet Lippman Abu-Lughod, to illustrate his point. Barrow thinks a new common ground can be found by relocating agency in people, who act as agent, instrument, or patient in different proportions and at different times.

However, many of these new historical perspectives have been catego-
rized under the general rubric of area studies. Indeed, one of the features
of these perspectives is that while they may differ from each other in
methodology, they are often constricted by post–Second World War political and cultural boundaries, which creates areas of study such as Latin
America, South Asia, or France. Until recently, for example, it was rare
for a historian to conduct research across areas, and even mutually antithetical approaches, such as rational choice and postmodern theories,
have been used predominantly within the area studies model. However,
both rational choice and postmodern studies have contributed to a pola-
rization within area studies, between those who consider that assumptions can be based on the predictive patterns of rational agents and those
who claim that there are no Absolutes, or standards for measuring
change, or any basis for systematically identifying patterns which conform to rational behavior. Therefore, the various approaches within area
studies have often differed in their modeling and conclusions. Yet for all
the discord there have been few challenges to the hegemony of area studies. Area studies has remained the predominant classificatory language
within which to study history in an academic setting.

Nevertheless, even though area studies has managed to subsume and
quell all manner of potentially hostile methodologies, it has begun to see
many of those historians, who are disaffected with the imposed categorical boundaries, search for a new form of classification. One of the most
apparent rifts within the discipline today is between area studies specialists, who have enjoyed fifty years of prominence and funding, and world
historians, who have begun to claim their rightful place as translators of
globalization processes. And it is world history, more than any other historical perspective or methodology, which has posed the greatest challenge to area studies.

World history is an enigma and a threat to many area studies specialists. It is an enigma because it is seen to generalize with impunity, ignoring local nuances and particularities. It is a threat because world historians often examine systemic or thematic processes on a global or
hemispheric scale, obliterating distinctions which characterize nations or
culturally discrete areas. In their own defense, world historians contend
that there are identifiable laws, cultures, economic processes, even dis-
eases which transcend single regions and which must be placed within a
vast temporal context. Thus, the gulf between area studies and world historians seems vast: on the crucial issues of time, place, and disciplinary
rigor, the two camps are worlds apart.

This essay argues that although world historians and area studies specialists are mutually mistrustful, they have something in common. What

they share is an assumption that the mechanisms of change can be located in substantialized and disembodied agents; that, in other words, civilizations and world systems—whether economic or cultural—nations and governments, unions, societies, even individuals are all capable of forcing and enforcing change. I argue that the common use of reified agency among world historians and area specialists, while a sign that their approaches are not as mutually exclusive as they might appear, is a hindrance to an analysis of how people effect and react to change.

A reexamination of agency, therefore, while initially disrupting disciplinary assumptions regarding change, might enable generalist and specialist historians to converse in a more common and relevant language. My hope is that by identifying an aspect of their histories which they share—namely, their reliance on disembodied agency—and by suggesting that a new theory of agency might be productive, I can initiate a dialogue between historians who are increasingly defensive and protective of their perspective. This essay begins by outlining a theory of agency, amenable to both area studies and a new world history; continues with a gentle critique of the leading models of world history and area studies, focusing on their use of agency; and concludes with an example of how to use the idea of agency as a way to bridge categorical differences.

Agency and a New World History

Outside the textbook arena, world history makes few claims to be a comprehensive accounting of the past in all regions of the earth. Instead, it has embraced a number of approaches—civilizational researches, systems analysis, or cross-regional thematic studies—much in the same way that area studies has fostered multiple, if often competing, theories. The great differences between world history and area studies are categorical, a subject which I will examine in detail in the following sections. But while world historians and area studies experts debate the relative utility of their categories, a crucial aspect of history has been ill-addressed, especially by world historians. This essay raises the question of agency and argues that a theory can be found which accommodates the seemingly divergent aims of world history and area studies, while at the same time perhaps initiating a rapprochement of sorts between the two warring paradigms.

Although agency is a largely forgotten subject for world historians, it has not been wholly neglected. Michael Adas, for example, a highly respected and innovative historian, has argued for a reconceptualization of agency in world history. In a recent article entitled "Bringing Ideas and

Agency Back In," Adas bemoans the fact that much of world history has relied so heavily on structuralist theories, resulting in an "impersonal and aggregate-oriented" body of scholarship, and argues, instead, that a focus on representation would allow historians to texture their analyses in a manner that would suit their approach.[1] Adas maintains that studies of representation would permit world-systems historians or locally oriented researchers to speak a common language of comparative or global history. A Gramscian understanding of hegemony and the possibilities of combining base (systems and structures) and superstructure (ideology), constitute one avenue for demonstrating how representational histories would enable historians to speak in broad but specifically nuanced terms. Representations are indeed an exceptionally important facet of agency, and studies which have examined representations have often been successful in attracting a broad readership. However, Adas's notions of agency allow for the continued existence of systems and structures as autonomous entities. For example, he notes that in order for ideas and agency to be adopted successfully, historians must connect "the various levels that world history must comprehend, from the workings of the world system to their impact on the lives of subaltern groups and individuals."[2] My argument is that world systems and other substantialized or disembodied agents cannot "impact" people in such a fashion that it is assumed that these entities have autonomous wills, capabilities, or powers. Agency must be relocated in people.

The theory of agency that I wish to propose as a means of reconfiguring the ties between area studies history and world history is based on the writings of Ronald Inden, who, in turn, was influenced by R. G. Collingwood.[3] Inden argues that historians, especially colonial and nationalist historians of India, have denied people agency by assigning powers to entities which are only made seemingly substantial or real through their expression of essences. For example, scholars have understood India as a category for research because it embodies certain unchanging and uniquely configured principles, such as caste, village republics, and divine kingship. These principles have been given such authority and weight that historians have often viewed people's actions and thoughts as being in accordance with or subject to them. Caste, therefore, is seen as prescriptive in that a Hindu is born into it and that he or she cannot, throughout life, escape its hegemonic influence: caste, as a self-regulating and powerful expression of an unchanging principle, partially orders and determines relationships and decisions.

How might world or area studies historians locate agency in people without having to refer to disembodied entities such as civilizations, systems, structures, or nation-states? Following Inden, one solution would be to disaggregate the term *agency* and to see it as composed of at least three aspects: agent, instrument and patient. Inden called this disaggregated agency, complex agency.

This preliminary definition of agency would entail a rejection of the individual as a fundamental category. The notion of the individual incorporates assumptions of autonomy, which function in the same way as the larger entities described above. What is important to note is that people do not act in isolation. They do not think without being influenced by their environment, their community, or their pasts. Inden proposes a "scale of forms," whereby people are, in differing proportions and at different times, part agent, part instrument, and part patient. Such multiple states in both degree and kind enable people to act and react rationally, coherently, effectively, or not, depending upon their own limitations and abilities. The significance of this definition is that people need not be regarded as unified, whole, essential. They do not represent some principle such as rationality, as is the case with the use of "individual," but are instead central actors in how they respond to or initiate action. Although this theory makes people more responsible for change, agents need not be aware of the implications of their actions. Nor need they be aware of how their own responses are shaped by external conditions. Nevertheless, if historians were to think of agency as embodied in people who act in a variety of ways (sometimes even in simultaneously contradictory ways), then a common language for world history and area studies might be generated.

Two additional questions with regard to this definition are, how do agents act, and how do historians begin to discuss governments, nations, or other corporate bodies? With regard to the first concern, Inden proposes that agents act dialectically and eristically. He defines dialectic as the process whereby two opposing parties eventually create common ground upon which they can both tread. Eristical behavior, on the other hand, occurs when two opposing parties vie with one another for ultimate domination, resulting in the loss of any mutually acceptable solution. Although these two ways of projecting agency are possible, they nevertheless leave the impression that agents, however configured, are too starkly portrayed in terms of their definitive action. In other words, most people do not always act in a definite and confrontational manner, whether dialectically or eristically. Moreover, this definition may also result in the assumption that people's intentions, characters, and beliefs are necessarily represented by their actions, which is rarely the case.

It seems more fruitful to return to Inden's original characterization of agents as having multiple meanings and expressions. Most people act confusingly and hastily, pushed by bias or pulled by prejudice. I would contend that people are not rational agents and that their actions, there-fore, cannot be predicted, precisely because they are at once agents, in-struments, and patients. People often have conflicting interests; they lie; they dissimulate and flatter; they represent themselves as more powerful or wiser, or richer than they are in fact. The point is that actions or changes, at the most intimate and human level, can rarely be interpreted neatly but are more commonly the result of a complex intermingling and fusion of ideas and influences.

The second question focuses on the issue of treating nations, govern-ments, societies, or other corporate entities. What is often the case, as I have suggested, is that scholars and policy makers see these institutional bodies as "bodies," as entities which function as individuals. They exist in that they have sovereignty, coherence, or independence from direct human control. The use of tropes, such as structure and system, also indi-cate that there are forces which impinge upon or partially direct and de-termine human lives. The advantage of introducing structures to a histor-ical study, for example, is that it enables a scholar to shift responsibility away from people, while explaining compliance to what may now be considered oppressive regimes or social mores. For example, how can one explain the fact that most women in the seventeenth century ac-cepted the privileges accorded to men? Social structure and culture seem to be viable means by which historians can explain conditions and ac-tions without suggesting that women were unaware of other possibilities. My argument, using this brief example, is that in relying on structures historians may tend to take them for granted, as existing, autonomous, self-directing entities, when I would suggest that they are reifications, or the treatment of abstractions as real entities. I do not wish to dispense with categories such as the individual, structure, nation-state, system, or civilization; instead, I hope to refocus attention onto the idea of agency by pointing out that what we often think to be real—institutions, struc-tures, civilizations—are reified entities. The government, for example, which can imprison dissenters and criminals or provide succor to the ill and the enfeebled, seems to be "real," but is it a complex of buildings, a series of constitutional documents, a community of workers, or an as-semblage of ideas? We chose to believe that nation-states, that govern-ments, that structures exist because they help to make the world compre-hensible, orderly, and productive.

The idea of agency that I am proposing, following Inden, as a bridge between area studies specialists and world historians may be summarized as follows. Instead of looking first at systems, nation-states, or civiliza-tions and analyzing how they may impact, condition, or determine human lives, historians should remember that those entities are reified in the sense that people, for very good reasons, imagine them to exist as autonomous expressions of defining principles. If historians were to begin with a definition of complex agency, located in people, and expand that definition to include reified agents, new and more common perspectives may be generated. By complex agency I mean that a person may simultaneously be his or her own agent, someone else's instrument, and a passive or argumentative patient. Moreover, a person may choose to share ideas or practices with others, and as a result, common languages and assumptions are created. The reified institutions, structures, nation-states, and civilizations that are created may then be seen to operate as if they had autonomous power. This would enable scholars to maintain categories of analysis. But instead of regarding world systems, for example, as entities which direct or constrict or initiate human action, these world systems would be examined and used as reified products of human agency expressed as a common assumption. The focus, therefore, is on how people create conditions which allow for the projection of agency onto seemingly autonomous entities.

Such an approach would direct attention to how people condition their lives while accepting the existence of organized and comprehensible forces which seemingly cause them to comply or conform to common practices. The additional advantage of locating agency in people and then seeing that agency transferred by people to reified entities is that one of the contentious issues between area studies and world history has been obviated. As I have mentioned, both camps of historians articulate their differences in terms of how the categories they use either constrict or enable them to conduct certain kinds of historical inquiries. Area studies scholars dislike the systems, civilizational or thematic approaches to world history, while world historians rebel at the idea of being forced to conduct research within the confines of area and national studies. They express their differences, therefore, as categorical. Thus, my argument is that a reevaluation of agency and a renewed commitment to theorizing agency as located in people who choose to ascribe powers to reified entities will place historians' categorical differences in a different perspective and result in a dialogue between area studies and a new world history.

World History and Civilizations

World history is a growing but undertheorized area of inquiry. Even among its practitioners there seems to be a consensus that there are few generally accepted guiding precepts or theories. The result has been that almost all historical approaches—including economic, environmental, and political studies—which are transnational in scope may be classified under the rubric of world history.[4] This lack of definitional specificity and theoretical approach has meant that world history could be likened to a ship without a chart, directed only by a few stellar luminaries. However, this freedom from the constraints of national and area studies, together with the lack of pressure to conform to a dominant methodology, has enabled world historians to pursue research on such varied subjects as diasporas, the environment, and scientific knowledge, which often implicitly critique area studies specialists' reliance on anachronistic political boundaries.[5] While this may suggest that there are fundamental differences between world historians and area studies scholars—in terms of theoretical sophistication and dependence upon a geographically or nationally defined area as the primary unit of analysis—I will argue that both parties rely upon definitions of agency which strip people of their capacity to effect change. The point to be made is that too many world and area studies historians explain change through the means of metaphors (structure or system, for example) or geographical, political, or cultural units which are expressions of an essence. The use of "civilization" is the first of several categories of analysis I wish to examine in order to demonstrate how historians and social scientists have extruded people by assigning agency to essences. This section will examine various scholars' definitions of civilization and critique them on the basis that they construct agents which have only spurious relations to individuals. Four aspects of their definitions will be highlighted: the idea that civilizations reflect singular cultural traits; the assumption that civilizations are real (some would even contend that they have life cycles and can die); the belief that, even if they are not living organisms, they can still be analyzed as if they were individuals, in the same manner that nation-states are often regarded as corporate bodies; and the argument that civilizations, even if not bounded in a cartographic sense, are nevertheless unified and complete.

The idea of civilizations has played a prominent role in world history. Both Oswald Spengler and Arnold J. Toynbee made use of the term *civilization*, although they both used it loosely and sometimes confusingly.[6] Spengler, for example, believed that large-scale cultures were organisms with cycles of birth and death and thus defined civilizations as moribund cultures: "*Pure* Civilization, as a historical process, consists in a progressive exhaustion of forms that have become inorganic or dead."[7] Moreover, Spengler asserted that cultures and civilizations were characterized by essences, or "natures," such as rationality, that were the primary means by which scholars could explain events or cultural products. Although

Spengler's idiosyncratic use of civilization has not been widely adopted, his assumption that civilizations were discrete organisms directed by essences has resurfaced in various forms since the first volume of his *Decline of the West* was first published in 1926.

More recently, Fernand Braudel, William H. McNeill, and Samuel P. Huntington have employed the term as part of a strategy to comprehend either long-term changes over time or rapid and momentous political reconfigurations in our time.[8] Braudel, McNeill, and Huntington differ from each other and from Spengler in their use of civilization, but they share an understanding that civilizations are unitary entities, differentiated by essential characteristics. Braudel, for example, wrote an important essay, "The History of Civilizations: The Past Explains the Present," in which he argued that Spengler's sealed cultural and civilizational units should be retheorized so that historians of civilizations would not contend that civilizations were either living organisms, subject to maturity and death, or teleologies, leading, through successive stages, to predetermined conclusions.[9] Instead, Braudel wrote, historians should see civilizations as "cultural areas," organized around a locus but actively borrowing and refusing cultural elements. He reinforced his point by suggesting that the best studies of civilizations and their changes are those which focus on frontiers and borders and use the anthropological term *diffusion* as the primary analytic principle. Although Braudel offered an important corrective to both Spengler and Toynbee, he nevertheless imagined a civilization to be "a collection of cultural characteristics and phenomena."[10] One problem with this definition, apart from the conflation of culture and civilization, is that civilizations are identifiable by their singular traits: occurrences, changes, events, therefore, are explicable in terms of the interaction—or diffusion—of attributes, rather than in the interaction of people.

Perhaps the most important exponent of the diffusion principle was William McNeill, who in his monumental *Rise of the West: A History of the Human Community* regarded early civilizations as societies which had sufficiently specialized labor to permit skilled occupations, while later civilizations exhibited distinct "styles of life."[11] McNeill concentrated on a sequential narrative of high cultural and political achievements which was organized around the principle of diffusion: after 500 B.C.E., for example, civilizations were increasingly interconnected, and McNeill argued that an examination of the areas of disturbance between civilizations permits an analysis of both characteristic elements and the forces of change within and among civilizations. McNeill admitted that his definition of civilization was sufficiently vague for him to include a vast array of culturally and administratively coherent societies, although he also suggested that a civilization was as much a process as a state—that an infant, for example, was educated into being a member of a civilization (thus the importance of diffusion), as well as being prescriptively born into one. The difficulty I have with his characterization of civilizations, a difficulty which applies equally to Braudel, is that McNeill thought that civilizations existed: they "do seem real to me," he wrote.[12] The danger of using such a category of analysis, therefore, is that it is tempting to see civilizations as entities which have autonomous or independent powers which affect human lives. Even if Braudel and McNeill did not see civilizations as sentient beings, capable of maturation and expressive of a will, they nevertheless necessarily granted them agency, or the power to condition people's lives.

McNeill's reliance on diffusion and his Eurocentric approach (though not his displacement of agency) have been criticized by numerous scholars, most notably J. M. Blaut and Marshall Hodgson, who thought that McNeill's work was "unpalatable."[13] Hodgson articulated his vision of world history in a series of essays as well as in his extraordinary three-volume work, *The Venture of Islam*,[14] published posthumously. Hodgson's quarrel with McNeill focused on the latter's Eurocentric focus and his belief that a major watershed in world history occurred in the sixteenth century. Instead of seeing the Portuguese discoveries as a fundamental alteration in power structures between East and West, Hodgson argued that internal cultural changes, together with increasing specialization, resulted in a new age of technicalism. Hodgson structured time into four ages—early civilizations, the Axial Age (800–200 B.C.E.), the post–Axial Age (200 B.C.E.–1800 C.E.), and the Modern Age—and noted that what distinguished the post–Axial Age from the Modern Age was that, beginning in the seventeenth century, the West witnessed a shift from a dependence upon agrarian surpluses for cultural efflorescences to an economy which was marked by technical expertise and industrial investment, which was in part based upon the adoption of Afro-Eurasian inventions. The importance of Hodgson's work is that he placed civilizations, such as the Islamic civilizations, into a hemispheric context and that he strenuously argued for a temporal schema and philosophical understanding of how civilizations were interconnected and interdependent upon one another in such a fashion that they could not be seen as wholly distinct, unique, or essential.

Although Hodgson attempted to problematize "civilization" by decoupling it from a European referent and by nuancing the term sufficiently to suggest that civilizations are neither essential nor impermeable, he nevertheless took it as axiomatic that civilizations were cultural realities, that they could behave as if they were individuals because they expressed certain human characteristics. Hodgson defined a civilization, for example, as "any wider grouping of cultures insofar as they share consciously in interdependent cumulative traditions."[15] In this quotation, Hodgson was clearly stressing the interdependence of cultures within a civilization, although his use of the words "share consciously" unconsciously reveal his assumption that cultures and civilizations acted as individuals, an assumption which strips people of their agency only to give it to disembodied historical categories.

Hodgson has not been the only scholar to criticize McNeill for his use of the diffusion principle within a Eurocentric scheme. In his recent book, *The Colonizer's Model of the World*, J. M. Blaut strenuously argues against prevailing assumptions that the West's rise was due to internal advancements—he dislikes the core/periphery paradigm—and that changes emanated from a European center. Blaut goes to the heart of one of the abiding debates within world history, a debate to which I will refer again in the next section on world systems theories. The debate is what may be called the equivalency struggle: when and how exactly did the West, or the European civilization, first equal and then rise above the East in terms of wealth, power, and intellectual capability? I term it the Equivalency Struggle because two of the major motivating factors behind this scholarship are the desire to prove that fifteenth-century Europe was not more advanced than the East—if the East was not more "advanced," then there was a certain parity between East and West—and that Europe's rise was not due to autonomous processes but was the result of global interactions and interdependencies. Blaut's argument is that Europe was in no way superior to or more advanced than Asia or Africa and that its greatest advantage, one which it aggressively pursued, was its location. Moreover, its conquest of the New World was successful because of pandemics and European technology, although Blaut's point is that a nondiffusionist and non-Eurocentric model of history does not regard Europe as innately superior: Europe's success lay in its implementation of colonialism, which resulted in the accumulation of wealth, the exploitation of worldwide capital markets, and the empowerment of Europe's capital class, the bourgeoisie.

While Blaut provides a cogent critique of Eurocentric, diffusionist theory, he nevertheless comes under the sway of the twin tyrannies of typology and topography. In his desire to prove that there is neither an inner sphere of discovery and innovation which exerts its influence on peripheral areas, nor an inherently superior area of the world, he treats both Europe and the rest of the world as fixed categories. I do not wish to quarrel with Blaut's fine critiques, but what is important to note is that even though he does not refer to civilizations, he nevertheless treats his geographical, cultural, and economic categories as if they constituted civilizations: that is, his categories, such as Africa, America, and Europe, exhibit internal coherences, which enable him to identify large-scale geographical units without having to disaggregate the various component elements. Thus, when he speaks of Europe, he assumes that there are consistencies between and within states which override or make less meaningful distinctions and differences.

One of the problems of employing geographical terms as historical categories is that each area must either represent distinct characteristics (even if two or more areas' differences are seen to be equal in value), or they must be self-regulating. There is no sense in referring to Europe, for example, or to a civilization, if the category is meaningless. Thus, civilizations are a device by which scholars can fruitfully compare vast areas of the world. However, as I have indicated, the tendency has been to regard civilizations as expressions of unique characteristics and thus to assign them powers to effect change. Many scholars who have chosen to use the civilizational model, such as Hodgson, point to the interconnections and interdependencies which they regard as most significant. However, they all assume that civilizations exist and that they operate as corporate bodies.

The final civilizational model that I wish to address is that of Samuel Huntington. Huntington's recent *Clash of Civilizations and the Remaking of World Order* has sparked heated debate. His argument is that the old Cold War bipolar political paradigm is now obsolete as a model for comprehending and predicting change and that scholars should retreat from their previous reliance on the category of nation-states since these are temporary political phenomena, whereas "human history is the history of civilizations."[16] Following Braudel, Huntington makes a distinction between civilizations in the plural and civilization in the singular: the singular usage implies cultural superiority, whereas his plural usage has little to do with etiquette or social refinement. When examining civilizations, the perceived level of culture is irrelevant. As he notes, civilizations could be barbaric: they denote cultural formations of several societies which have more in common with each other than they do with other societies. Huntington then rejects nineteenth-century German definitions of civilizations as industrial states and cultures as aesthetic and moral social groupings, arguing instead that civilizations are congeries of culturally similar societies.

The most important element of his definition, however, is that civilizations, as the common expression of several societies, are code words for great religions. For example, the map which he provides, "The World of Civilizations: Post-1990," shows nine civilizations, almost all of which are readily identifiable as religions. His civilizations include Western (which I interpret as Christian), African, Islamic, Sinic, Hindu, Orthodox (representing Russia), Japanese, Latin American, and Buddhist. He also notes that civilizations are "mortal," although they ensure their longevity by evolving and adapting.[17] Even though he implies that civilizations function, or live, as individuals, he nuances his definition by asserting that they have no fixed boundaries (despite the map) and that their populations are constantly shifting. The utility of breaking the world into these civilizations, he claims, is that it avoids reductionism while providing a predictive model for social scientists and public officials. If we know the composition of a civilization, its dominant traits, and its maturation trajectory, then it is possible to articulate policies which are informed and proactive.

Huntington's model is beguiling: it is simple and yet complex; it relies on a well-articulated historical category to predict patterns or behaviors; it establishes an order to change even as it acknowledges that there is a degree of uncertainty with regard to the ultimate outcome. However, Huntington's use of the term encapsulates many of the previous historians' definitions, all of which presuppose the existence of a disembodied agency which is expressive of an essence. Civilization theorists, as outlined above, range from Spengler, who equated civilizations with organisms, to Hodgson, who stressed the interconnections and interdependencies among civilizations; from McNeill, whose world history was patterned by levels of diffusion, to Blaut, whose global perspective was antithetical to diffusionist paradigms; and from Braudel who adopted a vast hourglass-like perspective, to Huntington, who compressed Braudel's perspective in order to provide both an explanatory and predictive political science model. These scholars and many others have resorted to differing theories of civilization in order to examine those momentous and far-reaching changes which are thought to be inexplicable through area studies approaches.

World Systems Theories

Despite the lack of attention given to agency, the civilization model has been attractive to many world historians. However, scholars have increasingly noticed patterns which cross cultural, national, or political boundaries and which cannot be explained adequately under most theories of civilizations. The patterns which were identified were predominately economic: it made sense to demonstrate how localities have rarely been autarkic, at least within the last millennium, but have instead relied upon and contributed to multiregional flows of capital. This section will examine the works of two influential scholars of world systems, Immanuel Wallerstein and Janet Lippman Abu-Lughod,[18] and demonstrate that their conception of world economic systems, while dissimilar to civilizational studies, nevertheless establishes metaphors—structures, systems—which are endowed with power.

Building on the dependency-theory scholarship of André Gunder Frank and other antimodernization theorists, Wallerstein identified common economic patterns, or structures, which helped explain the modern world. Wallerstein's concept of a world system is surprisingly close to the generally accepted ideas of civilization. In the above section, I argued that historians have identified civilizations as having singular traits, some form of complete (some would say discrete) existence, and the ability to alter people's lives as independent agencies. Wallerstein described his world system as "a social system, one that has boundaries, structures . . . coherence. . . . It has the characteristics of an organism, in that it has a life-span . . . life within it is largely self-contained.'[19] He went on to argue that it is important to distinguish between world empires (political structures) and world economies (which have no relation to political organizations). For him, world empires have succumbed due to their own success: the political powers extracted wealth from peasants and others so effectively that they caused revolt and turmoil. World economies, until recently, were always transformed into world empires (his examples are China, Persia, and Rome), which he equates with civilizations. In the sixteenth century, however, European technological improvements in transportation and communication, together with rising national culture and bureaucracy, enabled capital to organize core states into an integrated and extrapolitical world system. Wallerstein's world system, containing core states, was distinguished from peripheral and semiperipheral areas, which were weakly administered and, at least initially, unreceptive to the transformative powers of capital.

Although Wallerstein's definitions of the capitalist world system suggest bounded cores, peripheries, and semiperipheries (as a dependency theorist he did stress the interconnections and the way in which the peripheries have been immiserated by the cores, which brings to mind permeable boundaries), his reliance on capital rather than politics or culture as the principal component of the modern world system has inspired many to focus on economic patterns as a way of integrating cities and regions within larger trade or even cultural networks. One of the most successful exponents of world systems analysis is Janet Abu-Lughod, who, in her acclaimed *Before European Hegemony: The World System A.D. 1250–1350* and in numerous subsequent articles,[20] transformed her category of analysis into a critique of Eurocentric scholarship.

Abu-Lughod's use of world systems differs markedly from Waller-stein's, whose careful reading of the history of capital results in a work which is both biased toward Europe and blind to the idea that there could be viable world systems prior to the seventeenth century. Abu-Lughod's argument is that prior to the overresearched rise of the West there existed a complex and widespread network of commercial ties which spanned much of what we call the East. Moreover, this system was sufficiently vibrant and robust that, were it not for a series of calamities and decisions, the system might have continued beyond the fourteenth century. The questions to be answered, for her, are why this world system broke down and why the West became regnant soon afterward. Her answers are that a worldwide recession in the fourteenth and fifteenth centuries, the Black Death (the swift spread of which—from China to Europe in twenty years—only demonstrates the enormous reach of the trade networks), and the Chinese decision to abandon its navy in the 1430s all resulted in a breakdown of the Eastern world system before the rise of the Western one. As to the question of why the West rose when it did, she suggests that it could be because of the unique form of capitalism which was beginning to be practiced in Western Europe or because capitalism was emboldened by the discoveries of the New World and because of the recent demise of the previous world system. No matter what the correct answer may be, she concludes that there was a dynamic world system prior to the modern world system and that it collapsed before, not because of, the rise of the capitalist world system. The importance of this argument, of course, is that it contextualizes the subsequent success of Western capitalism by demonstrating that there are reasons for the West's success which lie beyond and before Europe's sixteenth-century capital innovations.

One of the exciting aspects of Abu-Lughod's work is that she describes three large circuits and eight subcircuits of the thirteenth-century world system as interwoven. Like a Venn diagram the various circuits overlap and share territory and practices. Thus, for example, parts of southeastern Turkey formed part of subcircuits which stretched over the eastern Mediterranean, and Arabian and Central Asian subcircuits. This classification adds a level of complexity that is often missing in civilizational studies, where civilizations are necessarily discrete. Moreover, her insistence on interconnections (on movement of capital, for example, which concentrates attention on the performance or function of the system) distinguishes her work from civilizational studies, where definitions often focus on the organization, or structure, of relations.

In a fascinating essay, "The World-System Perspective in the Construction of Economic History," Abu-Lughod playfully suggests that ec-

centricity (the simultaneous use of discordant or incongruous texts) results in "de-centered accounts" which may be regarded "ex-centrically."[21]
While Abu-Lughod is at pains to avoid core/periphery arguments and
while she advocates a history which considers systems as overlapping and
composed of numerous subcircuits, she nevertheless describes systems
which are concentric. Her systems may not focus on specific sites, but, as
graphically portrayed in her map of eight subcircuits in the thirteenth-
century world system, they are depictable zones which are characterized
by systematic economic forces. The important point to be made is that
political, cultural, and economic activities relate to the operation of the
system: individuals or groups may change their patterns of behavior, and
that may affect the health of the system, but the focus of her studies is on
extracorporeal entities. Systems, by definition, are self-regulating: they
signify logical and distinct arrangements of interrelated entities. It is true
that Abu-Lughod emphasizes the connection between the elements (she
favors, for example, the term *global* history over the more common
world history as a way of highlighting systemic linkages). However, the
focus is on the patterns and links which characterize particular regions.
Within this conceptual framework, agency becomes highly abstract: if
systems, economic or otherwise, are the defining thematic principle connecting subcircuits while still differentiating regions, the implication is
that these systems both express distinctive characteristics and operate on
the basis of those characteristics. The result is a history which examines
the connections between events insofar as they constitute systems, rather
than probing the ways in which people, as various kinds of agents, determine events and, with the help of metaphors, imagine connections and
reify entities.

Area Studies

The previous two sections have surveyed two of the leading theories of
world history. Civilizational studies and world systems analysis have attracted attention largely because of the ease with which disparate areas of
the world may be compared or connected in a meaningful and productive
manner. These two theories are obviously not the only approaches to
world history; others include diasporic and gender studies, environmental and military histories, and industrial and imperial accounts. Moreover, many historians apply perspectives, such as Marxism and postmodernism, in order to make local events, discourses, or representations
relevant to larger processes. While I cannot begin to examine each of
these approaches, one of their defining features is that they relate local

events to larger processes in such a way that these processes express commonalities: the focus, therefore, is on the structure of the connections, rather than in the form or origin of agency. The two theories of world history which I have addressed similarly create categories which, by expressing defining characteristics, are able to sustain their own structural coherence in the face of other civilizations or world systems. In this section I wish to highlight the ways in which area studies specialists have also resorted to disembodied agency in their attempt to maintain the integrity of their subject. I will focus on how area studies are indebted and often beholden to the post–Second World War national-state paradigm and demonstrate how such a framework often pushes an untheorized agency onto entities such as the state, the masses, or a particular class.

After the end of the Second World War, programs were established across the United States and funded by federal military grants to promote the study of non-Western areas and their languages. Partly because of the success of these programs (the funding of which was later transferred from the military to the federal education budget), partly because of the prominence of the United Nations, and partly because of the increasing political, cultural, and economic role of the United States in international affairs, area studies became a legitimate and widely adopted avenue for studying the non-Western world. Moreover, within designated "areas"—South Asia, Southeast Asia, Africa, for example—relatively rapid decolonization, beginning in the late 1940s and culminating in the transfer of Hong Kong to China in 1997, permitted historians, anthropologists, and political scientists to tailor their research to the confines of the new nation-states. Therefore, the double tendency to see the world in terms of areas and to parcel those areas into nation-states has trammeled ideas within a modern worldview.

It is because funding agencies, whether private, such as the Social Science Research Council, or federal, have until recently been organized around nation-states within areas that specialist research has tended to focus on projects which may have anachronistic boundaries. It is much easier, for example, to receive grants to study kingship in ancient India than the influence of the Cholas (a southern Indian empire) on kingship in Southeast Asia. Even the terms used in the previous example (India and Southeast Asia), which are necessary to situate the example, force us to use categories that had little meaning before the twentieth century. Moreover, the example serves to indicate that scholarly research outside of areas or nation-states is unusual.

It is indeed this disciplinary reliance upon anachronistic categories that has helped swell the ranks of world historians. However, many area studies historians have used methodologies or theories which are applicable to a broad variety of contexts across the world. Marxist research on peasants and industrial classes, postcolonial strategies to uncover subaltern forms of resistance while revealing hegemonic thoughts and institutions, or postmodern critiques of knowledge, power, and structure are all prominent ways in which historians have applied and adapted general theories to specific locations and events. In this section I cannot address these varied strategies since the literature is so vast. Nevertheless, the point to be made is that one of the reasons why world history has become an increasingly popular avenue for research is that scholars feel constricted by the category of the area or the nation-state. It is, in fact, the categories which separate world historians from area studies specialists: they may adhere to the same political philosophy or practice the same theory, but they disagree on both the degree and the kind of parameters which they establish for their writing.

The disagreements, therefore, between area studies and world historians are not necessarily rooted in radically different methodologies. It is quite possible, for example, to examine environmental history within India[22] by using techniques similar to those used by a world environmental historian.[23] Alternatively, it is possible for a generation of area studies historians to rely on an understanding of Orientalism, which may easily be classified as a world historical theory.[24] The contentious issue between the two camps is the utility of the categories they use: world historians claim that areas and nations are too restrictive and potentially anachronistic, while area studies scholars argue that global world systems or civilizational research is too general to generate nuanced and appropriate conclusions. The theory of agency which I have proposed reconfigures these categories in such a way that they are recognized as reified entities. Agency is located in people and is considered to be the ability to alter and respond to change while nevertheless being influenced by economic, political, or social conditions. The important point to make is that although many area studies scholars are committed to recovering initiative and power for people, especially subalterns and those who have been colonized, most studies have remained area-focused.

Conclusions

In the previous sections, I have briefly critiqued several models used by world historians and area studies scholars on the basis that these paradigms reflect either a general lack of interest in or cavalier use of agency. I have argued that civilizational research, world systems theories, and studies using the nation-state as a geographical or analytic parameter, all displace the capacity to effect change onto disembodied and unitary agents. Moreover, this displacement involves a notion of agency which is largely left untheorized. Civilizations, systems, and areas are remarkable because of the patterns, relationships, and connections of the various elements which constitute these complete categorical units. Historians, therefore, have tended to measure the significance of change in terms of the alteration of the constituent elements, not in terms of how people themselves manipulate economic, political, or social conditions. Thus, while historians see a gulf between area studies and world history, they similarly create disembodied agents.

In conclusion, I offer a brief example of how world historians and area studies specialists may approach a topic in a way that contributes to a more trenchant and nuanced analysis. The example I wish to provide focuses on a theoretical debate concerning the construction of "Britishness": was it created within Britain and Europe or was it the result of transnational and colonial participation? A traditional area studies analysis of the eighteenth- and nineteenth-century making of a British nation-state and sense of belonging might focus on internal economic, social, or political factors, while nevertheless suggesting that Britishness was also constructed in opposition to the making of France and other European nation-states. The category of the nation-state would be the dominant organizing principle and would be, in some sense, anachronistic. In other words, by looking at the end result (national pride within a nation-state), a historian might then examine how conditions and events within that nation-state resulted in Britishness. A world historian, by contrast, might explain how a general sentiment or economic process, such as the creation of a bourgeois class, shared over a large geographical area and extending over a long period of time, resulted in regionally inflected national pride. Therefore, the categorical differences between the world historian and the area studies expert—the former beginning with a transnational phenomenon and the latter remaining largely within the confines of the national space in question—result in two possibly distinct perspectives. While the world historian might stress the commonalities of national sentiment and argue that the burgeoning of the phenomenon of nationalism is more significant than its particular expressions, an area studies historian might locate the genesis of Britishness, for example, in a specific region and as a result of specific internal conditions.

An alternative approach, which does not begin from either the category of the nation-state or a transnational system, could be constructed from the basis of agency outlined above. As I have suggested, a complex agency located in people and recognized as being amenable to reification might enable world and area studies historians to speak a more common language. For example, the experiences, practices and representations of people are the means by which ideas, assumptions, and beliefs are circulated and accepted. The colonial endeavors of the eighteenth century were among the most influential ventures which shaped the British public's understanding of its attachment to Britain and its involvement within Europe and the world. As complex agents, as people who were capable of being at once instruments, agents, and patients, the eighteenth-century British public disseminated ideas and generated actions which contributed to assumptions about the nature of the state and its position within a colonial world. The point is that the creation of a sense of Britishness in the eighteenth century was the result of practices and ideas, such as the discovery of the Indo-European language family, the mapping of British and colonial boundaries, or the description of racial types, which had specific local resonances within Britain and which all formed part of larger economic and cultural trends.

The argument, therefore, is that the formation of Britishness can best be understood by examining the practices and ideas of people whose opinions and actions were both influential and influenced by others. By beginning with practices and representations and by showing how those activities stretched beyond the British nation-state, a historian might be able to demonstrate how they were received and responded to in such a fashion that a particular, distinct, and local sense of Britishness was created. Thus, in this example the categorical differences between area studies and world historical perspectives may be narrowed by examining agency first. Britishness is indeed particular to the nation-state of Britain, but it is also part of larger transnational and colonial phenomenon; however, to study its formation from the perspective of a category or an abstraction overlooks the ways in which people create many of the conditions of their existence. A study, therefore, of practices, ideas, and representations—of how people are interested in the results of the Battle of Plassey and yet sentimentally attached to the oak tree at the bottom of the garden—allows historians to work beyond categorical boundaries and to create new histories of the world and its areas.

Notes

1. Michael Adas, "Bringing Ideas and Agency Back In," in *World History: Ideologies, Structures, and Identities,* ed. Philip Pomper, Richard H. Elphick, and Richard T. Vann (Malden, MA: Blackwell, 1998), 81–104.

2. Ibid., 88.

3. Ronald Inden, *Imagining India* (Cambridge, MA: Blackwell, 1990).

4. The breadth of world history is impressive. The following is a brief selection of recent scholarship which indicates how varied and robust the literature

has become: Jerry H. Bentley's *Old World Encounters: Cross-Cultural Contacts and Exchange in Pre-Modern Times* (Oxford: Oxford University Press, 1993) is an excellent example of cultural approach to world history; Mary Louise Pratt's *Imperial Eyes: Travel Writing and Transculturation* (London: Routledge, 1992) and Stephen Greenblatt's *Marvelous Possessions: The Wonder of the New World* (Chicago: University of Chicago Press, 1991) are innovative historical examinations of cross-cultural contacts by scholars of literature; and Alfred Crosby's *Ecological Imperialism: The Biological Expansion of Europe, 900–1900* (Cambridge: Cambridge University Press, 1986) and Philip Curtin's *Death by Migration: Europe's Encounter with the Tropical World in the Nineteenth Century* (Cambridge: Cambridge University Press, 1989) present two very different world historical approaches to disease, migration, and imperialism.

5. Examples may include Ronald Segal, *The Black Diaspora* (New York: Farrar, Straus and Giroux, 1995); Clive Ponting, *A Green History of the World: The Environment and the Collapse of Great Civilizations* (New York: St. Martin's Press, 1992); Toby Huff, *The Rise of Early Modern Science: Islam, China, and the West* (Cambridge: Cambridge University Press, 1995).

6. Oswald Spengler, *The Decline of the West* (abridged ed. trans. by H. Stuart Hughes (New York: Oxford University Press, 1991); Arnold Toynbee, *A Study of History*, 12 vols. (Oxford: Oxford University Press, 1934–61).

7. Spengler, *Decline of the West*, 25.

8. Fernand Braudel, *On History* , trans. Sarah Matthews (Chicago: University of Chicago Press, 1980); William H. McNeill, *The Rise of the West* (Chicago: University of Chicago Press, 1991); Samuel P. Huntington, *The Clash of Civilizations and the Remaking of World Order* (New York: Touchstone, 1996).

9. Fernand Braudel, "The History of Civilizations: The Past Explains the Present," in *On History,* trans. Sarah Matthews (Chicago: University of Chicago Press, 1980), 177–218.

10. Ibid., 177.

11. McNeill, *Rise of the West*, xx.

12. Ibid., xxi.

13. J. M. Blaut, *The Colonizer's Model of the World: Geographical Diffusionism and Eurocentric History* (New York: Guilford Press, 1993); Marshall G. S. Hodgson, "On Doing World History," in *Rethinking World History: Essays on Europe, Islam, and World History*, ed. Edmund Burke III, Cambridge: Cambridge University Press, 1996), 93.

14. Marshall G. S. Hodgson, *The Venture of Islam: Conscience and History in a World Civilization*, 3 vols. (Chicago: University of Chicago Press, 1977).

15. Marshall G. S. Hodgson, "Historical Method in Civilization Studies," in *Rethinking World History: Essays on Europe, Islam, and World History* (Cambridge: Cambridge University Press, 1996), 84.

16. Huntington, *Clash of Civilizations,* 40.

17. Ibid., 43.

18. Immanuel Wallerstein, *The Modern World-System: Capitalist Agriculture and the Origins of the European World-Economy in the Sixteenth Century* (New York: Academic Press, 1974); Janet L. Abu-Lughod, *Before European Hegemony: The World System A.D. 1250–1350* (New York: Oxford University Press, 1989).

19. Wallerstein, *Modern World-System,* 347.

20. For example, Janet Lippman Abu-Lughod, "The World System in the Thirteenth Century: Dead-End or Precursor?" in *Essays on Global and Comparative History*, ed. Michael Adas (Washington, DC: American Historical Association, 1993).

21. Janet Lippman Abu-Lughod, "The World-System Perspective in the Construction of Economic History," in *World History: Ideologies, Structures, and Identities;* ed. Philip Pomper, Richard H. Elphick, and Richard T. Vann (Malden, MA: Blackwell, 1998), 76.

22. Madhav Gadgil and Ramachandra Guha, *This Fissured Land: An Ecological History of India* (Delhi: Oxford University Press, 1993).

23. Richard H. Grove, *Green Imperialism: Colonial Expansion, Tropical Island Edens and the Origins of Environmentalism, 1600–1860* (Cambridge: Cambridge University Press, 1995).

24. Edward W. Said, *Orientalism* (New York: Vintage, 1979).

References

Abu-Lughod, Janet L. *Before European Hegemony: The World System A.D. 1250–1350*. New York: Oxford University Press, 1989.

———. "The World System in the Thirteenth Century: Dead-End or Precursor?" In *Essays on Global and Comparative History*. Ed. Michael Adas. Washington, DC: American Historical Association, 1993.

———. "The World-System Perspective in the Construction of Economic History." In *World History: Ideologies, Structures, and Identities*. Ed. Philip Pomper, Richard H. Elphick, and Richard T. Vann. Malden, MA: Blackwell, 1998.

Adas, Michael. "Bringing Ideas and Agency Back In." In *World History: Ideologies, Structures, and Identities*. Ed. Philip Pomper, Richard H. Elphick, and Richard T. Vann. Malden, MA: Blackwell, 1998.

Bentley, Jerry H. *Old World Encounters: Cross-Cultural Contacts and Exchange in Pre-Modern Times*. Oxford: Oxford University Press, 1993.

Blaut, J. M. *The Colonizer's Model of the World: Geographical Diffusionism and Eurocentric History*. New York: Guilford Press, 1993.

Braudel, Fernand. *On History*. Trans. Sarah Matthews. Chicago: University of Chicago Press, 1980.

———. "The History of Civilizations: The Past Explains the Present." In *On History*. Trans. Sarah Matthews. Chicago: University of Chicago Press, 1980.

Crosby, Alfred. *Ecological Imperialism: The Biological Expansion of Europe, 900–1900*. Cambridge: Cambridge University Press, 1986.

Curtin, Philip. *Death by Migration: Europe's Encounter with the Tropical World in the Nineteenth Century*. Cambridge: Cambridge University Press, 1989.

Gadgil, Madhav, and Ramachandra Guha. *This Fissured Land: An Ecological History of India*. Delhi: Oxford University Press, 1993.

Greenblatt, Stephen. *Marvelous Possessions: The Wonder of the New World*. Chicago: University of Chicago Press, 1991.

Grove, Richard H. *Green Imperialism: Colonial Expansion, Tropical Island Edens and the Origins of Environmentalism, 1600–1860*. Cambridge: Cambridge University Press, 1995.

Hodgson, Marshall G. S. "On Doing World History." In *Rethinking World History: Essays on Europe, Islam, and World History*. Ed. Edmund Burke III. Cambridge: Cambridge University Press, 1996.

———. "Historical Method in Civilization Studies." *Rethinking World History: Essays on Europe, Islam, and World History*. Ed. Edmund Burke III. Cambridge: Cambridge University Press, 1996.

———. *The Venture of Islam: Conscience and History in a World Civilization*. 3 vols. Chicago and London: University of Chicago Press, 1977.

Huff, Toby. *The Rise of Early Modern Science: Islam, China, and the West*. Cambridge: Cambridge University Press, 1995.

Huntington, Samuel P. *The Clash of Civilizations and the Remaking of World Order*. New York: Touchstone, 1996.

Inden, Ronald. *Imagining India*. Cambridge, MA: Blackwell, 1990.

McNeill, William H. *The Rise of the West*. Chicago: University of Chicago Press, 1991.

Ponting, Clive. *A Green History of the World: The Environment and the Collapse of Great Civilizations*. New York: St. Martin's Press, 1992.

Pratt, Mary Louise. *Imperial Eyes: Travel Writing and Transculturalation*. London: Routledge, 1992.

Said, Edward W. *Orientalism*. New York: Vintage, 1979.

Segal, Ronald. *The Black Diaspora*. New York: Farrar, Straus, and Giroux, 1995.

Spengler, Oswald. *The Decline of the West,* abridged ed. Trans. H. Stuart Hughes. New York: Oxford University Press, 1991.

Toynbee, Arnold. *A Study of History*. 12 vols. Oxford: Oxford University Press, 1934–61.

Wallerstein, Immanuel. *The Modern World-System: Capitalist Agriculture and the Origins of the European World-Economy in the Sixteenth Century*. New York: Academic Press, 1974.

JON M. STROLLE

The American Way of Language Learning

∽∘∾

IN THE UNITED STATES, from long before the founding of the republic itself, the languages studied in colleges and universities have reflected the peculiarities of European culture transported to the Americas. The religious impulse of the first hispanophone and anglophone arrivals created a need to evangelize in the language of the Native Americans, and a long tradition of Bible translation ensued. Higher education and a study of the Greek and Roman classics were synonymous at the few institutions of higher learning that colonial America supported. Training clergy, lawyers, and others of the professional stratum of society derived from knowing the language and the philosophical, literary, and historical writing of Greece and Rome, with a nod to Hebrew for the theological student. But the status of language learning beyond the classical tongues follows an irregular path, intersecting with large new influences of technology, political disruptions and wars, and the rise of a middle class for whom the English vernacular was sufficient or even superior.

The contemporary role of World English and the long-standing dominance of English as the American national language provide a distinctive

Editor's note: What happens to language study if area studies are under attack and new technologies seem to indicate that English will be the predominant "lingua franca" in the future? "The American Way of Language Learning" by Jon Strolle of the Monterey Institute of International Studies recapitulates the history of the place of language study in American education. Strolle finds a possible answer in the long tradition of "practicality" shaping language education in the United States, manifested most recently in a call for "global competence." He points to the likelihood of a number of "lingua francas" emerging and the capacity of cheap and available communications equipment to bind together language groups "that were weakening but which can now regain strength through electronic association." On a note of what might best be called cautious optimism, Strolle implies that the perceived need for global competence is likely to require Americans, for practical reasons, to master other languages.

framework to many of the language issues debated within the American community of higher education. Calculations vary, but approximately 95 percent of the population of the United States speaks English, a degree of national uniformity unequaled in any other large continental nation. The educational system in place today is the creation of the English-speaking society that early became the dominant and is now the virtually exclusive sponsor of institutions of higher learning. In every era, the persistent influences of the national sense of distance and isolation from "foreign entanglements" (Washington's famous words), the buffer of great oceans, and fears of immigration and strange tongues have combined to form an erratic history of the place of language education in American society and culture. It is a history of odd and ill-fitting pieces, a mosaic that is always susceptible to rearrangement but always embedded in English.

Early Advocacy

On occasion a national leader has called for specific curriculum changes. Thomas Jefferson proposed the introduction of French and German to the College of William and Mary to assist in preparing the new nation's diplomats. Intellectual leaders of the generation after Jefferson's, such as George Ticknor, led an enormous national educational effort that included a vision of a broad yet clearly practical place for languages: they led to understanding the history, culture, and literature of the societies they represented.

Ticknor's part in creating the modern American university illustrates the lead that the field of modern language once provided in establishing the fundamental disciplinary and department-based structure that now prevails. In his letters on the subject of educational reform at Harvard University, he expressed concern for the then current practice of awarding a degree for an accumulation of studies taken across a number of topics. He proposed:

the division of the whole institution into *departments*, with the right of a limited choice of studies; the separation of members of a class for their exercises according to their proficiency so that each division might be carried forward as rapidly as was consistent with thoroughness, every man having a right to make progress according to his industry and capacity. (Ticknor, 1880, p. 362)

To achieve his ends, the department of modern languages was established in 1825 and was given the authority to create a curriculum based not on an accumulation of courses but on the development of proficiency—Ticknor's word—in a subject. One was to learn Latin, not just read Livy, for example. The quality of the teaching was established as the

measurement of the accomplishment. The examination of students via rec-
itation, the dominant model, he saw as sterile and structured on punish-
ment. The professor interacted little with students. Ticknor sought a vigorous intellectual involvement between student and teacher as the model for
the future. One might conclude from Ticknor's experience that humanistic
learning may not be susceptible to the dichotomous universe of teaching
and research; for one without the other makes very little sense. To do research apart from actual teaching of students is sterile, impractical (a word
that would not offend), and in contrast to his idea of a university.

Students were divided according to their backgrounds and levels of
proficiency, and adjustments were made during the course of the term to
provide for the most supportive setting for them to progress. The goals
for learners were clearly different then. Students were divided into
groups, and those that were successful "[were] sufficiently familiar with
French to read it anywhere, to write it decently, and to speak a little."
(Ticknor, 1880, p. 367). It was Ticknor's rigorous implementation of the
reforms promised by departmental organization that produced the results. Other parts of the university took longer to move to this model
that had its origin in Ticknor's experience of study in the great universities of Europe. The department had distinguished names, such as
Longfellow, as successors to Ticknor. And at the end of the nineteenth
century, discipline-based organizations emerged to set patterns for departments and fields that would dominate post–secondary learning for
the next one hundred years.

Founding the Modern Language Association

The leadership of the early nineteenth century did not translate into
flourishing programs of modern language instruction. The fascination
Spain and Mexico held for Irving, Prescott, and Longfellow was not
echoed in burgeoning enrollments for Spanish nor high prestige in other
modern languages. The early documents published by the Modern Language Association (MLA) strike many of the same notes heard in the
halls of departments at the end of the twentieth century: a melancholy
chorus. This statement of hope from the "Proceedings at New York, December, 1884" (1885) sums it up:

Considering the present low standing of the subject in the minds of most American educators, and the consequent neglect of it in our systems of education; considering the inferior position that many of our Modern Language professors hold
compared with their colleagues in other subjects; remembering that there never
had been before any attempt to unite the professors of Modern Languages, or in

any way stir up a feeling of common interest with them; noting the differences of educational requirements in different sections of our country, and bearing in mind that the representatives of this Conference came together without knowing, in many cases, anything of the nature of the subjects to be presented for discussion, and, hence, wholly unprepared on them;—taking into account these things—the meeting in New York must be considered a success and, perhaps, the most remarkable one of its kind ever held in the United States. (p. vii)

The "practical ends" that were to be pursued included recognition of sectional differences in the country, standards of study, and the role of language in the educational system. In the earliest meeting there was a split between practical language development based on the then current method of oral instruction, the Natural Method, and the notion that "intellectual discipline" was the end of college level work. Their resolution declared: "[T]he chief aims to be sought in the study of Modern Languages in our Colleges, are literary culture, philological scholarship and linguistic discipline, but . . . a course in oral practice is desirable as an auxiliary" ("Proceedings," p. iv).

The spirit of the proficiency movement in the 1980s and beyond would seem to be more in harmony with the idea of Ticknor than the essence of the early MLA. Ticknor meant reading proficiency rather than oral proficiency, but the practical spirit reigns in both approaches. The MLA in the 1880s was deeply affected by the shadow of the classics and was motivated to find an equal status for modern languages by imitating the classical curriculum. The report of the New York meeting confirms:

There was little disposition manifest to overthrow the existing state of things so far as the relation of Modern to Classical languages is concerned, in point of importance, but a serious, determined unity of sentiment to move with all possible energy towards the establishment, and legitimate maintenance of the claims of the Modern studies for the same rights and privileges as are now enjoyed by the Classics. ("Proceedings," p. vii)

The participants in that meeting would be astonished, no doubt, to see the disappearance of the great programs in classics from college and university campuses and would not want to share their fate.

Making the Argument

A list of justifications for language study became regular fare for teachers and program administrators to promote their programs. Professor Charles Kroeh wrote a particularly candid version in the 1887 *Proceedings*:

Modern Languages are studied, for example,
  1. As an accomplishment.

2. Because other schools offer them, and with no special ulterior object, or with a vague idea of some intellectual benefit.
3. To serve the purposes of a summer trip abroad.
4. As a means of improvement in the use of one's native tongue.
5. For general culture obtainable by reading foreign literature.
6. For philological research or amusement.
7. For acquiring the ability to consult foreign scientific and technical publications.
8. For business correspondence.
9. Because business, family, or friendly relations bring with them personal intercourse with foreigners.
10. To teach them.

From the beginning of the MLA, there have been regular summaries of justification, those of William Riley Parker most prominently among them. His pamphlet, *The National Interest and Foreign Languages. A Discussion Guide for the U.S. National Commission for UNESCO* was issued in three widely-used editions from 1954 to 1961. The educational is interwoven with the practical, the intellectual with the pragmatic. A representative list of arguments prepared by Wilga Rivers of Harvard in the 1970s was quoted by James Alaitis (1976) of Georgetown:

1. To develop the student's intellectual powers through foreign language study;
2. To increase the student's personal culture through the study of the great literature and philosophy to which it is the key;
3. To increase the student's understanding of how language functions and to bring him, through the study of a foreign language, to a greater awareness to the functioning of his own language;
4. To teach the student to read the foreign language with comprehension so that he may keep abreast of modern writing, research, and information;
5. To bring the student to a greater understanding of people across national barriers by giving him a sympathetic insight into the ways of life and ways of thinking of the people who speak the language he is learning; and
6. To provide the student with skills which will enable him to communicate orally, and to some degree in writing, with the speakers of another language and with people of other nationalities who may have also learned this language. (P. 448)

Finally, the latest pamphlets from the MLA (1999) have the following captions:

Knowing other languages brings opportunities.
Give yourself a competitive edge.
The job advantage in a global economy.
Learning other cultures: your world and beyond.
Go for the excitement: new ways of language learning.
Which language should you learn?

The answer to the last item is that "whatever language you choose, learning it will make a difference in how you see the world and in how the world sees you."

Enrollment Trends and Patterns

A graphic representation of language enrollment levels in secondary schools would show that the highest percentages were achieved around 1905, when Latin captured 54 percent of students; German 22 percent; and French, 10 percent. These figures, of course, reflect the limited number and elite status of people in high school at the time. As the classical languages fell out of favor, the modern languages did not become a broadly accepted substitute. Despite frequent efforts to encourage or require students to take language classes in hopes of acquiring useful proficiency, enrollments were modest successes. In a society that moves on two rhetorical impulses: to satisfy its idealism and to meet the practical demands of communication in a cost-effective way, a convinced public will act when either of these motives is high in its consciousness: to win a war, to spread the political or religious word, to win the contract, or for self-satisfaction.

The second peak of language enrollments came on the heels of the launch of Sputnik in 1957. An entire era of justification by security and defense needs led to legislation and funding, very clearly characterized as the National Defense Education Act (NDEA). Language learning via summer institutes, teacher training, graduate fellowships, and support for area studies and the relevant languages garnered substantial money for over a decade, and elements of the program continue to this day. The enrollments and dollars have never again equaled the mid-1960s figures, when a million-plus students out of six million in postsecondary education were studying a language other than English. After a precipitous bust in the 1970s as general enrollment projections declined and requirements were altered to allow larger choice, the one million level would not be reached again until the 1990s, by which time the overall enrollments had grown to more than fourteen million.

In addition to these numbers relating the mass consumption of language learning, there are other successes. The maintenance of programs for the less commonly taught languages and the encouragement given to scholars in African, Asian, and other languages with a low profile on the U.S. linguistic horizon are points of pride for the heirs to NDEA and its current incarnation as Title VI. The other changes are in attitude and in campus resources for international programs, cross-disciplinary courses, and other language-related support systems. After the Title VI grants were completed, a follow-up survey identified significant levels of participation in international internships and study abroad, in greater institutional planning for international programming, and in improved linkages with other U.S. institutions to facilitate transfers (Schneider and Burn, n.d., p. 21).

National Goals: Reform and Renovation

The whole national effort at language learning, whatever the stated and implied goals, involves large numbers of people and considerable investment by schools, colleges and universities, government agencies, and private sector initiatives. In a recent Harris poll commissioned by the National Foreign Language Center and reported in 1999, 80 percent of Americans recognized the value of second-language learning, and yet the national effort is highly diffuse and atomized (Brecht and Rivers, 1999, p. 209). In the current decade several state, regional, and national efforts at articulation have been proclaimed and at least have reached the level of initial action and broad proclamation of goals.

The Goals 2000 project of the U.S. Department of Education, which emerged from the national governors' meetings of the early 1990s for the purpose of identifying national educational goals initially did not make language one of the top priorities. With concerted political action, the study of language was moved from a list of desirable addenda to one of the core subjects. Still, the follow-up reports on articulation efforts most often confirm that the decentralized nature of American education will produce loose connections along the educational continuum from grade school through university. Rarely can a student progress from language acquisition in the lower grades to substantial study and not spend time in unfortunate duplication and repetition. Until a more powerful regional or national consensus forms, progress will be modest. ("Presentations," 1995).

The effort to define with clarity our national educational goals and to articulate the place of language learning among them has been aided by a number of steps over the past twenty years. The President's Commission on Foreign Language and International Studies, 1979, and its report, *Strength through Wisdom: A Critique of U.S. Capability,* was criticized for producing a list of goals that was undifferentiated and insufficiently focused on language. Nonetheless, a series of curricular and structural developments have brought the language learning field to a stronger position at the end of the twentieth century. The proficiency movement took advantage of the work done in federal agencies on standards of assessment and recast their metric in a form useful to language learners in high schools, colleges, and universities. The oral proficiency tests developed and administered through the American Council of Teachers of Foreign Language (ACTFL) are still the subject of debate and criticism, but there are now sufficient evaluators and numbers of tests administered to raise awareness in the general public about what should be expected. Moreover, other organizations, such as the Association for Testing of Materials (now known as ASTM), not normally associated with educational institutions, have published guidelines for language consumers.

Nevertheless, the very successes of post–secondary language education created problems for the field. The growth of departments in the boom years of the late 1960s had created numerous doctoral programs, and the production of Ph.D.'s outstripped the available positions. In addition, the nature of doctoral research rarely reflected the actual teaching load, especially of junior faculty people. With the exception of the large research universities, professors in a language program would expect that the first three years of language study would make up the bulk of their assignments throughout most of their careers. With singular exceptions, the graduate program did not offer language pedagogy beyond the training given to teaching assistants and the experienced gathered in the classroom while doing the doctorate. In the 1980s a series of efforts to redefine the profession of language scholars was undertaken by the leading national organizations of teachers and scholars. The imbalance of the situation was recognized in the MLA report on the profession that called for more preparation for the language classroom in addition to the research skills in literature and linguistics (MLA 1981).

At present, language courses continue to hold steady in overall enrollment, while in many languages fewer advanced students are available to take the classes in literature, culture, and history that the faculty member's research interests would allow. In other instances, language instruction has become the province of a group of teachers who have qualitatively different appointments from tenure-track faculty. The disjunction between professional training and the demands of the actual student enrollment profile place pressure on departments and institutions to create alternative solutions. The alternatives will derive from curriculum restructuring, professional training programs at the graduate level that reflect the restructuring, career tracks that reward all forms of learning sought by society, and ultimately by the learners' willingness to make the investment of self and energy in acquiring language competence for a large array of goals.

With the fall of the Soviet Union and the opening of commerce and communication across many frontiers, a variety of pushes for reform and revitalization materialized. One of the more serious movements, the Council for the Advancement of Foreign Language and International Studies (CAFLIS), proceeded to develop a proposal for a national endowment in these fields and to make recommendations for the states, elementary and secondary schools, and private sector relations. The proposal recommended in the CAFLIS report could not attract the level of congressional support to provide the funding required. The *Washington Post* editorialized that another federal office was not the solution to better language learning, and the effort faded.

From early in the 1980s through the present, a concerted national effort to keep Congress informed and active on language issues has succeeded through the combined efforts of teacher associations and other associations for international education. Acting together in the Joint National Committee for Languages (JNCL) and the National Council of Language and International Studies (NCLIS), JNCL was instrumental in bringing funding to Title VI, part B, the Centers for International Business and Research, the National Resource Centers, and the Foreign Language Assistance Program.

In addition, the federal budget provides large amounts of money for an equally large range of language programs only tangentially related to the work of the academic departments at colleges and universities. The largest of these appropriations goes to bilingual education, mainly for English language instruction. When programs for bilingual education were set up in the late 1960s they were specifically denied the opportunity to become second-language learning opportunities for anglophone students. In fact ambiguity was characteristic and intentional in much of the legislation (Shiffman, 1996, pp. 240–41). After a well-publicized defeat in 1998, specifically Proposition 209 in California, which limited bilingual education, the leadership of the bilingual education field is now talking about integrating students from different linguistic communities for the benefit of all.

The dangers of the comparative argument and an overreliance on national security as a justification are evident in the fate of Russian and other languages supported by the defense rationale. Pamphlets published in the 1980s by the American Council on Education's Commission on International Education warned that the Soviets were outspending the United States on student exchanges and language training and that the need for qualified language and area studies experts was far outstripping the supply (ACE, 1983). Of course, the linguistic strength of the Soviet Union was not enough to save it, and the shortcomings of the United States have not impeded its economic and political progress as the world's leading power. The higher education community has regularly given consideration to issues of security and defense in justifying the study of language. In times of war and international crisis, they will inevitably arise again, but to rely solely on them can only weaken the educational benefits when they are thus narrowly defined.

While educational institutions and their friends and advocates will continue to articulate reasons for studying one field or another, perhaps a long view and an eclectic philosophy ultimately will find society's purpose and convince a larger number of students. It has been instructive to look back to the early reforms of Ticknor and to see how often practicality was associated with education. Yet the emphasis on the practical element of education as a means to informed citizenship in the new republic had a sense of immediacy and currency that has dulled in the public imagination after more than 220 years. Nonetheless, the concept seems to have been reborn on a larger scale: the millennial urges of century's end and the collapse of international barriers have given strength to the idea that citizens must acquire "global competence."

At a Washington conference in 1993 (CIEE), Richard Lambert laid out the principal features of his definition for global competence: knowledge, empathy, approval, foreign language competency, and task performance. Foreign language was mentioned by most of the contributors to the discussion, but one can sense that Lambert was vexed by the imprecision of the kind and type of language learning required (Education Exchange and Global Competence, 1994, p. 291). In the end, however, language applied to task performance is the essence of its function in global competence. The variations are large and defined with extensive needs analyses and other assessments (Strolle, 1994, p. 216).

A test of global competence came with the Gulf War at the beginning of 1990s. Afterward, Congress reexamined national strategic and linguistic readiness for engagements beyond our usual security perimeters. From the perspective of the pamphleteers who warned of Soviet competition and called for more emphasis on the Russian language, it would be hard to imagine that the principal military engagements of the United States in this decade would be Iraq, Somalia, Haiti, Bosnia, and Kosovo. Senator Boren of Oklahoma, for example, found the lack of Arabic language expertise in the intelligence community and the military of sufficient concern to set aside $150 million and to create a National Security Education Program (NSEP). After subsequent alterations, NSEP was charged with helping to fill in the gaps in American knowledge of languages and cultures of critical strategic importance.

The language departments of colleges and universities, however, still find the bulk of their enrollment in the lower division courses and still in the more commonly taught languages—Spanish, French, and German. The next overall postsecondary enrollment survey from Association of Departments of Foreign Language (ADFL) will likely show flat numbers as compared with five years ago and thus a continuing drop in the percentage of college-level students taking language. In recent reports, the Center for Applied Linguistics did note an upsurge in students in kindergarten through eighth grade (K–8), and ACTFL has reported stronger enrollments in secondary schools. But as the efforts at cross-institutional articulation have shown, transforming these increases into more students ready to do college-level work, arbitrarily defined here as fifth semester and higher, has had mixed results.

There is reason to hope that a new willingness of language professionals to engage in broad discussions will see in the strong growth in K–8 enrollments and the steady increase in secondary numbers a basis for both strength and quality in college classrooms. The professional dialogue sustained in the relevant journals such as the *Modern Language Journal, The Bulletin of the ADFL, Foreign Language Annals,* and other publications of language-associated groups has broadened in the last two decades. The Presidential Commission of 1979 may not have produced a definitive program of action or, as its critics would have it, even given languages sufficient prominence, but the discussions and dialogues have extended the capacity of the teacher with increasingly sophisticated tools. Teachers and scholars examine a great diversity of approaches, techniques, and methods, and these are then assimilated and subsequently framed in eclectic educational, cultural, and theoretical contexts.

The profession of language teaching in colleges has benefited from a broadening of the scope of post-secondary programs and a recognition of the distinctive needs of the American cultural context (Kramsch, 1995). In large measure the articulation issue turns on the great diversity of the national culture on the one hand and on the monochrome aspect of the country and its linguistic uniformity on the other (Campbell, 1996).

The publication of national standards has brought the effort at program articulation to its first plateau. With standards, the various segments can undertake the planning required for measurable implementation. It may be assumed for the time being that the K–16 education system will be the primary provider of language learning for the next twenty years. But it also may be time to ask whether expanding communication alternatives and the large amount of information available to the individual might not imply more changes than are currently being contemplated. With good evidence of improved teacher preparation and materials availability, the tools of the trade for language teachers are richer and more varied than at any time, and the opportunity for students to experience language, at least electronically mediated language, are swelling (Foreign Language Standards, 1999, p. 98).

Despite the many assessments of language programs discussed at conferences and in print, the assumption that there will continue to be large numbers of students for lower division instruction does not seem to be examined closely. Some scholars, such as Russell Campbell, do point to the new learner profiles of students arriving in college with language backgrounds very different from those of the student population that dominated the second half of the twentieth century. Especially in the recent immigrant communities, heritage speakers of languages such as Korean, Mandarin, and Vietnamese dominate in the classroom. The National Council of Less Commonly Taught Languages (NCOLCTL) has learned that the heritage communities and their schools are increasingly the largest provider of instruction, sometimes at a ratio of ten to one over what colleges and universities offer. Eighty thousand students of Mandarin in community-run schools compare to eight thousand in university classes.

Good data are not accessible, unfortunately, for the levels and quantity of instruction offered through private sector schools. "Berlitz" can jar academic ears in language departments. To many in higher education, the lowest denominator of language learning is the casual offering given to tourists and occasional business travelers. There is fear that academic classrooms will become more like them, but Berlitz and other private and proprietary language programs have no trouble attracting student/clients. After some of the proprietary schools agreed to modify their advertising and state outcomes in more realistic terms, some of the distrust held by the teacher associations was allayed. In 1995 ASTM, a national standards association for business and industry, published their *Standard Guide for Use-oriented Language Instruction*. It is the result of discussions among government, academic, and proprietary organizations that lead to a consensus on requirements for curriculum, materials, teacher qualifications, and other aspects of a quality program of language instruction (ASTM, F-1562–95, pp. 1–7).

Standards such as those published through ASTM are recognized internationally. Those of educational groups are just now getting national stature. One of the implications of globalization is establishing international standards, and industry and other professional associations are used to looking to guidelines such as those of ASTM for their international quality accreditation. It is an open question whether the academic world will find its version of standards to be the ones ultimately accepted by the larger society.

Making the Agenda for the Future

Who is offering a concrete proposal for large changes in national language policy? At a 1999 conference at Stanford on the study of foreign languages in the next century, Leon Panetta (1999), long a champion of language learning, voiced his concerns about the strategy for bringing about real change in the schools. For him, language is the fourth *r*, *reality*, and an imperative for the kind of change that the twenty-first century requires. As someone skilled in political change he prescribes strong medicine:

1. That by 2010, 100 percent of all schools, colleges and universities should require all of their students to study a foreign language; and
2. This requirement should be a condition for the receipt of federal funds for education. (p. 10)

How will language departments fare, especially those in higher education? An imminent disappearance does not appear likely, but in confidential discussions with college administrators, even those who are sympathetic, a realignment of resources appears likely. The momentum of the language department created long ago by Ticknor is too strong to stop in the near term. The decline of Latin and Greek, however, is an emblem of how total change can be when society renders a judgment. The study of modern languages may be compelling because the trend to having one lingua franca is not as clearly pointed to English as many currently believe.

At the Language in the Twenty-First Century conference at Yale in 1999, William Mackey outlined the perils of predicting language dominance or demise (p. 8). David Graddol at the same meeting suggested that four or five languages will dominate intercultural communications by midcentury. English does and will continue to lead in worldwide communications. And though the American public, according to a recent Harris survey (NFLC), believes that up to one-half of the world's population speaks English, a more likely scenario may be that a number of linguas will emerge and English will be principal among them. It is also possible that communication media, available cheaply and widely in twenty years, will bind up language groups that were weakening but that can now regain strength through electronic association. Esther Dyson, a frequent commentator on the Internet, noted in a C-Span interview that smaller language communities get new sustenance from greater interaction and access, a concept that Mackey supports as well, especially as it pertains to orality.

Among the cultural trends of the times, technologically facilitated individual choice appears to be an emerging distinctive characteristic of society. Where, when, and how to acquire language will be determined from a greater field of institutional and technological choices than academic institutions are used to providing. A peripatetic use of language— that is, language that follows the topic, field, or cultural location— could in effect attract a larger number of learners into the classroom. The classroom here is not necessarily a dedicated language classroom.

Content-based instruction has found its way into a number of institutions, not to replace the study of literature, history, and philosophy but to give opportunities to the scientist and social scientist to reach into the cultural corners that English-mediated experiences do not illuminate. There is a logic to a course in U.S./Latin American affairs that uses both Spanish and English as the day and topic demand.

Higher level language skills are difficult to acquire without direct experience of the countries and cultures where the target language is spoken. Students going abroad nowadays find themselves sometimes negotiating to use the language of the country they are visiting because their counterparts' motivation to learn English is as strong as the Americans', say, to learn Spanish. When they return to campus in the United States, students urge that their own progress may have been enhanced through more authentic situations and materials. In the end, no one program design will meet the variability of experience of all students, and the greatest hope is for a core of learning that includes language to be spoken, read, written, and heard beyond that of the student's native tongue. The subsequent curriculum choices at the college/university level can be built on this core designed to a national standard.

Whether international studies programs will continue to promote language learning actively and integrally can be questioned. When greater accountability for the funds spent on language learning in Title VI programs was requested in the 1980s, there was some reluctance even within the U.S. Department of Education to change the allocation of resources into more extensive and verifiable examination of language-learning outcomes. In point of fact most classes in international studies are conducted entirely in English, and there is an assumption on the part of some that the language investment is of marginal importance. This sentiment is often seen when curriculum discussions equate *language* with all languages other than English. A supercategory has been created for English, never precisely defined but understood by its believers to be the most efficient medium of intellectual activity, adequate to all purposes. The advocates of this posture showed their hand and their vote in faculty debates over language requirements. While some have been reintroduced, few have the breadth of those that were in place thirty years ago.

To provide a counterweight to the English-dominant view, a large change for colleges and universities and perhaps the healthiest would be to focus language learning for the adult student on the second foreign language and to conduct these classes in centers and institutes that specialize in the task. The faculty would be trained, managed, and rewarded for language teaching and would articulate with departments of literature, history, philosophy, and culture. The teaching assistant could be imperiled by such an arrangement or have his or her training enhanced thereby. It will take imaginative and creative leadership to bring out the most beneficial results. Such an arrangement would depend on strong, widely available programs in the K–12 system. Twenty years of planning and implementation are probably the minimum to effect such a change. It may be unusual, but an analogy to sport and the long-term effects of Title IX on women's athletics might suggest the time it may take to reorient the schools to successful second language learning.

As society decides where education leads, language studies will find their place. What can be predicted is only that change will come more quickly than most can imagine. Between idealism and practicality, the practical impulse will most likely shape language education in the United States. The expression of that impulse in terms of global competency, together with the development of communication technology and the growing willingness of language professionals to experiment in both public and private venues, may constitute a note of hope. A unified vision of the field, one that ties learning at all points along a career of lifelong linguistic exploration, may be of greatest benefit. The professional, applied, intellectually and scholarly approaches to language study need not war with each other. A new love of language—a *neophilogy* that includes the work of teachers, writers, and researchers with mutual respect, tolerance, and understanding would be an appropriate and positive prescription for the profession's future practitioners.

Works cited

Alaitis, James 1976. "Teaching Foreign Languages—Why? A Look at an Old Question." *Foreign Language Annals* 9.5 (October): 448.

American Council on Education (ACE). 1983. *What We Don't Know Can Hurt Us: The Shortfall in International Competence.* Washington, DC: ACE.

American Society for Testing and Materials (ASTM). 1995. *Standard Guide for Use-oriented Foreign Language Instruction* (No. F1562–95). Philadelphia: ASTM.

Brecht, Richard D., and William P. Rivers 1999. *Language and National Security for the 21st Century: The Federal Role in Supporting National Language Capacity.* Washington, DC: The National Foreign Language Center.

Campbell, Russell N. 1996. "New Learners and New Environments: Challenges and Opportunities." Pp. 97–118 in *National Standards: A Catalyst for Reform.* Ed. Robert C. Lafayette. Lincolnwood, IL: National Textbook Company, in conjunction with the American Council on the Teaching of Foreign Languages (ACTFL).

Education Exchange and Global Competence. 1994. Ed. Richard D. Lambert. New York: Council on International Educational Exchange (CIEE).

Foreign Language Standards: Linking Research, Theories, and Practices. 1999. Ed. June K. Philips. Lincolnwood, IL: National Textbook Company, in conjunction with the American Council on the Teaching of Foreign Language (ACTFL).

Kramsch, Claire. 1995. "Embracing Conflict versus Achieving Consensus in Foreign Language Education." *ADFL* 26.3: 6–12.

Kroeh, Charles F. 1887. "Methods of Teaching Modern Languages," *PMLA* 3: 169.

MLA. 1981. "Profession 81" (pamphlet). New York: Modern Language Association.

MLA. 1999. "Why Learn Another Language?" (pamphlet series). New York: Modern Language Association.

Mackey, William F. 1999. "Forecasting the Fate of Languages." Paper read at the conference on Language in the Twenty-First Century, Yale University, New Haven, CT, June.

Panetta, Leon E. 1999. "Foreign Language Education: If 'Scandalous' in the 20th Century, What Will It Be in the 21st Century?" Paper read at the Stanford University Language Center Conference on the Study of Foreign Languages in the New Century, Palo Alto, CA, June.

"Presentations from the Foreign Language Coalition Conference 'Achieving Consensus on Articulation in Foreign Language Education.'" 1995. *ADFL Bulletin* 26.3: 6–43.

"Proceedings at New York, December, 1884," 1885. *PMLA* 1: iv–vii.

Schiffman, Harold F. 1996. *Linguistic Culture and Language Policy*. New York: Routledge, 210–247.

Schneider, Ann Imlah, and Barbara B. Burn. n.d., [1999]. *Federal Funding for International Studies. Does it Help? Does it Matter?* American Association of International Education Administrators.

Strolle, Jon M. 1994. "Language Competency as a Component of Global Competency." New York: CIEE, 215–220.

Ticknor, George. 1880. *Life, Letters, and Journal of George Ticknor*, vol. 1. Boston: Houghton Mifflin and Co.

INDEX

AAASS (American Association for the Advancement of Slavic Studies), 99n.2, 100n.5, 101n.21

AAS (Association for Asian Studies), 99n.2, 100n.5, 101n.21

Abstraction, 167–68

Abu-Lughod, Janet Lippman, 203–5

Accuracy, 111–12, 126

ACTFL (American Council of Teachers of Foreign Languages), 219, 222

Adas, Michael, 192–93

ADFL (Association of Departments of Foreign Language), 222

Africa: agricultural marketing boards in, 56; arbitrary colonial boundaries in, 73–74, 100n.11; colonialism and "traditional" structures in, 93; country-specific studies and decolonization in, 73; decolonization in, 206; division into smaller segments, 75; the equivalency struggle, 200; immigration to Western Europe, 101n.22; national and liberation movements arising in, 68; North Africa, 69, 71; studies separated from those for Asia and Middle East, 72; tribalism in, 77, 78, 101n.13. See also Sub-Saharan Africa

African Americans, 90

African Studies Association (ASA), 99n.2, 100n.5, 101n.21

Agarwal, Bina, 55

Agency: aspects of, 194; complex agency, 194, 196, 208–9; disembodied agents, 192, 193, 206, 208; as located in people, 207; a new theory of, 192–96, 207; reified agents, 192, 196; representations in, 193; in world history, 190–212

Agency slack, 36–37, 43, 58

Agrawal, Arun, 55

Agricultural production, economic and anthropological methods in study of, 164–65

Alaitis, James, 217

Altruism, 48

America. See United States

America-centrism, 7

American Anthropological Association, 121

American Anthropologist, 121

American Association for the Advancement of Slavic Studies (AAASS), 99n.2, 100n.5, 101n.21

American-British-Dutch-Australian (ABDA) command, 100n.8

American Council of Teachers of Foreign Languages (ACTFL), 219, 222

American Council on Education, 69, 221

American Economic Review, 169, 173

Americas: Caribbean, 69, 75; records maintained in metropolitan languages, 75; unity of, 74. *See also* Latin America; North America

Anderson, Benedict, 73

Annales school, 190